D0929720

GRAYBACKS AND GOLD:
CONFEDERATE MONETARY POLICY

GRAYBACKS AND GOLD: CONFEDERATE MONETARY POLICY

By

James F. Morgan

Volume II
SOUTHERN HISTORY AND GENEALOGY SERIES
The Perdido Bay Press
Pensacola, Florida
1985

Copyright 1985 by James F. Morgan

Renton, Washington

Library of Congress Cataloging in Publication Data

Morgan, James F., 1945-
  Graybacks and gold.

  (Southern history and genealogy series ; v. 2)
  Bibliography: p.
  Includes index.
  1. Money--Confederate States of America.
2. United States--History--Civil War, 1861-1865--
Economic aspects. I. Title. II. Series.
  HG526.M67   1985   332.4'975   85-16913
  ISBN 0-933776-22-5

CONTENTS

Page

ILLUSTRATIONS vi
MAPS viii
TABLES ix
PREFACE x

CHAPTER

    I   The Monetary Situation 1
    II   Coinage 11
   III Treasury Notes 23
   IV Eastern States' Paper Money 42
    V   Contrasts in Eastern States' Paper Money Issues 56
   VI The Trans-Mississippi Monetary Situation 70
  VII The Cherokee Scrip of 1862 85
 VIII The Choctaw Warrants of 1863 95
   IX Supremacy of Paper Money 104
    X   The Demise of Paper Money 115
   XI An Epilogue on Monetary Policy 127
BIBLIOGRAPHY 139
  Abbreviations 139
INDEX 154

ILLUSTRATIONS AND PHOTOGRAPHS

Figure		Following or on Page
1	$500 Confederate Stock Certificate	10
2	A Corporate Certificate	10
3	Four Per Cent Registered Bond. Unregistered	10
4	Four Per Cent Registered Bond. Registered	10
5	Confederate Half Dollar, 1861. Obverse	22
6	Confederate Half Dollar, 1861. Reverse	22
7	Confederate One Cent, 1861. Obverse	22
8	Confederate One Cent, 1861. Reverse	22
9	Confederate Cabinet Officers	22
10	Confederate Treasury Department Officials and Building	22
11	Robert Tyler, Register of the Treasury	22
12	Confederate Treasury Notes, $500 & .50¢	39
13	Confederate Treasury Note, $1,000	39
14	Interest Bearing Notes, $100	39
15	Counterfeit Confederate Note, $20	39
16	Alabama—One Dollar Bill, 1863	44
17	Alabama—Fifty Cents Bill, 1863	44
18	Mississippi—Three Dollar Bill, 1862	44
19	Mississippi—Fifty Cents Bill, 1864	44
20	Tennessee—One Dollar Bill, 1863, Smithville Issue	50
21	Tennessee—One Dollar Bill, 1863, Kingston Issue	50
22	Virginia—One Dollar Bill, 1862	50
23	Virginia—One Hundred Dollar Treasury Note, 1861	50
24	Georgia—Fifty Dollar Note, 1862	60
25	Georgia—Five Dollar Bill, 1864	60
26	North Carolina—One Dollar Bill, 1863	60
27	North Carolina—Seventy Five Cents Note, 1863	60
28	Florida—Three Dollar Note, 1863	60

29	Florida — Twenty-Five Cents Note, 1863	60
30	Pensacola, Florida — Fifty Cents Scrip, 1862. Obverse	69
31	Pensacola, Florida — Fifty Cents Scrip, 1862. Reverse	69
32	Arkansas — Five Dollar Treasury Warrant, 1862	74
33	Arkansas — One Dollar Treasury Warrant, 1861	74
34	Louisiana — Five Dollar Bill, 1862	74
35	Louisiana — Three Dollar Note, 1862	74
36	Texas — Fifty Dollar Treasury Warrant, 1862	80
37	Texas — Five Dollars, 1862	80
38	Missouri — Five Dollars, 1862	80
39	Missouri — Five Dollar Bill, 1862. Reverse	80
40	Cherokee Nation. One Dollar Note, 1862	90
41	John Ross, Principal Chief of the Cherokee Nation	90
42	Brigadier General Stand Watie	90
43	Elias Cornelius Boudinot	90
44	Choctaw Nation One Dollar Treasury Warrant	100
45	Samuel Garland, Principal Chief of the Choctaw Nation	100
46	Peter P. Pitchlynn, Principal Chief of the Choctaw Nation	100
47	W. W. Wilbur Token, 1846. Obverse	110
48	W. W. Wilbur Token, 1846. Reverse	110
49	Marshall House Token, 1859-62. Obverse	110
50	Marshall House Token, 1859-62. Reverse	110
51	The Wealth of the South Token, 1860. Obverse	110
52	The Wealth of the South Token, 1860. Reverse	110
53	Beauregard "Dime," 1861. Obverse	110
54	Beauregard "Dime," 1861. Reverse	110
55	The First Confederate Postage Stamp, Five Cents — Green	110
56	The First "American" (U.S. Area) Stamp, Produced Abroad, Five Cents — Pale Greenish Blue	110
57	The First Recessed-Engraved Confederate Postage Stamp, Ten Cents — Blue	110
58	Twenty Cents — Green	110
59	Merchant Scrip — Shinplasters Louisiana. Crosley Fifty Cents Scrip, 1862	110

60   Merchant Scrip—Shinplasters Louisiana. Arent
         Fifty Cents Scrip, 1862 110
61   Southern Bank Notes. One Dollar Note,
         Bank of Augusta, Georgia, 1861 110
62   Southern Bank Notes. One Dollar Note,
         Bank of Chattanooga, Tennessee, 1863 110
63   Northern Bank Note. Five Dollars Note, 1861, The
         Egg Harbor Bank, Egg Harbor City, New Jersey . . .126
64   Chemicograph Backs, 1863. $20 Note 126
65    $1000 Non Taxable Certificate, 1864. Unregistered 126
66    $1000 Non Taxable Certificate, 1864. Registered 126
67   Confederate Call Certificate. Fifty Thousand
         Dollars Call Certificate, 1863 138
68   Foreign Loan Bond. Seven Per Cent Cotton Loan Bond . . .138

MAPS

Following
or on Page

1.   Locations East of the Mississippi River
         (Mentioned in Text) xii

2.   Locations in Trans-Mississippi West
         (Mentioned in Text) 69

TABLES

Page

1 CONFEDERATE STOCKS AND BONDS 10

2 CONFEDERATE GOLD 22

3 TREASURY NOTES I 40

4 TREASURY NOTES II 41

5 TREASURY NOTES III 41

6 GEORGIA TREASURY NOTES AND CHANGE BILLS,
   1861-1865 60

7 GOLD PRICES IN CONFEDERATE BILLS,
   JANUARY 1, 1861 TO MAY 12, 1865 119

8 CONFEDERATE FUNDED DEBT, JANUARY 1, 1864 . . . 136

9 CONFEDERATE FUNDED DEBT, 1861-1865 137

10 CONFEDERATE NATIONAL DEBT, 1865 138

ix

PREFACE

When the Confederacy was organized, Southerners assumed that the monetary policy used by the Federal government would continue. Coinage would serve as change and be legal tender in the payment of small debts. Large debts would be settled with bank notes of the state-chartered banks — designated the circulating paper medium. But changes came with the war and the exigencies produced by the four-year conflict. This study surveys and evaluates the role of money in the Confederate States of America. It involves not only the issuances of the central government, but the issues of the various states and the Indian nations as well.

My deep love for numismatics led me to study monetary policies, and when my interest in the Confederacy developed, it seemed only natural to combine the two. When I began this research I had no preconceived notions about what I would find, except that I knew the Confederacy had relied primarily on paper money and that it had inflated at a rapid rate. I was surprised to find that the Confederate government had only thought of paper money as an internal currency and used precious metals to purchase equipment and other supplies abroad. I also discovered that the central government and the state governments virtually forbade private citizens from obtaining specie from banks while reserving the right to do so themselves; the United States government did the same thing with gold in the 1930s. But these policies could not be enforced indefinitely. Perhaps the will of the people is too strong to be controlled for a long period of time.

My research took me to many parts of the United States and nearly every state that composed the Confederacy. The fact that the Indian nations also issued paper currency during this period was another surprise, and I decided to devote a separate chapter to each of these forgotten people. Perhaps this will inspire additional research into these neglected areas.

I found many people throughout the country eager to help with my research. I am particularly indebted to Mr. James Walker of the National Archives; his continual help went far beyond the requirements of assisting a researcher. I also gratefully acknowledge the help of the late Dr. Vladimir Clain-Stefenelli of the Smithsonian Institution in finding materials about the tokens issued in the Confederacy. Washington, D. C. proved to be a treasure trove in my attempt at unraveling the story of Confederate monetary policy.

I cannot begin to list all of the friends I made in the many state archives. I thank them for their help and for making the task a little less formidable. In particular, I am indebted for the assistance of Ms. Connie J. Beane of the Florida State Archives.

I would be remiss if I did not acknowledge the help and direction which I received from the members of my doctoral committee at Oklahoma State University: Professors Norbert R. Mahnken, Neil J. Hackett, Jr., and James H. Howard, and especially Professor LeRoy H. Fischer, my graduate adviser and the director of my dissertation, who was also a friend and confidant.

Finally, I extend special thanks to those who financed my travels, comforted me when I was depressed, and encouraged me to go forward with research and writing. These wonderful persons are my parents, Mr. and Mrs. La Verne E. Morgan.

James F. Morgan

LOCATIONS EAST OF THE MISSISSIPPI RIVER

(Mentioned in Text)

✦ State Capitals
◉ National Capitals
■ Mints

xii

Chapter I

THE MONETARY SITUATION

The monetary system of the Confederate States of America developed largely from the banking and credit systems of the South. State banks and property banks constituted the two main types of banks in the South prior to the war. Most Southerners, however, had little contact with either of these banks. Instead they dealt with merchants who extended them credit from year to year. Even the planter class often dealt with a third party, a factor, who sold their commodities, made purchases for them, and kept balance sheets for them too. The factor did all of this for a percentage of the sales. The factor might be located in Europe, or more often than not might be a Northern merchant.

When President Andrew Jackson failed to renew the charter of the Second Bank of the United States in 1832 and withdrew federal funds from it, numerous state banks increased their activities. This also affected the South; nearly every Southern state had a state bank at one time or another.

Property banks were unique in the South. Established by the states in order to attract foreign capital for agriculture and internal developments, property banks could issue notes and many of them—like the state banks—overissued them. Louisiana led in establishing property banks, but soon other Southern states followed. Even Arkansas permitted one property bank, and the only bank in the State of Texas was a property bank, the Commercial and Agriculture Bank of Galveston.

When Texas entered the Union in 1845 it outlawed banks, but some private firms circulated notes. In all of the other Southern states the state banks began to overprint their currency and to speculate on land and cotton. The prolonged depression of cotton prices had by 1841 forced loan

1

foreclosures and caused the crash of many state banking houses. Nearly all property and state banks in the South failed, except in Virginia and Louisiana, but they began to rebuild in the 1850s. When the states again chartered property and state banks in the 1850s, they were under stricter state control. Only Arkansas lacked a state or property bank in 1861 when Southerners formed the Confederate States of America at Montgomery, Alabama.

Most Southerners had little contact with money. Farmers in the interior established their own "factorage system" comparable to the planters. But for them the factor was the local merchant, who extended them credit on their crop, sold them their necessities, and traveled to the North for merchandise — often using his own credit to purchase goods. This system made the South virtually a colony of the North — unacceptable to an independent nation.

When the Confederate government began operations in February 1861, the monetary and economic system of the seceded states was already in extreme disorder. Some banks suspended the redemption of their notes for specie, and the little specie in circulation quickly began to disappear. Only in the cities of New Orleans, Louisiana, and Mobile, Alabama, was there a quantity of specie. In place of coinage, bank notes — in volume nearly equal to the amount of gold and silver held by banks and private individuals in the South — were allowed to circulate. Even though bank notes circulated throughout the Confederacy, the banks issuing them were few in number and were located only in the most developed areas. Arkansas, without such banks within its boundaries, began issuing state treasury warrants almost immediately. South Carolina, with its great commercial center at Charleston, never issued a state note until after the Confederacy collapsed in April 1865. Many banks in the Confederacy were authorized to issue additional bank notes at the beginning of the conflict and continued normal operations during the war. Although the banks experienced mild inflation, the situation was less severe than the crisis of the central government.[1]

Notes issued by the Confederate States were referred to as either state treasury notes or state treasury warrants, which differed in the way funds were drawn from state treasuries. When the state paid its debts, the auditor first verified the amount and then issued a warrant directing treasury payment. If there were insufficient funds in the treasury, the treasurer issued a warrant to the bearer, payable at a future date with interest. Arkansas, Texas, and the Choctaw Nation continued the practice of issuing treasury warrants. The other states and the Cherokee Nation issued treasury notes funded largely in stocks and bonds as well as specie and Confederate treasury notes. They usually paid interest during the early war years, but the war crisis forced an end to this practice.

Confusion clouded the Confederate monetary situation at the beginning; order had to be found. Coins of all descriptions were hoarded, and the small amount of bullion owned by the Confederacy went for supplies from foreign countries. Lacking any great quantity of bullion, the Confederacy's attempt at coinage seemed impractical. In fact, only four coins were ever struck within the Confederacy. Some bullion came to the authorities from mints at New Orleans, Louisiana; Charlotte, North Carolina; and Dahlonega, Georgia, but far less than needed.

The mints were soon closed and their materials diverted to war needs: copper was converted to musket percussion caps; other materials were also given to the states. All mints were eventually converted into assay offices, with only the Dahlonega mint remaining open during most of the war. The quantity of precious metals that passed through Dahlonega was never very great, with the largest shipment coming from New Orleans in the third quarter of 1862 in a probable attempt to avoid Union capture.[2]

The only other form of metallic currency in circulation was copper-based, privately issued tokens, appearing in limited distribution in Alabama, South Carolina, and Virginia. But the tokens passed quickly from the scene. The Confederate Congress discussed token coinage, but legislation was never enacted by both chambers.

With the beginning of the war, Southerners viewed paper as the only logical solution to Confederate monetary problems. Produced quickly and inexpensively, paper currency's final day of reckoning could be delayed until after the war. In April 1861, Secretary of the Treasury Christopher G. Memminger committed the Confederate government to a policy of paper currency, as one way to save bullion from local use and to allow it to be employed elsewhere.[3]

Memminger was born in Nayhingen, Württemberg, presently a part of West Germany, on January 9, 1803. He was orphaned in Charleston, South Carolina, where his mother had moved in 1807 following the death of his father. After several years in an orphanage, he was raised in the home of Thomas Bennett, who later was elected governor of South Carolina. Educated as a lawyer, Memminger served in the South Carolina House of Representatives. In 1832, as chairman of the Ways and Means Committee, he waged a long campaign to disassociate the state from banks and to force the banks to maintain specie payment. Memminger's legislative service won him a considerable reputation as a sound financier. He lived until well after the war and died in Charleston, South Carolina, on March 7, 1888.[4]

Because the Confederate government needed time to print the required bills, Memminger felt bank notes could be used in the interim. These notes were quickly loaned by the state banks in return for Confederate stock, which was interest-bearing paper, without coupons, usually purchased by banks. The notes were then sent either to the Confederate Treasury or kept for Memminger in a special account in the banks. Delays in printing the notes produced an acute situation, and Memminger asked the Confederate Provisional Congress—a unicameral legislature that served until the permanent government was inaugurated in February 1862—to grant him authority to print a government guarantee of payment on any bank note. Yet the Provisional Congress never acted. After Confederate bills were finally produced in sufficient quantities, they were the standard of value as well as the usual medium of exchange. The banks even kept a quantity in their vaults to back their own issuances of currency and circulated them beyond state boundaries.

Confederate notes suffered from never being accorded legal-tender status, because they did not have to be accepted for private transactions and could not be tendered for every debt (export duties were specifically exempted on the notes themselves). Several attempts in Congress to correct the flaw were unsuccessful. Early in the war, Memminger was particularly opposed to this effort, believing there was no need to force acceptance of Confederate notes since most people were already using them voluntarily. However, later in the war, large numbers of people refused to accept the notes.

Further complicating the delicate monetary situation, the states began issuing their own notes. Only South Carolina and Kentucky declined to issue notes. South Carolina already had a large number of state bank notes with an established reputation for stability, and money from its commercial centers. Kentucky, a border state, never had a permanent state government within the Confederacy. Generally, state notes had only local acceptance and were not circulated beyond the state.[5]

State issuances were printed for two reasons: to help finance state military activities, and to relieve the confusion caused by private issuances of scrip in lieu of small change, known collectively as "shinplasters." But regional reaction divided the later monetary situation. Throughout the war, the Eastern states relied solely on paper money and by the end of the war began exchanging it for commodities against its potential value on the open market. There was even a little direct selling of cotton and tobacco commodities to United States authorities, but in no great quantity.

The Trans-Mississippi Confederate states pursued a different policy. With a foreign outlet available through Mexico, the western states began to export their products, later using the pounds sterling which they received to buy imported supplies. Instead of only distributing money to their destitute citizens, these states began to give them commodities as well. In the end, therefore, they were relying less on paper than were the other states.

Some of the smaller issuances of notes came from Florida, the Cherokee and the Choctaw Nations. In addition, the treasury warrant issuances of Texas and Arkansas were relatively orderly. Two of the worst offenders were North Carolina and Georgia, where the governors tried to keep more control over military and political affairs that affected their states.

The Confederacy also faced an early monetary problem when small change quickly disappeared and governmental expenses rose rapidly. The acute shortage of change was one of the major sources of complaint; a variety of remedies were attempted.

In late 1860, the banks of the South began stopping payment in specie for their notes. Not all of the banks followed this early lead. The banks of Mobile, Alabama, did not suspend specie payment until August 1861; only after September 1861 did New Orleans banks follow suit. Thereafter the gold and silver remained hidden in private hands or in bank vaults; slowly reappearing shortly before the end of the conflict. Coins, however, were sold at auction throughout the war. Brokers dealt in gold coins, but they were not circulated for a long time. In fact, much of the bullion held by the central government eventually found its way abroad.

A number of substitutes were offered to alleviate the chronic small change shortage. Copper tokens saw some use, but these did not remain in circulation long and were confined mostly to large commercial areas. Soon even the copper tokens were hoarded. In New Orleans, five cent omnibus tickets were used instead of coins. Eventually postage stamps issued by both the Confederate States and Washington — together with privately issued shinplasters, pieces of paper issued by individuals with little backing — gained widespread circulation. Shinplasters circulated from one area to another, but they usually remained near the area of issue. Eventually the states outlawed these private issuances, instead printing their own change notes. In 1863, the Confederate States issued a fifty cent note and paper soon replaced the coins in chronically short supply in all of the Confederate states.[6]

Paper poured forth from many govermental sources, yet failed to serve fully the early needs of the Confederate economy. Prior to the war, the lowest denomination bank note was generally five dollars, for the United States had not issued legal tender paper money. Gold, silver, and copper coins were used for transactions below the sum of five dollars. But the disappearance of these coins limited payment for small transactions and change-making. The earliest Confederate Treasury note issuances — none below the sum of five dollars were authorized until 1862 — failed to correct the inconveniences. Instead of small denominations, the central government concentrated on issuing the same values as banks before the war. Many states quickly empowered their banks to issue notes between the values of one dollar and five dollars. Still many complained because of the lack of small bills. By the time that the Confederate government moved to remedy this situation, the states also had begun to issue notes in these denominations.

It was soon obvious that the Confederacy would use paper as its domestic currency. Inexpensive and fairly easy to produce, paper fit in with the crisis, and its delayed redemption date postponed demands on specie until after the war. If people wished to redeem paper money before the end of the war, bonds were the only thing that most states and the central government offered in exchange. Essentially paper issuances were supported solely by faith in the government and the people's belief that the Confederacy must eventually triumph. While Confederate armies were victorious early in the war, the value of the bills remained close to that of gold. However, after several major defeats, the loss of morale and overprinting of the currency caused the notes to become virtually worthless.[7]

When inflation gripped the beleaguered Confederate States and the notes quickly began to decline in value, the central government sought ways to stabilize the currency. Far more paper was being printed than could ever be absorbed by the Confederate economy, motivating planners to try to reduce the surplus without harming the economy. Taxes were considered, but Congress was reluctant to enact such measures.

A law enacted in 1864 required retirement of old Confederate notes and circulation of new notes. The old issues were converted into bonds at full face value until April 1, 1864, for those states east of the Mississippi River, or until July 1, 1864, for western states and the Indian nations. After 1864, the old notes could be exchanged for the new issue only at a rate of three dollars of the old bills for two dollars of the new. The measure provided some aid and the prices of many items in some areas briefly declined, but no permanent relief resulted. The new law passed Congress in early 1864, but no major battlefield victories occurred to reinforce it after passage. The public seemed confused about the workings of the law and hesitant to give up the old notes; instead they continued to use them, working out a rate of exchange for each transaction.

The new issue of notes with its accompanying exchange rate of three for two alienated a segment of the population. The Indian nations loyal to the Confederacy feared that in such an exchange they were being required to pay at least in part for the cost of the war, although the treaties which they had negotiated with the Confederate States government stated that they were to assume none of the costs. Some Southerners saw the new issue as a default by the Confederate States on a part of its debt; they questioned whether the CSA would honor the rest of its debt. Values continued to decline and prices in Confederate notes soared, especially after the Confederacy allowed circulation of old and new paper money issues together instead of forcing the planned retirement of the old issues.

The depreciation of paper money throughout the Confederacy caused hardship for many. Gold, jewelry, and silverware were sold in an attempt to survive. Gold coins were continually purchased throughout the war by the public and the governments. In Richmond, gold was peddled in the black market, with some people purchasing gold coins as a hedge against inflation. Even the Confederate government stepped into the gold market towards the end of the war in a vain attempt to bolster the value of its notes.[8]

In order to slow inflation, security was needed for the people of the Confederacy. In the East, the only alternatives were trading with the United States or running the blockade. A number of patriots viewed Yankee trading as unthinkable, and blockade-running was so expensive that only the government of North Carolina organized a state blockade-running trade. But the Trans-Mississippi River area offered another alternative for both the state government and the private citizen, for its residents had easy access to foreign trade by way of Texas and Mexico. This route was continually employed by the state governments, private individuals, and Confederate authorities. Trade became so widespread that officials of the central government limited the number of bales of cotton that the Choctaw Nation could export. Among its last acts, the Confederate Congress authorized payment to the various Indian nations for their annuities in cotton at specie value instead of Confederate bills. In this way, the Trans-Mississippi River area moved toward commodities and specie and away from paper money as its medium of exchange.

Beset with inflation and inconsistent policies, the Confederate monetary system suffered from currency which was not tied to anything of intrinsic value and was fundable only in bonds of the Confederate States. Although bullion was in short supply during the war, there were other items with which the currency could have been backed, especially cotton. Cotton provided good results in the Trans-Mississippi River area towards the end of the war and the South's major crop could have been utilized by the government long before the Confederacy's demise became imminent. Yet the government needed to export cotton to foreign markets. Mexico provided access to foreign trade until the capture of the Mississippi River in 1863 cut off much of the Confederacy from its Mexican connection. Blockade-running became the only other answer, but Union gunboats continued to close Southern ports as the war intensified. Perhaps blockade-running would have been viable earlier in the war, but in its early expectations the Confederacy was committed to a policy of withholding cotton from Europe in hopes of forcing intervention by England and France.

Another major flaw in the Confederacy's monetary policy was the lack of legal tender status for its notes. Not only did the United States have more commercial activities which absorbed greater amounts of its paper issuances, but it gave its notes legal tender status which forced their acceptance by the public for all debts. The Confederacy, however, depended on the patriotic zeal of its people and the necessity of the war to force acceptance rather than legislative action. This worked well during the early years of the war when morale was high, but the zeal eroded into economic chaos as Union forces encircled the withering Confederacy.

Confederate shinplasters added to the chaos, but the cental government took no action to regulate them. Suggestions for copper token coinage to relieve this plague fell on a disinterested Southern Congress. The states were left to act, but their issuances to replace the shinplasters were not regulated by a central policy. The central government and the various state governments appeared more interested in meeting their immediate expenses than planning for the future. Planning was not coordinated, applying to the immediate emergency only. The Confederate notes may have become the standard within the states, but they never supplanted state issuances. The central government, therefore, failed to meet the circulating medium needs of the country.

With the exception of bank notes, paper money depended upon faith in the Confederacy's future, and little thought was given to meeting distant and uncertain obligations. Future authorities, it appeared, could take care of this problem. Bank notes declined very little in value compared to other bills, because they were the most regulated of all the paper money.[9]

The Confederacy made use of money unsecured with anything of intrinsic value. Unbacked paper currency can be used successfully for a time, but will not last indefinitely. Eventually events undermined the public's trust in its government, and money declined in value, further increasing public mistrust. Confederate currency appeared sound as long as the people believed in their government. When faith was shaken, the value of the money declined; neither could be sustained. Had the war been of short duration, with either a negotiated peace or Southern victory, the Confederacy's monetary policy might have succeeded. Yet fate dealt cruelly with the Confederate experience, despite its military stamina and will against the inevitable Federal triumph. And paper money, printed in large amounts to meet increasing economic obligations, fed the rampaging inflation. Backed only by the people's faith in the Southern cause, the Confederate monetary system was soon as penniless and threadbare as many of the Southern soldiers who saw their dream of an independent nation vanish in the chaos of Confederate mismanagement.

The Confederacy's effort to establish a satisfactory monetary system is a story of mistaken judgment, poor management, declining morale, confusion, and failure.

[1]Edward A. Pollard, *The Lost Cause: A New Southern History of the War of the Confederates* (New York, 1867), p. 421; Grover C. Criswell, Jr., *Criswell's Currency Series: Confederate and Southern States Currency* ([Iola, Wisconsin], 1964), pp. 105-286.

[2]Quarterly reports of Lewis W. Quillian to the Secretary of the Treasury, Confederate Secretary of the Treasury (CST), Letters Received, 1861-1865, NARG 365, Washington, D. C.

[3]Christopher G. Memminger to William A. Elmore, April 13, 1861, CST, Letters Sent, April 3, 1861-June 25, 1861, NARG 365.

[4]Richard C. Todd, *Confederate Finance* (Athens, 1954), p. 201, note.

[5]George W. Johnson to Wife, Bowling Green, Kentucky, February 15, 1862, George W. Johnson, "Letters of George W. Johnson," *Register of the Kentucky State Historical Society* (October 1942); 40(133):347.

[6]Clara Solomon, "Diary of a New Orleans Girl, 1861-1862," Louisiana Room, Louisiana State University Library, Baton Rouge, Louisiana, p. 125; F. A. Nast, "History of Confederate Stamps," p. 78; George E. White to Andy Nave, April 13, 1862, Nave Papers, Cherokee Room, Northeastern Oklahoma State University Library, Tahlequah, Oklahoma.

[7]Pollard, *The Lost Cause*, pp. 425-28.

[8]Mary Boykin Chesnut, *A Diary from Dixie* (Boston, 1949), p. 403; Pollard, *The Lost Cause*, p. 425; John B. Jones, *A Rebel War Clerk's Diary at the Confederate States Capital*, 2 vols. (Philadelphia, 1866), 2:393-94.

[9]John C. Schwab, *The Confederate States of America, 1861-1865: A Financial and Industrial History of the South during the Civil War* (New York, 1901), p. 133.

TABLE 1

CONFEDERATE STOCKS AND BONDS*

To avoid confusion stocks of the Confederate States of America are described in this work as non-coupon interest-bearing bonds. On the surface, this definition is correct, but the differences between Confederate stocks and bonds go beyond this. Depending on the individual's investment strategy and reasons for investing, he could have elected to purchase either stocks or bonds. Each had advantages and disadvantages.

The stocks of the Confederate States were a registered security of the central government. The certificates themselves bore the name of the purchaser and, like the stock certificates of modern corporations, had to be endorsed on the back in order to be transferred from one person to another. In addition, the interest on the stocks was paid to some central point in each state and the amount due each person was forwarded by check. Any bond could be converted to stock upon application by the holder.

But the bonds differed from this. They were bearer bonds sold unregistered to purchasers and in that way were more readily transferable and less secure. Interest was paid only upon presentation of the attached coupons, thus requiring the person to travel to some central point in his state. Since coupons did not carry the bearer's name, they could pass as easily as money until someone finally exchanged them.

Stocks were registered, thus more secure, and the interest was paid to the holder by the issuance of a check. While the bonds were less secure and more easily stolen, they did have the advantage of being readily transferable and were often used in making large purchases; the coupons could be used like money and the holder did not need to await the arrival of a check. For the most part, banks primarily purchased stocks, but some private parties also bought them. The general public usually invested in bonds.

*Grover C. Criswell, Jr., *Criswell's Currency Series: Confederate and Southern States Currency* ([Iola, Wisconsin], 1964), throughout; North Carolinian to Robert Tyler, May 28, 1862, COR, Letters Received, March 20, 1861-June 18, 1862, Confederate Museum, Richmond, Virginia; Matthews, *Statutes at Large*, pp. 191-92.

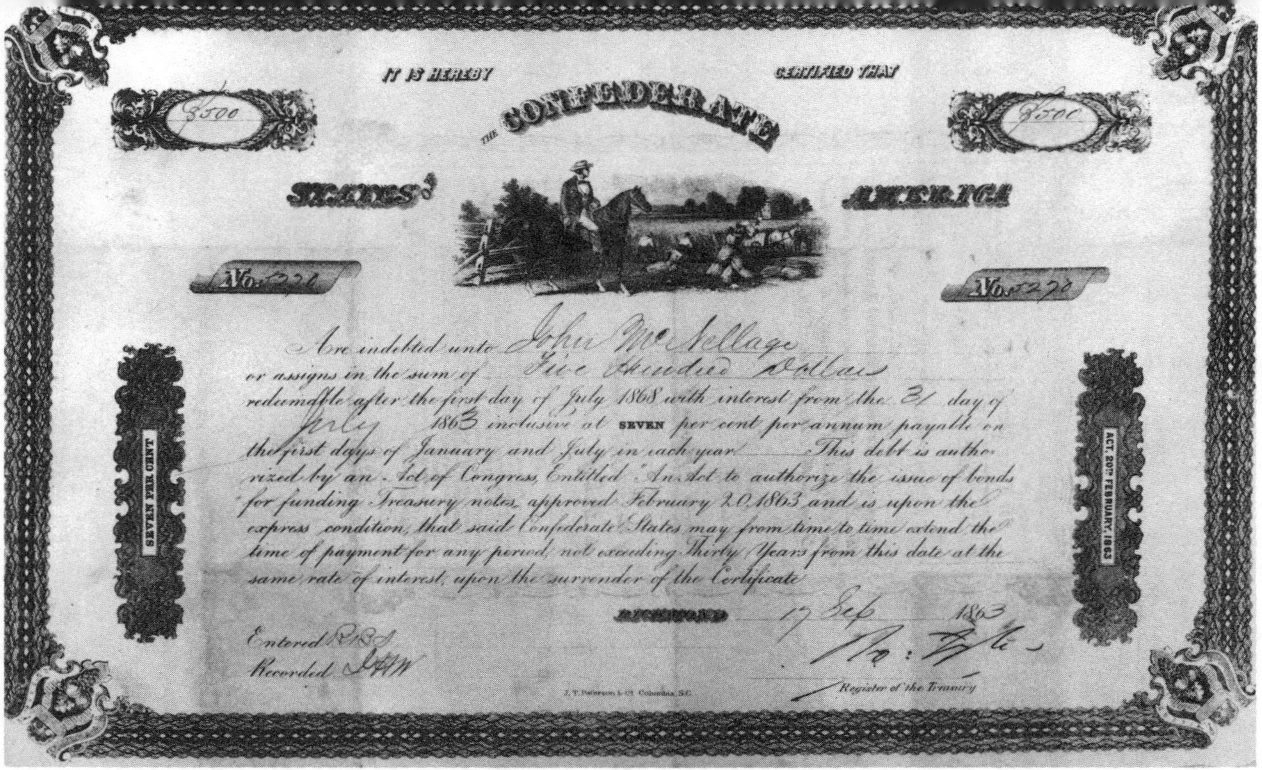

IT IS HEREBY CERTIFIED THAT

THE CONFEDERATE STATES OF AMERICA

$500 $500

No. 228 No. 228

Are indebted unto John McNellage or assigns in the sum of Five Hundred Dollars redeemable after the first day of July 1868 with interest from the 21 day of July 1863 inclusive at SEVEN per cent per annum payable on the first days of January and July in each year. This debt is authorized by an Act of Congress, Entitled "An Act to authorize the issue of bonds for funding Treasury notes, approved February 20, 1863 and is upon the express condition, that said Confederate States may from time to time extend the time of payment for any period, not exceeding Thirty Years from this date at the same rate of interest, upon the surrender of the Certificate

SEVEN PER CENT

ACT, 20TH FEBRUARY, 1863

RICHMOND 17 Sep 1863

Entered RBS

Recorded JHW

Register of the Treasury

J. T. Paterson & Co. Columbia, S.C.

$500 CONFEDERATE STOCK CERTIFICATE. An investor had a choice between stocks and bonds. The stock certificate, like its corporate counterpart on the reverse side, was registered to a particular owner. In order to transfer title, the owner had to fill out the form on the back side of the certificate. Since it bore interest, a stock certificate was little more than a registered bond, which replaced it in 1864.

Figure 1

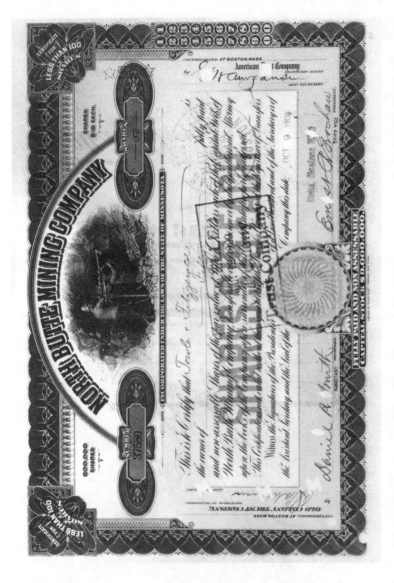

A CORPORATE CERTIFICATE. This certificate was the corporate counterpart of the Confederate stock certificate on the preceding page. Issued by the North Butte Mining Company, the certificate was for fifty shares valued at $15.00 per share.

FOUR PER CENT REGISTERED BOND. Registration stub on left side. This bond was unregistered.

Figure 3

FOUR PER CENT REGISTERED BOND. This bond was issued to R. H. Maury & Co. The registration stub (left side) was removed when the bond was issued.

Chapter II

COINAGE

Beginning the arduous task of organizing a government, the Confederacy faced the vital issue of money. Logically the monetary policy of the United States would be continued, but Southern pride in the new nation dictated a different system. Key questions centered on form and circulating medium. The Confederacy turned to coinage for answers.

Branch mints of the United States were located in New Orleans, Louisiana; Dahlonega, Georgia; and Charlotte, North Carolina. Almost as soon as the Confederate government was organized, Southern states seized and transferred the mints and other former Federal property to the new authorities. On March 7, 1861, Louisiana instructed its state depositor, Anthony J. Guirot, to transfer the bullion fund of the New Orleans mint and all customs receipts to the Confederate government. In reporting this action to the Provisional Congress of the Confederate States, member Duncan F. Kenner of Louisiana called upon all the other states to do likewise, especially if war came. On March 25, 1861, Louisiana authorized the transfer of all former United States government property within the state to the control of the central authorities. This was accomplished the next day.[1]

Prior to this time, William A. Elmore, the superintendent of the New Orleans mint, had opened negotiations with Secretary of the Treasury Memminger in expectation of the actual transfer. On March 6, 1861, Elmore asked Memminger if he should begin preparing for Confederate coinage before completion of the transfer. The same day, the Provisional Congress passed a resolution to keep the mints open and to prepare dies for a new coin. Elmore told Memminger on March 25, that dies could be ordered from private concerns at an average cost of one hundred dollars

11

and required three week's preparation time. Elmore cautioned, however, that there was no insurance against counterfeits if this method were employed.[2]

On April 1, 1861, Memminger asked Elmore for designs for a half-dollar coin, emphasizing his desire for a totally new design that would break with the past. Elmore soon found a qualified die-sinker to prepare the coinage dies, but he doubted if the man "would be willing to work in time."[3] It was April 22, 1861, before Elmore was able to provide designs for the new coin. On April 29, he submitted another design to Memminger, one produced by the New Orleans architectural firm of Gallier and Esterbrook. The obverse of this design resembled that used on the coins of the United States, but the reverse was a chain of fifteen links with the names of the states then a part of the Confederacy inscribed within some of the links. The remaining links could be filled in with the names of states that joined later.[4]

Finally, Memminger selected a design, and A. N. M. Peterson engraved the dies for the fifty cent coin. Only the reverse differed from the one-half dollar coin of the United States. Conrad Schmidt, the foreman of the coining room at the New Orleans mint, prepared the dies for the press and a total of four specimens were struck. Why they ever made the pieces, however, is unclear. On April 13, 1861, well before designs were even submitted, Memminger informed Elmore that war had begun and expressed the view that not "much coinage will be required while it is certain that the Government will need the Bullion." He ordered Elmore to reduce his expenses.[5]

Elmore may have commissioned the pieces on his own authority, but there are reasons to believe that this might not be the case. In accordance with Memminger's order of April 13, Elmore planned to suspend operations at the mint on April 30, 1861. But on April 19, he pointed out that "there are parties who wish some coining done" and that the facility could profitably remain open through May. Because of this, the mint was able to strike the four coins, but whether it was on Memminger's orders or not is uncertain. B. F. Taylor, the coiner of the Confederate States, later said that among the several designs submitted to Memminger, "the one approved" was the one for which specimens were prepared. Approval would imply that Memminger authorized the patterns.[6]

In addition to the fifty cent piece, a one-cent coin was commissioned. Robert Lovett, Jr., of Philadelphia, Pennsylvania, an employee of a local jewelry firm, Baily and Company, prepared the dies. Twelve specimens were struck but never delivered. Lovett later claimed that he feared arrest by Federal authorities, and he hid the dies until after the war. We have only Lovett's word to substantiate this story. The first of the coins did not surface until 1874, nine years after the close of the war.[7]

While early attempts at a coinage system proved unsuccessful, Confederate interest in coins did not end. On March 16, 1861, the Provisional Congress passed an act regulating the value of foreign coins, including those of the United States, that could pass as current money within the Confederacy. This act was amended on August 24, 1861, to raise the value of English gold sovereigns and French gold Napoleons by three cents, and Mexican and Spanish gold doubloons by seven cents. The value of these coins remained at this level throughout the war for official purposes, while the United States silver dollar was fixed at $1.02. An attempt to raise the value of various silver coins in the same act was defeated.[8]

In addition, there were attempts to establish the weight and fineness of the nonexistent Confederate coins. Memminger on August 7, 1861, said that "we should start with a new unit which would assimilate our coins to those of France and relieve some of the confusion which prevails on this subject."[9] On March 26, 1862, Representative William P. Miles of South Carolina introduced a resolution in the House of Representatives to investigate a coinage system, but the resolution never passed. Finally, on April 17, 1862, Senator George Davis of North Carolina introduced a bill in the Senate to provide coins for the Confederacy. This bill passed the Senate the same day, and was sent to the House of Representatives where it died in the Ways and Means Committee. The main objection to this bill was that it tied coinage standards to those of the United States. As early as April 10, 1862, one correspondent in North Carolina wrote to the *Daily Richmond Enquirer*, calling for Confederate coins to conform to European rather than United States weights and values. On April 18, 1862, the editor of the *Daily Richmond Examiner* complained about the Davis bill because he feared that coins of the same fineness and denominations as those of the North would mean that commercial intercourse with that nation would be reintroduced after the war. Senator Davis resubmitted his bill to the Senate in late August minus the section making the value of the coins equal to those of the United States, but it met the same fate as before in the Ways and Means Committee of the House.[10]

The year 1862 also saw the only active attempt by the Confederate Congress to alleviate the nuisance of shinplasters, pieces of paper issued by traders, merchants, railroads, and private parties in lieu of increasingly scarce small change. Senator Thomas J. Semmes of Louisiana introduced a bill on September 2, authorizing the Secretary of the Treasury to strike copper tokens in denominations of one, five, ten, and twenty-five cents to the total of $5,000,000. Passing the Senate on September 25, 1862, the bill then went to the House of Representatives where it was referred to the Ways and Means Committee, like the coinage bills before it. On October 13, 1862, Louisiana Representative Duncan F. Kenner of the Ways and Means committee, recommended that the Semmes bill lie upon the table—a suggestion quickly approved. No further attempt ever came before the Congress to establish a system of token coinage.[11]

Even though tokens were not reconsidered, the question of a standard for Confederate coins did not disappear. On January 22, 1863, Judah P. Benjamin, the Secretary of State, contacted Senator Clement C. Clay of Alabama, chairman of the Senate Committee on Commerce, proposing the issuance of a five-dollar gold coin, which he called a cavalier, of the exact value of the English gold sovereign. Benjamin argued that this would facilitate direct commerce with Europe rather than the United States. He also proposed ten and twenty dollar gold pieces called double and quadruple cavaliers respectively, in a system tied to European standards. Interest in Benjamin's proposal appeared strong enough to have forced its acceptance had the Confederacy survived the war. Benjamin may have been the last Confederate official to discuss the subject, although earlier a number of Confederate citizens were anxious to have their silver coined as a patriotic gesture.[12]

As it became apparent that coinage would play only a minor role in the Confederate States, leaders had to settle the question of what to do with the mints at New Orleans, Louisiana, Dahlonega, Georgia, and Charlotte, North Carolina. Eventually, all three were to suffer a similar fate.

On March 6, 1861, the Confederate Provisional Congress passed a resolution to keep the mints open and working. Only the New Orleans mint produced silver coins on any large scale before the transfer, but all of its dies were destroyed by United States officials before they fled. Both Louisiana and Georgia turned their mints over to the central government prior to the war, but North Carolina, which did not secede until May 20, 1861, did not transfer the Charlotte mint until June 27 of that year. On May 14, 1861, Congress voted to close the mints on June 1, 1861.[13]

The New Orleans mint had been the most active mint in the South before the war. On March 30, 1861, its total count of coins on hand amounted to $431,954.86. With the outbreak of war, Elmore set April 30, 1861, as the closing date, but an additional deposit of bullion enabled him to keep it open during May. On April 17, 1861, he begged Memminger to permit him to keep his staff together if there was a possibility of the Confederacy resuming minting at a later date. But on August 7, 1861, Memminger went on record as considering coins "a waste of means and money" because he thought most of the coins would be exported and remelted outside of the nation. Little possibility existed that minting operations would be resumed in the near future, and even if they did, Memminger wanted only the amount of coins needed for the Confederacy's internal commerce.[14]

While the New Orleans mint began to wind down operations, supplies were used for other purposes. In late April 1861, Governor Thomas O. Moore of Louisiana asked Memminger if he could use the mint's copper for percussion caps for his soldiers' guns, and on May 3 Memminger telegraphed such permission to both Moore and Elmore. On May 16, Memminger instructed Elmore to close his doors on June 1, in accordance with the act of the Provisional Congress. He also asked Elmore to dispose of all perishable items, retain his dwelling in order to look after the property, and dismiss all other workers. The mint closed on the appointed day, and all the gold and silver coins and bullion were transferred to Assistant Confederate Treasurer Anthony J. Guirot in New Orleans.[15]

John H. Gibbon, the Assayer of the Charlotte mint, proposed to North Carolina Governor John W. Ellis that the gold be used to make 1,000 five-dollar gold pieces, a state coin impressed with a design unique to the state. He also suggested bronze and copperproof specimens for libraries and colleges. Apparently, the governor never took the suggestion seriously, for there is no evidence that the matter was considered further.[16]

The central government was slow to assume control over the Charlotte mint. Although the ordinance of the North Carolina Secession Convention transferring the property was approved by the convention on June 27, 1861, no formal transfer of control had taken place as late as September 30, 1861. Green W. Caldwell, the superintendent of the mint, reported to Memminger but also continued to correspond with the governor. In the meantime, the employees received their pay from the coins on deposit, following instructions from Governor Ex-Officio Henry T. Clark. Former Governor Ellis had died shortly before. In July 1861, coins and bullion totaled $28,195.04. By the time of the actual transfer of the property on October 18, 1861, this amount had decreased to $26,229.61. The difference probably represents the salaries paid the employees from the fund.[17]

To further complicate matters, on August 24, 1861, the Provisional Congress voted to keep the mints at Charlotte and Dahlonega open as assay offices. On January 27, 1862, New Orleans was added to the list. But little assaying seems to have ever been done at Charlotte, and the mint's facilities were used for other functions. On October 18, 1861, the Charlotte office turned over its coins and bullion to Benjamin C. Pressley, the assistant treasurer of the Confederate States at Charleston, South Carolina, and by October 26, copper pipe was being sent to the mint for rolling into copper wire. In early 1862 the mint also manufactured percussion caps for the use of the Confederate States Army. Finally on May 27, 1862, assayer John H. Gibbon received instructions to turn over the buildings to the Navy Department and to store his equipment. Thus ended the operations of the Charlotte Assay Office.[18]

One other question, however, needed to be settled: who had the right to the mint's bullion fund? Governor Clark maintained it belonged to North Carolina; the funds were not mentioned in the act transferring the property to the central authorities. Clark so informed Memminger on December 20, 1861, asking for return of the bullion to the state. Memminger, replying on December 23, said it would take an act of Congress to release the funds, and that the bullion had already been exchanged for coin at Charleston banks. Clark then decided to accept the accomplished fact and assented to the transfer. But he made it clear to Memminger on January 18, 1862, that the state had not relinquished all claim to the funds. He asked that North Carolina be credited with the amount transferred, but he also seems to have had hopes of recovering the coins and bullion after the war.[19]

At Dahlonega, affairs continued in a fairly normal manner at first. Superintendent George Kellogg reported for the first quarter of 1861 that the total amount of precious metals on hand, coined in bars, totaled $27,526.46. On May 16, 1861, Memminger contacted Kellogg as well as Elmore in New Orleans, instructing them to close their mints, discharge all employees as of June 1, and ship all coins and bullion on hand to the assistant Confederate treasurers at Charleston or New Orleans. Memminger also asked Kellogg if he could find someone to take care of the Georgia property in exchange for the free rent of the superintendent's residence. Kellogg indicated on May 21 that he would comply with Memminger's wishes as best as he could, but he did not feel that he would be able to get the bullion and coins ready for shipment that quickly.[20]

But this was not to be the last precious metal to pass through Dahlonega during the war. The Georgia mint became the only Confederate Assay Office to remain active for any significant period of time. On June 10, 1861, Kellogg informed Memminger, in answer to his communication of

June 4, that an assay office could be run profitably at Dahlonega, but not if the gold was shipped elsewhere to be coined. He also noted that mint assayer Lewis W. Quillian, would assume this duty. The mention of coining was obviously an attempt to get Memminger to keep the entire facility open — something the Confederate Treasurer did not wish to do. Kellogg said the people desperately needed the mint for the gold being mined in the area.[21]

Memminger told Congressman Robert W. Barnwell, chairman of the Committee on Finances of the Provisional Congress, that an assay office could be made to pay only if the gold was cast into bars and the whole expense of the office was borne by the assayer. His suggestions became the guidelines for legislation establishing the assay operations. On September 25, 1861, Memminger asked President Jefferson Davis to appoint Quillian as assayer at Dahlonega; and on October 1, Memminger told Quillian that his position was confirmed.[22]

Working quickly and dutifully, Quillian assayed $8,235.09 in the first quarter of 1862. Reports continued through the first quarter of 1864, when he handled $1,040.76. The largest amount processed, $41,945.76 in bullion, came in the third quarter of 1862 when New Orleans and its mint fell to Federal troops.[23]

The idea of sending the precious metals to Dahlonega seems to have originated with Assistant Confederate Treasurer Guirot, who was by then at Jackson, Mississippi. On May 28, 1862, Memminger telegraphed Guirot to "send the bullion as you propose to dahlonega [sic.] . . . with orders to assay and cast into bars and hold subject to my order."[24] All in all, a total of $29,571.61 was sent by Guirot to Quillian, who assayed it and dispatched the final product, as bars, to Augusta, Georgia, in late September 1862. By the end of November, the gold was still there; later, it probably found its way overseas through the port downriver at Savannah.[25]

Although bullion from New Orleans may have been dispatched to Europe, coins from that city, especially the bank's coins, were not. On July 2, 1862, Guirot informed Elmore that he was transferring $20,000 in coin to an undisclosed destination. It is not clear whether these coins came from the New Orleans mint, the banks of New Orleans, or from other sources, but it shows that there was some activity there. If the coins came from the banks, they must have been transferred for safekeeping, because the Treasury Department's estimate of appropriations for the first half of 1864 included $559 "to defray Expenses incurred in the transportation and safe keeping of Coin belonging to the New Orleans Banks." Nothing was said about the coins from the New Orleans mint, which could have been dispatched anywhere, or used within the Confederacy prior to the fall of New Orleans.[26]

Quillian assayed a minimum amount of gold from sources other than the Confederate government. The mining of other types of ore provided one source of precious metals, and some gold mines continued to operate on a small scale. The central government dispatched most of the gold and silver that was refined. On August 23, 1862, Representative Hardy Strickland of Georgia presented a resolution to the House of Representatives, asking the Ways and Means Committee to explore the possibility of beginning coining and operating the Dahlonega mint once again. The resolution, however, never came up for a vote.[27]

So, Confederate coinage never developed momentum. Despite early interest in a coinage system, Memminger opposed it on a large-scale; preferring precious metals in bars. This was probably wise; coins would not have been circulated effectively due to the uncertainty of Confederate success and the hoarding of precious metals prevalent in wartime. While the government needed precious metals, the people held onto them as security against governmental collapse. What would have been done after the war is a matter of speculation, but it is reasonable to assume that had Memminger remained treasurer he would have continued upon the groundwork he had built.

The interest in coinage shown by Confederate lawmakers indicated the people favored and trusted the system used in the United States. Some favored United States standards for new coins, but most preferred European weights and values, such as those of England or France. It seems likely the European standards would have been adopted had the new nation won independence.

Memminger was the behind-the-scenes influence against coinage. Apparently, it was only through pressure by Elmore and the Provisional Congress that he even gave the slightest consideration to coins. Even the four coins that had been struck as patterns might not have been done on his orders. He quickly ended the idea of coinage when war came; he was openly hostile to coins in general, as though he felt specie had no place in commerce. After the war he might have been more supportive of a token coinage — definitely preventing coin export — than a precious metals system. He approved the assay offices grudgingly, perhaps feeling that by requiring the assayer to bear all costs would make it impossible to find any man to take this position. If this was the case, Quillian must have disappointed him. Memminger wanted to use bullion and coins abroad, and make very limited use of coins at home. In some way, he must have gained the support of the Ways and Means Committee of the House of Representatives, because this committee killed every coinage bill, including the one for tokens. Eventually the realities of the war halted the calls for a coinage system. By 1864, within a year of the close of the war, people seemed to have forgotten about coinage.

Coins were kept by the banks and to a lesser extent by the governments. After the mints closed, only Dahlonega played any significant role as an assay office; it sent the refined precious metals to other locations, likely including points abroad. The people and the central government of the Confederate States needed a circulating medium to be used internally while precious metals were exported and used for foreign purchases. Thus they turned to paper money, and with it opened the Pandora's box of symbolic worth.

¹*Proceedings of the Louisiana State Convention . . . together with the Ordinances passed* (New Orleans, 1861), p. 265; *Montgomery Daily Advertiser* (Alabama), March 12, 1861; *Proceedings of the Louisiana State Convention,* pp., 281, 929; William A. Elmore to Thomas O. Moore, March 26, 1861, Letters Received, Executive Department, State of Louisiana, 1860-1865, Louisiana State Archives, Baton Rouge, Louisiana.

²Elmore to Christopher G. Memminger, March 6, 1861, CST, Letters Received, 1861-1865; James M. Mathews, ed., *The Statutes at Large of the Provisional Government of the Confederate States of America* (Richmond, 1864), p. 93; Elmore to Memminger, March 25, 1861, CST, Letters Received, 1861-1865. Before a coin can be made or struck, master dies must be engraved from which working dies are later produced. Working dies are used to strike the actual coins.

³Memminger to Elmore, April 1, 1861, CST, Letters Sent, March 1, 1861-October 12, 1861, NARG 365; Elmore to Memminger, April 8, 1861, CST, Letters Received, 1861-1865.

⁴Elmore to Memminger, April 22, 29, 1861, ibid.

⁵B. F. Taylor to Marcus J. Wright, April 7, 1879, Gray Box, NARG 109; Memminger to Elmore, April 13, 1861, CST, Letters Sent, April 3, 1861-June 25, 1861.

⁶Elmore to Memminger, April 17, 19, 1861, CST, Letters Received, 1861-1865; Taylor to Wright, April 17, 1879, Gray Box, NARG 109. Patterns are struck specimens of proposed designs that are not fully adopted. They are made in order to show what the finished product would look like. Mintage figures on patterns are always very low. It is possible that the Confederate half dollars were not patterns but presentation pieces for key officials.

⁷Don Taxay, *Comprehensive Catalogue and Encyclopedia of United States Coins* (Omaha, 1971), p. 191.

[8]An act to repeal the Fourth Section of "An act to Regulate Foreign Coins in the Confederate States," Confederate States Congress (hereafter cited as CSC), Legislative Papers, February, 1862-March, 1865, NARG 109; Mathews, ed., *Statutes at Large*, pp. 62-63.

[9]Memminger to Robert W. Barnwell, August 7, 1861, CSC, Legislative Papers, February, 1861-March, 1865.

[10]U. S. Senate, 58th Cong., 2nd Sess., *Journal of the Congress of the Confederate States*, 7 vols. (Washington, 1905), 2:179; 5:145, 194, 265-67; *Daily Richmond Enquirer* (Virginia), April 22, 1862; *Daily Richmond Examiner* (Virginia), April 18, 1862; A bill to be entitled, "An act to make provision for coins for the Confederate States," CSC, Legislative Papers, February, 1862-March, 1865; *Confederate Congressional Journals*, 5:194.

[11]A bill to be entitled, "An act to provide for the coining of Copper Tokens," CSC, Legislative Papers, February, 1862-March, 1865; "Proceedings of First Confederate Congress," Southern Historical Society Papers (January 1928), 46(1):242; *Confederate Congressional Journals*, 5:442, 555.

[12]U. S. Department of the Navy, *Official Records of the Union and Confederate Navies in the War of the Rebellion*, 31 vols. (Washington, 1894-1922), Ser. II, 3:669; Jefferson Davis to Mrs. Sarah E. Cochrane, June 5, 1862, Dunbar Rowland, ed., *Jefferson Davis, Constitutionalist: His Letters, Papers, and Speeches*, 10 vols. (Jackson, 1923), 5:269.

[13]Mathews, ed., *Statutes at Large*, p. 93; U. S. Director of the Mint, Annual Report, October 27, 1862, in U. S. Senate, 37th Cong., 3rd Sess., *Executive Document No. 1*, "Report of the Secretary of the Treasury . . . for the Year ending June 30, 1862" (Washington, 1863), p. 45; "An Ordinance to cede to the Confederate States, the property . . . in North Carolina," CST, Letters Received, 1861-1865; Mathews, ed., *Statutes at Large*, p. 110.

[14]Elmore to Memminger, March 30, April 17, 19, 1861, CST, Letters Received, 1861-1865; Memminger to Barnwell, August 7, 1861, CSC, Legislative Papers, February, 1862-March, 1865.

[15]Memminger to Moore and Memminger to Elmore, May 3, 1861, CST, Telegrams Sent, February 23, 1861-July 30, 1864, NARG 365; Memminger to Elmore, May 16, 1861, CST, Letters Sent, March 1, 1861-October 12, 1861.

[16]John H. Gibbon to John W. Ellis, May 20, 1861, John W. Ellis Papers, 1859-1861, North Carolina State Archives, Raleigh, North Carolina.

[17]Henry T. Clark to Green W. Caldwell, September 30, 1861, Caldwell to Memminger, August 7, September 14, October 9, 1861, CST, Letters Received, 1861-1865.

[18]Mathews, ed., *Statutes at Large*, pp. 192, 253; Receipt, Benjamin C. Pressley, October 18, 1861, CST, Letters Received, 1861-1865; Clark to Caldwell, October 26, 1861, Henry T. Clark Letter Book, 1861-1862, North Carolina State Archives; Caldwell to Memminger, April 21, 1862, CST, Letters Received, 1861-1865; Memminger to Gibbon, May 28, 1862, CST, Letters Sent, April 3, 1861-August 2, 1864, NARG 109.

[19]Clark to Memminger, December 20, 1861, CST, Letters Received, 1861-1865; Memminger to Clark, December 23, 1861, Clark to Memminger, January 9, 1862, Henry T. Clark Letter Book, 1861-1862; Clark to Memminger, January 15, 1862, CST, Letters Received, 1861-1865.

[20]George Kellogg to Memminger, April 17, 1861, ibid.; Memminger to Kellogg, May 16, 1861, CST, Letters Sent, March 1, 1861-October 12, 1861; Kellogg to Memminger, May 21, 1861, CST, Letters Received, 1861-1865.

[21]Kellogg to Memminger, June 10, 1861, ibid.

[22]Memminger to Barnwell, August 7, 1861, CSC, Legislative Papers, February, 1862-March, 1865; Memminger to Davis, September 25, 1861, CST, Letters Received, 1861-1865; Memminger to Quillian, October 1, 1861, CST, Letters Sent, March 1, 1861-October 12, 1861.

[23]Quarterly Reports, Lewis W. Quillian, CST, Letters Received, 1861-1865.

[24]Telegram, Memminger to Guirot, May 25, 1862, Confederate Office of the Comptroller (hereafter cited as COC), Letters Received, April 15, 1861-January 10, 1862, Confederate Collection, Library of Congress, Washington, D. C.

[25]Quillian to Guirot, October 21, 1862, ibid.; Quillian to Memminger, September 25, October 1, November 22, 1862, CST, Letters Received, 1861-1865.

[26]Guirot to Edward C. Elmore, July 2, 1862, CST, Letters Received, February, 1861-December, 1862, NARG 109; "Estimates of Appropriations . . . January lst to June 30th . . . 1864," CST, Estimates of Appropriations, January, 1863-February, 1865, NARG 365.

[27]Smith Stansburg to Edward C. Elmore, June 25, 1862, CST, Letters Received, February, 1861-December, 1862.

TABLE 2

CONFEDERATE GOLD*

Early Specie Receipts

Transferred by Louisiana Convention	$ 536,787.72
Transferred from New Orleans Mint	457,559.48
Transferred from Charlotte Mint	26,299.61
Transferred from Dahlonega Mint	23,716.01
Total Received	**$1,044,292.82**

CASH ON HAND — DECEMBER 4, 1861

At New Orleans		
Gold Coin	$ 328,600.00	
Bullion	18,851.91	
Silver Coin	228,303.00	
Bullion	21,282.32	
Three Cent Pieces	6,795.00	
Total at New Orleans		$ 603,832.23
At Charleston		
Gold & Silver Coin	$ 59,917.72	
Bullion	42,648.12	
Total at Charleston		102,565.84
At Richmond		
In Gold	$ 16,461.00	
Silver	13,609.00	
Total at Richmond		30,070.00
Total Cash on Hand		**$ 736,468.07**

*Official reports of the mint officers, CST, Letters Received, 1861-1865, NARG 365; Confederate States Treasurer, Miscellaneous Office Records, June 5, 1861- March 8, 1865, ibid.

CONFEDERATE HALF DOLLAR, 1861. Obverse. Courtesy American Numismatic Society (No. 73-2462).

Figure 5

CONFEDERATE HALF DOLLAR, 1861. Reverse. The reverse of this coin was a new design by the young Confederacy. Only four specimens were struck. Courtesy American Numismatic Society (No. 73-2462).

Figure 6

CONFEDERATE ONE CENT, 1861. Obverse. The Confederate cent is steeped in mystery. The designer claimed after the war, that a contract for the one cent coin had been made with a Philadelphia jewelry firm. He had cut the dies and struck twelve specimens before he hid them. He did so for fear of what the United States authorities might do to him. No copy of this contract has ever surfaced. Courtesy Smithsonian Institution. (No. 66/82).

Figure 7

CONFEDERATE ONE CENT, 1861. Reverse. Courtesy Smithsonian Institution (No. 66/82).

Figure 8

CONFEDERATE CABINET OFFICERS. Secretary of the Treasury: Christopher G. Memminger (1861-64), George Trenholm (1864-65), and John H. Reagan (Acting Sec., 1865); also Post Master General (1861-65). Attorney General: Judah P. Benjamin (1861), also Sec. of War (1861-62); Thomas Bragg (1861-62); Thomas H. Watts (1862-64). Secretary of State: Robert Toombs (1861); Judah P. Benjamin (1862-65). From Varina Davis, *Jefferson Davis*.

Figure 9

CONFEDERATE TREASURY DEPARTMENT. 1. Alexander B. Clitherall, Register (1861). 2. Bolling Baker, Auditor (1861-65). 3. Edward C. Elmore, Treasurer (1861-65). 4. Treasury Dept. building. Courtesy of Richard C. Todd, *Confederate Finance.*

Figure 10

ROBERT TYLER. Register of the Treasury (1861-65). Robert Tyler was the son of John Tyler, tenth President of the United States. John Tyler, a peace advocate and president of the Peace Convention in February 1861, soon abandoned hope that the U. S. Congress would adopt the Peace Convention resolutions. Subsequently he was elected to the provisional Confederate Congress. He was then elected to the permanent Congress, but died before he could be seated. From Lyon S. Tyler, *The Letters and Times of the Tylers.*

Figure 11

Chapter III

TREASURY NOTES

On March 9, 1861, the Confederate Provisional Congress authorized the first issuance of Treasury notes: $1,000,000 printed in denominations of $50, $100, $500, and $1,000, with interest of one cent per day for each $100. The entire amount was to be retired at the end of one year. But because of their high face values, these bills were not intended to serve as the general circulating medium. At first bank notes and coinage served that purpose. Unfortunately, the war changed this. Congress soon passed laws which permitted a virtual flood of non-interest bearing paper and Treasury notes became the medium of exchange.[1]

Once paper money began to come from the printing presses, the people quickly accepted it. As early as October 15, 1861, Memminger declared that "treasury notes have become the currency of the country."[2] But certain difficulties had to be surmounted before the bills were released. The first issue of March 1861, ordered from New York before the outbreak of hostilities, had not been released by April 1, 1861. As war drew nearer, Memminger contacted the Bank of the Republic in New York City on April 11, asking that all impressions and plates for the Treasury notes be shipped. Apparently there was little demand for the $1,000 notes, because Memminger mentioned that he intended to order more $50's and $100's and to suppress the $1,000's. The printing of these notes, according to Memminger, would be resumed at New Orleans after delivery of the plates.[3]

With the rapid disappearance of specie, Memminger decided that the best way to alleviate the shortage was to issue Treasury notes for general circulation. An act quickly passed on May 16, 1861, authorized $20,000,000 in small denominations, with five dollars being the smallest,

23

as in the case of the bank bills. But it required time for these bills to be printed and, in the interim, Memminger decided to use bank notes to meet the existing emergency. In May 1861, he contacted the directors of several banks asking for a loan of their bills, not to exceed $300,000 from each bank. Memminger planned to secure the loans with the interest bearing $1,000 and $500 Treasury notes then available, followed eventually by the return of the bank paper or the small denomination Confederate Treasury notes. Memminger also planned to distribute the Confederate issue to the public in Pensacola, Florida; Charleston, South Carolina; and Richmond, Virginia, and contacted only the banks whose bills were circulating in those places at the time.[4]

The banks quickly responded to Memminger's call, and circulation occurred soon thereafter. Bank notes received for the first Confederate loan of April 1861, were even sent back to the banks, and made subject to Memminger's orders so that an open account might be established at the same banks. Except at Mobile and New Orleans Confederate paper currency was eventually received by most banks and paid out at par with gold before the end of July 1861. The amounts lent to the government by the banks were reportedly large and liberal, and as late as August 28, 1861, one bank still offered notes to the central authorities, in one and two dollar denominations, to a total of $60,000.[5]

At first the Confederate issue could not be produced fast enough. The government not only used bank bills continuously during 1861, but on August 23, 1861, Memminger, who was also a member of the Provisional Congress, introduced a bill into Congress to allow him, as Secretary of the Treasury, to endorse bank bills to make them an obligation of the central government. Confederate authorities would then be obliged to pay such notes and not the issuing bank, and they would be retired with Confederate currency. In essence, this would produce a national currency in a short amount of time. Congress placed the bill on the calendar but never acted upon it. A shortage of paper may have been one cause for the delay in distributing paper money.[6]

Memminger looked upon Confederate Treasury notes as a way for the government to meet its obligations at a minimum of expense. He turned down a proposal to have the government lend cotton planters money on their crops, stating that his department would then have no money to use and would not receive its notes back from the planters until the crops were sold. He proposed that planters go to the banks instead, and invest their excess crops in Confederate produce loan bonds. He told the planters that this situation existed only at the time, but in truth, it did not.[7]

Memminger felt that if his monetary plan was to work, all banks in the Confederacy must accept national bills as currency. Although most banks quickly suspended specie payment and received Treasury notes at par with coin, the Mobile and New Orleans banks did not fall into line so easily. Because of this, some merchants accepted notes at par only from these banks, and discounted notes from other banks. Some banks in Mobile discounted Confederate paper because it was not readily convertible into specie. Memminger then brought pressure to bear on these banks, and by August 1861, some of the Mobile banks served notice to their depositors that Confederate currency would be received for all debts made after September 10, 1861. Any creditor who had accepted debts before this time could choose the currency he would accept in payment.[8]

As early as June 15, 1861, Memminger had contacted J. D. Denegre of the Citizens Bank in New Orleans, asking him to accept Confederate notes as currency, but this did not help the situation. Therefore, on September 11, 1861, Memminger informed the directors and presidents of the banks in New Orleans as well as Louisiana's governor, Thomas O. Moore, that the value of the Treasury notes depended upon their acceptance as a circulating medium throughout the nation. Calling upon the bank officers' patriotism, Memminger urged them to suspend specie payment immediately and receive the notes of the central government as money. He stated that President Davis and the entire cabinet concurred in this request.[9]

Memminger asked Governor Moore for his cooperation in gaining the desired results, and urged him immediately to convene the necessary people and give them whatever assurances were needed. Louisiana laws prohibited the banks from suspending specie payments but Moore acted on his own initiative. On September 16, 1861, he issued a proclamation, which may have been necessary before the banks would act, asking them to cease specie redemption and to accept Confederate paper money. The banks then moved quickly, and specie disappeared rapidly because people hoarded it. One newspaper reported that a considerable number of large and small speculators engaged in this practice, but no doubt many others did too. Another newspaper feared that shinplasters would soon appear in daily commercial life and urged municipal authorities to issue change notes. By November 2, 1862, change proved virtually impossible to obtain and some even used five-cent omnibus tickets in lieu of specie.[10]

Banks were not the only ones troubled; some individuals refused to accept Confederate Treasury notes. While Mobile banks were still paying silver, Memminger notified Major J. D. Leadbetter, the paymaster at

Fort Morgan on Mobile Point, that if public creditors refused to accept either Treasury notes or the bank bills he had on hand, they could wait for payment until after the war. Previously Secretary of the Navy Stephen R. Mallory had pointed out to Memminger that merchants in Florida would not accept Confederate paper. Memminger retorted that if sutlers and storekeepers at Pensacola refused to accept the bills, then new suppliers should be found. Obviously, Memminger intended to use the power of necessity to force acceptance of the notes.[11]

But no matter how much pressure Memminger applied, he did not resort to Congressional action, the enactment of legislation conferring legal tender status on Treasury notes. The main support for legislation that would force acceptance of the bills for the settlement of all public and private debts came in 1862. Nevertheless, on July 26, 1861, Augustus H. Garland of Arkansas introduced a resolution in Congress calling for an investigation to make Confederate paper money legal tender. The Provisional Congress took no action at that time. On March 4, 1862, Senator Robert W. Johnson, also of Arkansas, introduced a bill in the Senate to make Treasury notes legal tender, but the Senate never voted on Johnson's bill. The House of Representatives considered a similar idea, and Memminger contacted Representative Lucius J. Gartrell, chairman of the House Judiciary Committee, outlining his views on the subject. Memminger stated that everybody now accepted Treasury notes. Even the courts made awards in that medium, so there was no need for a statute to force people to accept them. He also felt that creditors opposed the legislation because debts could then be settled with an inflated currency.[12]

Even with Memminger's opposition, supporters in Congress of legal tender status for the bills continued the debate. Apparently some felt that legal tender status would halt depreciation of the paper. Thus a bill to this effect introduced in the House of Representatives on August 18, 1862, was referred to the House Judiciary Committee, which recommended on September 20 that it should not pass. Consideration of the bill was postponed and it never came up for debate. On September 24, Senator Landon C. Haynes of Tennessee presented a petition from his constituents asking for legal tender status. The next day, the Senate Committee on Finance asked for further consideration of the petition, but further consideration was denied.[13]

While Congress flirted with the issue of legal tender, the country's citizens actively debated it. John B. Jones, a clerk in the War Department in Richmond, recorded in his diary on October 14, 1862, that because

Congress failed to pass the bill he felt "there will be a still greater depreciation."[14] Even General Robert E. Lee indicated he favored legal tender, but President Jefferson Davis echoed Memminger when he stated that the courts could not enforce payment in anything other than Treasury notes. So the notes were already substantially legal tender. Others also opposed the measure. One anonymous writer, using the pseudonym "Cato," argued that those who depended on a fixed income, such as widows, people who invested most of their capital in bonds, salaried people, and others were entitled to receive the best money possible. He also made it clear that while inexpensive legal tender money might appeal to a debtor, "a debtor to-day may be a creditor to-morrow." Apparently, Congress agreed with this opinion.[15]

In 1863, several state legislatures took up the debate on legal tender. On January 11, 1863, the Virginia legislature passed a resolution to investigate the legal tender status of Confederate notes and to prescribe the punishment for those who did not accept them. Even the Texas legislature introduced in November 1863, a resolution urging Congress to make the notes legal tender for debts. The editor of the Austin, Texas, newspaper the *Tri-Weekly State Gazette*, however, felt that if a similar law passed in Texas, the public would not sustain it. One correspondent in Alabama argued that legal tender would not help solve the problem of depreciation of the currency because it would not reduce the amount of paper in circulation, nor lower prices, and he urged a tax instead.[16]

Before the legal tender debate, a plan was developed to subordinate Confederate Treasury notes as a circulating medium. This was likely done in early 1861. Not only is a cut-off date of January 1, 1863, mentioned in the document, but it also speaks of Treasury notes as being about to be issued and recommends reliance on bank bills as the main currency. By 1862, Confederate paper money was called "the only medium of exchange," and had assumed this role by late 1861.[17]

The journals of the Confederate Provisional Congress show two possibilities for the introduction of a plan to subordinate Confederate Treasury notes as a circulating medium. On July 23, 1861, member John Perkins, Jr. of Louisiana, presented a memorial to the Provisional Congress "containing suggestions as to the financial resources of the Confederate States." At a later date, a communication from Mississippi presented to Congress was reported to contain statements about finances.[18] At the time cotton planters wanted to obtain loans on their crops from the government; the Mississippi communication may have involved this idea because planters dominated the state. Later, they obtained the desired loans from Mississippi authorities.

Apparently the plan suggested by Congressman Perkins was to provide "a Currency of known and certain value." The banks would pay into the Treasury, for some consideration, an amount of notes and collateral by using coupon and non-coupon bonds of the Confederacy. The non-coupon bonds were referred to as stocks at the time. The Treasury would then affix a statement to the bill indicating that it was backed by the deposit of the stocks and bonds, and so these notes could be used for Confederate governmental debts. This paper would then be receivable for debts due the central government. The arrangement would continue until January 1, 1863, or longer, if required. Face values of the bank notes were to be five, ten, and twenty dollars, "leaving the larger denominations of the general circulating medium to be furnished by the Treasury notes about to be issued."[19] The first issue of Treasury notes which appeared in April 1861, was of the values recommended but was not intended for general circulation. This requirement was deleted from the original plan, perhaps because both the higher and lower denominations were already contracted by the Confederate government. The plan might have worked for a time, but it was never enacted by Congress.[20]

Although the Confederacy was committed to a policy of paper money, the government continued the use of specie with the methods of procurement and the use to which it was put tied to paper money. Even Memminger, who was totally loyal to the power of the printing press, was not about to turn his back on coins.

On April 17, 1861, the first Confederate loan was offered to the general public. But prior to this date, Memminger had advised the banks that had already suspended specie payment that the value of their notes had declined against specie as well as the bills of those banks that still redeemed their paper. Memminger felt that this would create a hardship for those who used the depreciated bank notes, and asked the banks to redeem any of their bills for specie which could be received by the government in subscriptions to the loan. If Memminger's interest was to avoid problems for the public, it is curious that he declared only two months later that drafts drawn by the government were to be paid in current bank notes, and the banks "need pay no coin unless advised by me."[21]

The banks responded quickly to Memminger's request. The Commercial Bank of Columbia, South Carolina, the Commercial Bank of Alabama in Selma, the Central Bank of Alabama at Montgomery, and others agreed to redeem in coin their notes received for the loan, although some set a maximum to be exchanged. If the circular that Memminger sent gave his true thoughts, and the banks affirmed his request, why did he still tell government officials to receive notes at their specie conversion rate? Memminger told E. Stames, the chairman of the loan officials at Augusta, Georgia, that he was trying to get the banks there to redeem the notes, but it is not clear that he made this point known to the general public. The banks likely tried to disseminate this information, but it is also fairly obvious that Memminger seemed more interested in securing coin than he was in obtaining bank paper.[22]

But the loan was not the only source of specie for the Confederate government. In June 1861, Memminger instructed the customs collectors at Augusta, Georgia, that only coins or Treasury notes could be accepted in payment of customs duties. A generous amount of silver was received when Confederate authorities first assumed control of customs, but that source declined drastically soon afterwards. In 1861 alone, ninety-nine percent of the funds received were in Treasury notes and the remainder in silver. This ratio would continue for the remaining years of the war.[23]

Postal receipts provided another source of specie both from those turned over by former United States postmasters and those earned before Treasury notes began to predominate in commerce. Postmaster General John H. Reagan later maintained that fees "were paid in coin alone up to the date at which postage stamps were furnished [October 16, 1861]." Reagan continued: "Most of the post offices were not furnished with postage stamps . . . and they continued to receive and pay in specie until a long time after this."[24] Indeed, Reagan asserted that within the first few months of 1863 the postmaster at Savannah, Georgia, had deposited $3,000 in gold, and a total in excess of $68,000 was placed on account up to the middle of 1863. Although this amount was small when compared to governmental expenses, it was an additional source of specie.[25]

Taxes also brought in some gold and silver. On August 19, 1861, the Confederate Congress authorized a new issue of Treasury notes: a limit of $100,000,000 was placed on all issues of these bills, and a war tax was levied on all citizens in the country in order to redeem these notes. The tax was intended to be paid in Treasury notes, but some specie was apparently also received in payment. In August 1862, John Handy, the chief collector of the war tax for Mississippi, submitted to the assistant treasurer of the Confederate States, Andrew J. Guirot (then in Jackson, Mississippi, after the fall of New Orleans) the amount that he had collected, a total of $30,033.99, of which $64.05 was in gold and silver. Later on, other taxes were assessed. The Confederate Congress on February 17, 1864, levied a five percent tax on gold and silver coin, gold dust, or gold or silver bullion held by any citizen within the Confederacy or abroad. On March 4, Memminger ordered that coin was to be taxed in kind, but on July 29, Attorney General George Davis decided that because an amendatory act had been passed on June 14, the tax could be paid in Confederate Treasury notes *at their specie value*. This probably cut down on the total coinage received by the central government, but the tax must have brought in some specie.[26]

Undoubtedly the largest source of coin came from direct purchase, for notes or bonds, or the sale of commodities such as cotton, which had either been purchased for Confederate paper or received from the produce loan. Throughout the war, James D. B. DeBow, Produce Loan Agent for Mississippi and Louisiana, bought cotton with bonds and Treasury notes and sold the cotton for pounds sterling and gold, which was then used to make purchases in Mexico or overseas. Confederate money could not be used in payment of foreign contracts, and because of this the War and Navy Departments set up their own system. They used the paper within the Confederacy to purchase steamers and cotton, then shipped the commodities to depositors overseas to be sold and the funds kept in trust. The Post Office Department used some of the specie it received in payment of foreign contracts, but by 1863 Memminger insisted that even this department had to buy coin on the open market for Treasury notes.[27]

The local purchase of coin appears to have been the only other major source of specie for the needs of the government. In June 1862, a Virginia concern offered to sell gold and silver for a ten percent premium on gold and five percent on silver. In December of 1862 silver coin was purchased in Augusta, Georgia, for the Confederate depository. In calendar year 1862, a total of $162,087.99 was expended for the purchase of specie, and in the first half of 1863 the Treasury Department estimated it would need $4,000,000 for the purchase of hard money. This state of affairs continued throughout the rest of the war, and by its close in 1865 the need for hard money was so great that drastic measures had to be taken by the government.[28]

Without legal tender status, no statutory requirement obligated the people to accept Confederate bills for debts, and by 1865 many individuals declined to accept them. In order to combat this, various schemes were tried, especially by the new Secretary of the Treasury, George A. Trenholm.

Trenholm's policies, although slightly different from Memminger's, were essentially a continuation, for Memminger was Trenholm's early adviser. Trenholm was born in Charleston, South Carolina, on February 25, 1807. He was a leading merchant of that city and enjoyed almost unlimited credit at home and abroad. He joined the firm of John Fraser and Company and soon rose to the position of senior partner and, finally, owner. His firm engaged in blockade-running and even permitted the central government to use its vessels. Known as a staunch supporter of secession, he had a hand in shaping the fiscal policy of the Confederacy. When he entered the cabinet on June 18, 1864, he was hailed as the one man capable of bringing order to the situation. The Liverpool, England, branch of his company, Fraser, Trenholm, and Company, became the European financial agent of the Confederacy. He served as Confederate Secretary of the Treasury until forced to resign in 1865 due to ill health. He died in Charleston, South Carolina, on December 10, 1876.[29]

In 1865, Trenholm began to sell specie in an attempt to bolster the volume of the Treasury bills, and the Confederate Congress passed an act on March 13, 1865, to allow Trenholm to borrow specie from any source, up to a limit of $30,000,000, "to be applied to the redemption and reduction of the currency."[30] But the attempts proved fruitless, and the value of paper money continued downward. Four days later another bill, introduced by Representative Francis S. Lyon of Alabama, became law which attempted to raise coin in order to supply the army. Like the March 13, 1865, act, this law also provided for bonds for the $3,000,000 that was further authorized to be loaned. While this bill was being debated, Representative Charles M. Conrad of Louisiana attempted to have the coin in the New Orleans banks added to the coin to be lent, but this failed. The House of Representatives then decided that if the money was not lent, a special tax of twenty-five percent, payable in kind, would be levied to obtain it. Apparently this tax, due April 1, 1865, was fully anticipated because on March 24, 1865, Attorney General George Davis clarified an obscure section of the act for Trenholm. Such clarification would not have been needed so quickly, if it were not felt that the tax would be required.[31]

But what of the specie from the New Orleans banks? Confederate authorities had kept close watch over the specie since its removal prior to the fall of the city. As early as April 30, 1862, Memminger had telegraphed the Confederate Comptroller to determine what had happened to the coin. After that, the authorities of the central government kept a part if not all of the coin in trust. As noted, an attempt in early 1865 to transfer the coin to the Confederate government failed. A law passed on March 17, 1865, allowed the Secretary of the Treasury to accept specie from the states in return for Treasury notes at market rate. This time the coin from New Orleans was included in the specie to be transferred, a last desperate effort by a government whose faith in paper money had undoubtedly been shaken to the core.[32]

The Confederacy needed specie and used it in various ways, especially during the early part of the war. It was Memminger's intention to pay the interest on the bonds of the first loan in specie, as well as any bonds issued for the conversion of Treasury notes. He hoped to do this with funds received as export duty on cotton, the only duty for which Treasury notes could not be used. Apparently this was carried out, even though the expected revenue did not materialize, for in December 1861, Assistant Treasurer Guirot reported that he continued to pay the bond interest in specie, even though he had to draw it from the New Orleans banks. In January 1862, Memminger still advertised interest payments on certain bonds in specie, even though he was buying it at a fifty percent premium, and the bonds themselves were being sold for Treasury notes. John B. Jones commented on this action: "What sort of financiering is this?"[33] But specie payment on those bonds eventually ended, and the Treasury issued non-interest bearing paper in lieu of coin under authority of a law passed on February 11, 1864. This non-interest bearing paper was receivable for all debts due the government, including the export duty on cotton, and was, in essence, coin. The first issue of Treasury notes, which bore interest, was to expire in 1862, and the public asked if the notes were being redeemed that year in specie? The answer was no, because a total of $2,000,000 plus interest, twice the amount originally authorized, was eventually due and on December 14, 1861, the Confederates had only $736,468.07 in specie. Indeed, in January 1862, the customs collector at New Orleans had to borrow specie from the banks to settle a contract.[34]

Gold was also shipped abroad to satisfy various obligations. During the first year of the war, the success of the foreign loan did not require the shipment of quantities of coin overseas. But Guirot had been forced to draw on Richmond's supply in 1862 for $20,000, so gold was already in short supply. By June 1863, James Spence, the Confederate financial agent in Europe, advised shipment of the government's gold to England, and John B. Jones recorded that Memminger started sending weekly shipments of $75,000. In August of the same year Jones noted $20,000 being shipped on each steamer sailing from Wilmington, North Carolina. On July 19, 1863, Major Thomas L. Bayne of the Ordnance Department, reported that $10,000 in coin was to be sent to Bermuda; July 25 he affirmed that it had been shipped and the entire amount was in gold coin.

In 1864 some army commanders such as General Joseph E. Johnston received gold, which they probably used to buy supplies.[35]

The year 1862 witnessed other major monetary events. The first of these was the issuance of an interest bearing Treasury note not intended for general circulation. The government authorized a total of $165,000,000 in the act of April 17, 1862, all in $100 bills; but only issued $122,640,000. Some people hoped to use these bills like money and attempted to deposit them in their bank accounts. But the banks refused to accept them, and Memminger defended the banks' actions. He explained that these certificates were designed as investment media and that it was neither intended nor desired that the banks should accept them for deposit. Both interest and principal on this paper were not payable until six months after a treaty of peace between the United States and the Confederate States, but the Treasury had refused to exchange these bills for non-interest bearing notes. Some of those notes found today have endorsements on the back showing that interest was paid during the war, so some of the rules must have been relaxed. The bills could only be used to pay debts owed to the government, except export duties, or exchanged for coupon bonds after November 1864. By April 30, 1864, a total of $22,658,100 had been received by the central authorities.[36]

With the government obtaining all of the coin it could, and the public hoarding as much as possible, a scarcity of small change soon existed in business circles. They tried shinplasters, but these proved to be a nuisance. Even so shinplasters were used mostly for values below one dollar and did nothing to alleviate the shortage between one dollar and five dollars. In April 1862, the Confederate Congress moved into the void. On April 7, 1862, Congress accepted a bill to allow the printing of notes below the denomination of five dollars. When enacted into law on April 17, only one and two dollar bills were included, but the original wording would have provided for values of $1.50, $2.50, $3.00, and $3.50 as well as the $1.00 and $2.00 bills that survived. Not until March 23, 1863, was the first fifty cent note issuance authorized. Interestingly, only the fifty cent bill in the Confederate series was not signed by hand; the signatures were printed. On August 27, 1862, Robert W. Barnwell of South Carolina introduced into the Senate legislation to allow printed signatures for all Treasury notes, and it quickly passed. But the legislation died in the House of Representatives. Thus, all currency above the denomination of fifty cents continued to be signed by hand.[37]

In addition to the flood of paper money coming from the government, authorities had another monetary problem with which to contend.

Counterfeiting proved to be a great annoyance, compounded by the economic warfare practiced by some citizens of the United States. By August 1862, the problem had become so great that Senator Barnwell introduced a bill to allow the Secretary of the Treasury to appoint a person at all places where public moneys were kept, whose sole job would be to examine bills to determine if they were genuine. The legislation also provided for a stamp to be placed on issues known to be widely counterfeited. This bill passed the Senate, was amended in the House of Representatives, and finally tabled in the Senate, where it died. The means used to combat counterfeits were either to have the differences in the notes explained to bank tellers, or to send people to examine them. In the summary of appropriations, the total requested for travel expenses connected with this activity increased from $5,000 to $10,000 during the course of the Confederacy's lifetime.[38]

In addition to local Southern counterfeiting, it became a business in the United States. Samuel C. Upham, a Philadelphia printer, stated that from March 12, 1862, to August 1, 1863, he printed notes, public and private, with a total face value of $15,000,000, and in denominations from five cents to one hundred dollars. He also counterfeited Confederate postage stamps. Prior to Upham's efforts, a five dollar Confederate note appeared in the pages of a March 1862 issue of the *Philadelphia Daily Inquirer*, and a ten dollar bill was reproduced in the March 1862 issue of Frank Leslie's *Illustrated Newspaper*. Upham sold his products as souveniers for one cent each or fifty cents per hundred, without regard to face value, and many of these found their way into circulation in the Confederacy. The Confederate government was well acquainted with Upham's endeavors, and the Confederate Congress condemned him for them. President Davis reportedly offered a reward of $10,000 for him, DEAD OR ALIVE, and Congress passed an act making the importation of such bills into the Confederacy punishable by death. Some of the counterfeits circulating within the nation proved to be so good that the Treasury Note Division of the Confederate Treasury Department sometimes unknowingly redeemed them; in one such case over $200 was redeemed.[39]

In addition to counterfeit Treasury notes, theft and forgery undermined the credit of the Confederate government. As early as September 1861, sheets of the bills were stolen and falsely signed and then passed. On November 13, 1862, authorities arrested one of President Davis's Negro slave servants for stealing $5,000 in unsigned Treasury notes. On August 27, 1863, Memminger told Comptroller Lewis Cruger about forgeries of quartermaster's checks that had been paid, stating that the only recourse for recovery was to institute a lawsuit. Widespread counterfeiting in the United States and the Confederate States, plus theft and forgery helped to erode the government's credit base.[40]

Confederate printing presses worked hard, and by April 1864, a total of $1,097,942,963.50 in paper money had been placed in circulation, of which $851,582,125.25 was still outstanding by the last day of the month. But on April 1, a new currency law went into effect. Under the law all old issues of notes were to be redeemed for a new series at a rate of three dollars old for two dollars new. It was hoped thereby to reduce the volume of currency and increase its value. But at the end of the first month of full operation east of the Mississippi, only $246,360,838.25 had been redeemed, and some of this may have been redeemed before the law was passed. The law did not take effect until July 1 in the Trans-Mississippi Department. In addition, $48,076,000 of the new notes had been issued by April 30, 1864. Understandably, by March 1865, the government was forced to resort to specie.[41]

When Confederate Treasury notes appeared, the patriotic people accepted them as currency. Those individuals who did not receive them at first were easily sidestepped. Memminger succeeded so well that paper money became virtually legal tender, but because Congress never enacted a law to that effect, it became increasingly difficult to use paper money later in the war. At first, even the Secretary of the Treasury found the notes to be an inexpensive way to secure specie needed for overseas trade, but eventually this became more difficult as the war progressed.

The image of Memminger pervades the entire story of Confederate Treasury notes. The first to endorse making paper the circulating medium, he went on to push and pressure to get paper accepted as money, and to oversee the results. Memminger seemed obsessed with the example of Great Britain and used it when he advocated the idea of keeping gold in the form of bars. England had issued paper money through the Bank of England, and Memminger now wanted to imitate that novelty with the Confederate States issuing their own paper money. He was even openly hostile towards the idea of coinage, especially during the war, and seemed to be possessed by paper money. But the history of the Confederate Treasury notes shows what happens to most governments that issue paper currency, for they tend to overprint and the value declines. Even Memminger could not halt this, and eventually "paper specie" had to be issued in the form of non-interest bearing paper receivable even for export duties. But nothing replaced hard money in people's minds, and the central government finally used every means available to obtain the coveted item.

The monetary policy of the Confederacy was paper money backed solely by faith in the government. The Confederates used paper money to pay their internal debts. However, as the debt grew, paper currency swelled to a level that could not be absorbed by the economy, or could not be redeemed for many years, even with Confederate success and independence.

[1]Mathews, ed., *Statutes at Large*, pp. 54-55.

[2]Memminger to the Committee appointed to receive subscriptions to the produce loan, Richmond, Virginia, October 15, 1861, Davis Papers, Tulane University Library, New Orleans, Louisiana.

[3]Memminger to Edward C. Elmore, April 1, 1861; Memminger to C. B. Lamar, April 11, 1861, CST, Letters Sent, March 1, 1861-October 12, 1861.

[4]Memminger to George W. Williams, April 27, 1861; Memminger to William Knox, May 27, 1861, ibid.

[5]William C. Riees to W. B. Johnston, May 8, 1861; John Gill Shorter to Memminger, May 31, 1861, CST, Letters Received, 1861-1865; *Charleston Daily Courier* (South Carolina), August 27, 1861; Memminger to G. B. Lamar, August 28, 1861, CST, Letters Sent, March 1, 1861-October 12, 1861.

[6]*Confederate Congressional Journals*, 2:377; A bill to be entitled, "An act to provide a temporary substitute for engraved Treasury notes," CSC, Legislative Papers, February, 1862-March, 1865; Correspondence with Blanton Duncan, CST, Letters Received, 1861-1865.

[7]Memminger to Charles T. Lowndes, June 20, 1861, CST, Letters Sent, March 1, 1861-October 12, 1861.

[8]Memminger to L. W. O'Bannon, June 29, 1861, ibid.; Notice from Bank of Mobile and Southern Bank of Alabama, Confederate Office of the Register (hereafter cited as COR), Letters Received, March 20, 1861-June 18, 1861, Confederate Museum, Richmond, Virginia.

[9]Memminger to Denegre, June 15, 1861, CST, Letters Sent, March 1, 1861-October 12, 1861; Memminger to the Presidents and Directors of the Banks of the City of New Orleans, September 16, 1861, CST, Letters Sent, April 3, 1861-August 2, 1864.

[10]Memminger to Moore, September 11, 1861, ibid.; *Daily Picayune* (New Orleans), September 17, 1861; *New Orleans Bea* (Louisiana), September 17, 1861; *Daily Picayune*, afternoon issue, September 17, 1861; Solomon, "Diary," p. 125.

[11]Memminger to Leadbetter, June 29, 1861; Memminger to Mallory, June 21, 1861, CST, Letters Sent, March 1, 1861-October 12, 1861.

[12]*Confederate Congressional Journals*, 1:285; 2:31, 58, 62, 89; Henry D. Capers, *The Life and Times of C. G. Memminger* (Richmond, 1893), pp. 488-89.

[13]A bill to be entitled, "An act to make Treasury Notes a legal tender in the payment of debts," CSC, Legislative Papers, February, 1862-March, 1865; *Confederate Congressional Journals*, 2:325, 329.

[14]Jones, *Diary*, 1:170.

[15]Ibid., pp. 174, 176; Anonymous, *"Cato" on Constitutional "Money" and Legal Tender* (Charleston, 1862), pp. 34-35.

[16]Frank Moore, ed., *The Rebellion Record: A Diary of American Events*, 11 vols. (New York, 1861-1868), 6:33; *Tri-Weekly Gazette* (Austin, Texas), November 16, 1863; *Montgomery Daily Advertiser* (Alabama), December 5, 1863.

[17]Anonymous, *"Cato" on "Money,"* p. 35.

[18]*Confederate Congressional Journals*, 1:277, 367; Memminger to Charles T. Lowndes, June 20, 1861, CST, Letters Sent, March 1, 1861-October 12, 1861.

[19]A plan for a currency of known and certain value, CSC, Memorials and Petitions, 1861-1865, NARG 109.

[20]*Daily Picayune*, April 19, 1861.

[21]Memminger to the Presidents and Directors of the Banks which have suspended Specie Payment, March 26, 1861, CST, Regulations and Circulars of the Treasury Department, March, 1861-July, 1864, NARG 365; Memminger to Edward Frost, May 15, 1861, CST, Letters Sent, March 1, 1861-October 12, 1861.

[22]J. A. Churfort to Memminger, April 9, 1861; Thomas C. Daniel to Memminger, April 12, 1861, COR, Letters Received, March 20, 1861-June 18, 1862; Resolutions of the Central Bank of Alabama, CST, Miscellaneous Office Records, February, 1861-March, 1865; Memminger to C. Stames, April 10, 1861; Memminger to George P. Beime, April 21, 1861, CST, Letters Sent, March 1, 1861-October 12, 1861.

[23]Memminger to W. P. Carmichal, Conley, Froce, and Company, and others, June 24, 1861; Lloyd Bower to Memminger, June 4, 1861, CST, Letters Received, 1861-1865; Deposit Receipts, various dates, COC, Records of the Custom Service, August, 1847-March, 1865, NARG 365.

[24]Reply of Reagan to Memminger's July 25, 1863, letter to President Davis, Confederate Post Office Department (hereafter cited as CPOD), Letters Sent, March 7, 1861-October 12, 1863, Confederate Collection, Library of Congress.

[25]Ibid.; Reagan to Memminger, June 27, 1863, ibid.

[26]Mathews, ed., *Statutes at Large*, pp. 177-83; John Handy to A. J. Guirot, August 18, 1862, COC, Letters Received, April 15, 1861-January 10, 1862; Memminger to J. L. Orr, March 4, 1864, CST, Telegrams Sent, February 23, 1861-July 30, 1864; Rembert W. Patrick, ed., *The Opinions of the Confederate Attorneys General, 1861-1865* (Buffalo, 1950), pp. 473-75.

[27]James D. B. DeBow to the Secretary of the Treasury, various dates, CST, Letters Received from James D. B. DeBow, February 5, 1862-January 20, 1865, NARG 109; Judah P. Benjamin to Memminger, Seddon, and Mallory, September 15, 1863, *Official Records, Navy*, Ser. II, 3:897-99.

[28]Thomas Branch and Sons to E. C. Elmore, June 13, 1862, CST, Letters Receiv-

ed, February, 1861-December, 1862; M. G. Goodman to Memminger, December 23, 1862, Letters Received, 1861-1865; Estimates of Appropriations . . . February 1-June 30, 1863; January, 1863-February, 1865; Report of the First Auditor's Office, January, 1863, CST, Letters Received, 1861-1865.

[29]*Dictionary of American Biography*, 22 vols., and three supplements (New York, 1922-1973), Supplement I, pp. 689-90.

[30]Charles W. Ramsdell, ed., *Laws and Joint Resolutions of the Last Session of the Confederate Congress* (Durham, 1941), pp. 121-22.

[31]An act to raise coin for the purpose of furnishing necessary supplies to the Army, CSC, Legislative Papers, February, 1862-March, 1865; *Confederate Congressional Journals*, 7:764, 767; Patrick, ed., *Opinions of the Confederate Attorneys General*, pp. 579-80.

[32]Memminger to Lewis Cruger, April 30, 1862, COC, Letters Received, April 15, 1861-January 10, 1862; Ramsdell, ed., *Laws*, p. 150.

[33]*Daily Picayune*, April 11, 1861; A. J. Guirot to Robert Tyler, December 9, 1861, COR, Letters Received, March 20, 1861-June 18, 1862; Jones, *Diary*, 1:106.

[34]Grover C. Criswell, Jr., *Criswell's Currency Series: Confederate and Southern States Bonds* (St. Petersburg Beach, 1961), pp. 139-40; Thomas A. Adams to A. J. Guirot, May 9, 1862, COC, Letters Received, April 15, 1861-January 10, 1862; Memorandum of cash at New Orleans, Charleston, and Richmond, Treasurer's Office, December 14, 1861, CST, Miscellaneous Office Records, March 23, 1861-December 16, 1861, NARG 365; J. H. Hatite to Memminger, January 3, 1862, CST, Letters Received, February, 1861-December, 1862, NARG 109.

[35]Guirot to E. C. Elmore, June 17, 1862, COC, Letters Received, April 15, 1861-January 10, 1862; Jones, *Diary*, 1:351, 2:11; Thomas L. Bayne to Memminger, July 19, 25, 1863, CST, Letters Received, 1861-1865; Memminger to A. J. Guirot, March 22, 1864, CST, Telegrams Sent, February 23, 1861-July 30, 1864.

[36]Criswell, *Confederate and Southern States Currency*, pp. 35-37; Statement of the Amount of *Treasury Notes* issued . . . up to and including the *30th of April, 1864*, COR, Letters Sent, March 18, 1861-April 1, 1865, NARG 109; *Daily Richmond Examiner*, July 19, 1862, November 28, 1864.

[37]An act authorizing the issuance of Treasury notes under the denomination of five dollars, CSC, Legislative Papers, February, 1862-March, 1865; *Confederate Congressional Journals*, 2:242, 249; 5:347.

[38]A bill to be entitled "An act to increase the provisions for detecting Counterfeit Notes,' CSC, Legislative Papers, February, 1862-March, 1865; *Confederate Congressional Journals*, 2:245, 249, 401; J. G. M. Ramsey to Memminger, September 5, 1862, CST, Letters Received, 1861-1865; Estimates of Appropriations . . . July 1-December 31, 1863, and others through December 31, 1865, CST, Estimates of Appropriations, January, 1863-February, 1865.

[39]Samuel C. Upham, "Counterfeit Confederate Circulation," pp. 102-103; *Confederate Congressional Journals*, 2:476, 483; Memo to Mr. White from Ott, undated, Confederate Treasury Note Bureau, Miscellaneous Records, August, 1861-March, 1865, NARG 365.

[40]*Daily Picayune*, afternoon issue, September 7, 1861; Jones, *Diary*, 1:189; Memminger to Cruger, August 27, 1863, COC, Correspondence, 1861 and 1863, NARG 109.

[41]Statement of the amount of *Treasury Notes* issued . . . up to and including the *30th of April, 1864;* Statement showing amount of *Treasury Notes* issued under Act of *February 17th 1864*, up to and including the *30th of April 1864*, COR, Letters Sent, March 18, 1861-April 1, 1865.

CONFEDERATE TREASURY NOTES. The largest denomination issued for general circulation by the central government was the $500 note of 1864. The smallest note issued was for fifty cents.

Figure 12

CONFEDERATE TREASURY NOTE. This interest bearing $1000 note issued in Montgomery, Alabama, in 1861, was the largest denomination issued by the Confederacy. Most of these were taken by banks in exchange for their notes. Courtesy of the Smithsonian Institution (No. 83-7880).

Figure 13

INTEREST BEARING NOTES. Secretary of the Treasury Memminger stated that these 1862 interest bearing notes were not meant to be accepted by the banks for deposit. They were designed for investment and to discharge debts to the central government.

Figure 14

COUNTERFEIT CONFEDERATE NOTE. The Confederacy was plagued by counterfeit currency, much of which came from the United States. There is evidence that this note, which bore no resemblance to any genuine Confederate bill, actually circulated.

Figure 15

TABLE 3

TREASURY NOTES I*

AMOUNT OF TREASURY NOTES ISSUED UNDER ALL ACTS
(EXCEPT ACT OF FEBRUARY 17, 1864)
UP TO AND INCLUDING APRIL 30, 1864

Act of	Issued	Redeemed	Outst
March 9, 1861, Interest Bearing Notes — $3.65	$ 2,021,100.00	$ 1,495,150.00	$ 525,
May 15, 1861, 2 Years After Date	17,347,955.00	9,172,580.00	8,175,
August 19, 1861, General Currency	291,961,830.00	141,034,709.00	150,927,
April 17, 1862, Interest Bearing Notes — $7.30	122,640,000.00	22,658,100.00	99,981,
April 17, 1862, $1 & $2 Notes	5,600,000.00	1,102,382.00	4,497,
October 13, 1862, General Currency	138,056,000.00		
October 13, 1862, $1 & $2 Notes	2,344,800.00	26,159,960.50	114,240,
March 23, 1863, General Currency	514,032,000.00		
March 23, 1863, $1 & $2 Notes	3,023,520.00		
March 23, 1863, 50¢ Notes	915,758.50	44,737,956.75	473,233,
Total	$1,097,942,963.50	$246,360,838.25	$851,582,

*Official report of the Register's Office, April 30, 1864, COR, Letters Sent, March 18 1861-April 1, 1865, NARG 109.

40

TABLE 4

TREASURY NOTES II*

AMOUNT OF TREASURY NOTES ISSUED UNDER ACT OF FEBRUARY 17, 1864, UP TO AND INCLUDING APRIL 30, 1864

Denominations	Amount
Tens	$13,280,000
Twenties	1,936,000
Fifties	8,460,000
Hundreds	14,400,000
Five Hundreds	10,000,000
Total Amount Issued	$48,076,000

*Official report of the Register's Office, April 30, 1864, COR, Letters Sent, March 18, 1861-April 1, 1865, NARG 109.

TABLE 5

TREASURY NOTES III*

APPROXIMATE VALUE OF NOTES ISSUED UNDER ACT OF JANUARY 17, 1864

Denominations	Value
Fifty Cents	$ 523,606.50
Ones	598,400.00
Twos	1,644,784.00
Fives	27,626,784.00
Tens	91,359,200.00
Twenties	85,940,080.00
Fifties	83,572,200.00
Hundreds	89,664,400.00
Five Hundreds	75,214,000.00
Total	$456,142,990.50

Note: The Confederate registers near the end of the war are incomplete. This Table is only an approximation. The actual amounts issued may have been higher.

*Raphael P. Thian, *Register of the Confederate Debt* (Boston, 1972), p. 178.

41

Chapter IV

EASTERN STATES' PAPER MONEY

Military considerations made the Confederate government institute a policy of internal paper money to obtain specie to be used elsewhere. But the state governments also faced wartime emergency needs, and they coveted hard money as much as the central government. For the most part, the Eastern states of the Confederacy issued state treasury notes throughout the entire war. Most of these outpourings were fairly large in volume, but Georgia and North Carolina far exceeded the others in total amount. Florida, however, pursued a more orderly policy. Of the thirteen states considered by central authorities to be a part of the Confederacy, all except South Carolina and Kentucky issued some form of paper currency. The remaining states resorted to the printing press for money at one time or another. Each of the states apparently hoped to gain a wide circulation for its issuances, but for the most part they received only local use. In the end, state officials had to face the same problems as the authorities at Richmond, and the ways that they found to deal with them were very much the same.

Non-Issuing States

SOUTH CAROLINA

This state served as an island of restraint awash in a sea of paper money. At the beginning of the Confederacy's history, South Carolina elected to use the notes of its banks (which survived most of the war unscathed), as well as those of the central government. The banks not the government provided small change notes when specie disappeared. The funds used by the state during the war came from the sale of bonds and the collection of taxes. South Carolina, unlike many of her Eastern sister states, continued to receive tax revenue during the war.

KENTUCKY

The only other state that did not issue currency was Kentucky. The special situation there resulted from the fact that the state possessed only a provisional Confederate state government which fled the state shortly after being inaugurated. Thus, Kentucky required few state funds. The provisional governor, George W. Johnson, could have siezed the state funds on deposit at various banks throughout the state, but he chose not to do so. Instead, he availed himself of the millions of dollars placed at his disposal by the Confederate central government.[1]

Issuing States

ALABAMA

Long before war came to Alabama, the state government was concerned with monetary matters. A shortage of small change was evident as early as February 1860, because on February 8, the legislature authorized all of the banks conducting business within its borders to issue notes in denominations between one and five dollars. As hostilities came ever closer, Governor Andrew B. Moore began to worry all the more about specie. On December 4, 1860, he told the president and directors of the Central Bank of Alabama that the suspension of specie payment by the banks of the neighboring states of South Carolina and Georgia was imminent, and such an action would cause a run on Alabama's banks. In order to prevent this, and to keep all gold and silver in the vaults of banks in Alabama, Moore requested all banks within the state to suspend specie payment at the same time. But only three banks heeded Moore's urgings, even though he assured them that he felt confident the secession convention and legislature would sustain the action.[2]

In the beginning, Alabama seemed to be more interested in securing specie held by the banks than in issuing paper money. To this end, the secession convention authorized $1,000,000 worth of bonds, and on February 2, 1861, gave permission for the banks to suspend specie payment provided they purchased the bonds. On April 9, Governor Moore informed James J. Donegan, president of the Northern Bank of Alabama in

Huntsville, that he was sending him fifty bonds of five hundred dollars denomination. In the $25,000 due the state for these bonds, Moore wanted $10,000 in bank notes upon receipt and the rest in weekly shipments of specie in $5,000 units. As of January 1, 1861, the Bank of Selma had $70,926.10 in its specie fund and much of this probably went into the state treasury.[3]

Apparently Moore's efforts to secure coin proved fruitful. As early as January 1861, he dispatched $200,000 in coin to the Citizens Bank of Louisiana, which was to be used for state purchases. By March 1861, the bonds were nearly ready to be issued, and they were to be sold for specie or its equivalent; the notes of unsuspended banks were valued the same as specie. The banks responded well to the offerings and by October 18, 1861, the government's account at the Southern Bank of Alabama in Mobile totaled $90,316.38, of which $51,040.38 was in hard money. On March 31, 1862, the new Governor, John Gill Shorter even turned away a Richmond, Virginia, investor when he informed him that Alabama had "sold all the bonds I wish to dispose of for the present."[4]

On February 8, 1861, the first issuance of Alabama treasury notes was authorized. The state set a limit of $1,000,000 for these bills, which could be no greater in denomination than one hundred dollars and would bear six percent interest. They were to be receivable for all sums due to the state and could be reissued with the same interest requirement; however, there is no evidence that these bills were ever issued. The bonds were sold, but bank notes and specie were used. In August 1861, Governor Moore stated that only suspended bank paper remained in the treasury and offered to pay public debts with these or a bank draft. As late as February 1, 1862, Governor John G. Shorter, resisted a plan for the state to suspend the collection of all taxes and to issue treasury notes, redeemable by a future tax to meet its obligations.[5]

If Alabama hesitated to issue paper money, the merchants did not. Shinplasters began to appear quickly when the Northern Bank of Alabama, among the last of the banks to suspend specie payment, did so on September 18, 1861. Problems associated with these shinplasters continued to grow until the state was finally forced to act. On November 8, 1862, Alabama voted its first issue of $3,500,000 change bills, redeemable for Confederate Treasury notes. On November 11, Governor Shorter sent a man to J. F. Patterson and Company at Augusta, Georgia, to authorize that company to design these bills, but the first proofs were not sent until January 13, 1863, having been delayed by the engravers. The private shinplasters were declared illegal on December 9. 1862.[6]

ALABAMA

)NE DOLLAR BILL. Issued in 1863, this bill bears a portrait of Governor John
:. Shorter.

Figure 16

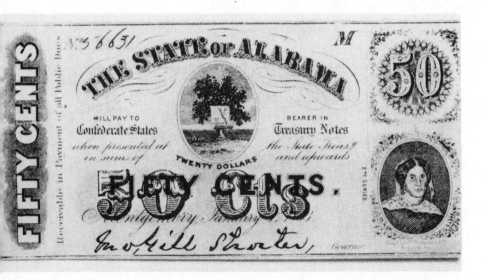

'IFTY CENTS BILL. Engraved by J. F. Patterson and Company of Augusta,
;eorgia, these bills were issued in 1863.

Figure 17

MISSISSIPPI

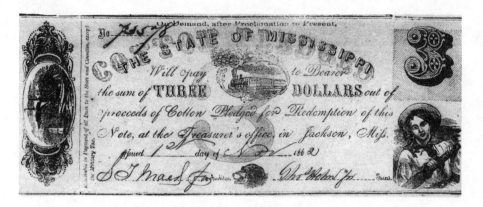

THREE DOLLAR BILL, 1862. Proceeds of cotton sales were pledged for its redemption.

Figure 18

FIFTY CENTS BILL, 1864.

Figure 19

Apparently, Alabama's resistance to state treasury notes was overcome, for on the same day that the state authorized the change bills, it also provided for an unlimited issue of six percent state bonds to meet deficiencies in the treasury. But this law provided that instead of bonds, only state treasury notes could be issued, redeemable in either state bonds or Confederate Treasury notes at the state's option. This time the state printed the treasury notes which it paid out the next year.

This opened the floodgates and paper money poured forth. In August 1863, a law provided for the support of destitute families of Alabama's soldiers, and if there were not sufficient funds in the treasury, the governor could use the December 1862 issue of notes. On December 13, 1864, the final step was taken. The state gave blanket authority to the treasurer to issue paper for any and all deficiencies. These notes, and all old issues except for the change bills, could be redeemed only with the new issue of Confederate Treasury notes. Nothing suggested that a bond could be obtained for state paper. The same act also empowered the governor to borrow up to $1,000,000 at no more than eight percent interest.[7]

Apparently, the only other problem faced by the state government of Alabama was that people did not want to accept Confederate bills at first. In order to combat this, a law passed on November 17, 1862, provided that if any creditor refused these notes in payment, he could collect only one-quarter of one percent interest per year on his debt. This might have made the paper more attractive to many persons.[8]

In summary, Alabama had the authority to issue paper money in 1861, but the bills authorized bore interest, and none seem to have been issued. Perhaps the reason for this was that until nearly mid-year, the seat of the Confederate government was also in the state; this changed after Virginia seceded, and the government moved the Confederate capital to Richmond. After authorizing a non-interest note in late 1862, there was no halt to the printing presses. The continual need for more bonds and loans suggests an unsound monetary policy.

MISSISSIPPI

Although Alabama delayed printing paper money, Mississippi did not. The secession convention of January 26, 1861, voted for the issuance of paper money. The first issue of $1,000,000 worth of notes, bearing ten percent interest, was to be redeemed (⅓ each year) until they were fully retired in 1864. In order to withdraw them from circulation, the same act levied a special tax.[9]

Not all of these notes were issued in 1861; a reduced number appeared in 1862 and an even smaller amount, in 1863. In November 1861, the state treasurer was authorized to receive these notes at all times, both before and after the redemption date, for the satisfaction of amounts owed to the state. And on January 29, 1862, the state permitted the treasurer to pay out again any bills received by him but not due for redemption until 1863 or 1864. In a move to cut down on interest payments, Governor John J. Pettus issued a proclamation on December 9, 1863, that all notes that had been due in June 1862, would be redeemed in specie upon presentation; but all interest would cease sixty days after the date of the proclamation. By virtue of a December 5, 1863 law, the remaining convention bills were to be exchanged for eight percent bonds or notes; payable in ten years from the date of exchange. By October 1865, an estimated $641,000 was still outstanding in convention notes and bonds.[10]

The convention notes were not the only bills issued by Mississippi. The cotton planters had failed to get the central government to lend them money on their crops in 1861, but they were more successful in Mississippi. On December 19, 1861, the state authorized a series of treasury notes with a limit of $5,000,000, to be lent on stored cotton at a rate of no more than five cents per pound. The bills were issued in denominations of one, two and one-half, three, five, ten, twenty, fifty, and one hundred dollars. The notes were to be redeemable whenever sufficient gold and silver came into the treasury from the sale of the cotton or after the blockade had been raised. The amounts loaned to the planters could be repaid only in specie or these notes, and they were receivable by the state for all sums due it, except the tax levied by the convention for the redemption of its paper.[11]

It appears that the demand for these Mississippi cotton notes was great. On January 29, 1862, before the bills were even printed, the Mississippi government allowed an advance with the stipulation that one-half of one percent was to be deducted to cover the cost of the printing plates. This paper, however, was not designed to circulate very long. The original law provided for the cancellation of all bills redeemed in gold and silver. But on December 5, 1863, it was further ordered that all cotton notes received or to be received by the treasurer were to be destroyed. At least in Mississippi the cotton planters had their way, and the state tried to keep some control over these issues.[12]

On January 29, 1862, the Mississippi legislature authorized an issue of $2,500,000 in non-interest bearing notes, known as military notes, to be used for military expenses only. The law provided for denominations of five, ten, twenty, fifty, one hundred, and five hundred dollars, but the last two values do not seem to have been printed. The state pledged to redeem the notes, and they could be exchanged for eight percent bonds. Any of the notes so exchanged were to be cancelled, but this intention was defeated on August 12, 1864, when the state treasurer was permitted to reissue any military notes that had been redeemed. The same law also provided for an additional $2,000,000 of military notes. By October 1865, these acts and others that provided for reissuance managed to keep a total of $2,500,000 outstanding, $180,000 of which was in 1864 notes.[13]

The final type of bill issued by Mississippi concerned the problem of small change. In 1861 the banks were allowed to suspend specie payment until after the blockade was raised, and shinplasters soon made their appearance. The state also permitted some companies and municipalities to issue small change bills, and the situation grew critical. On January 3, 1863, a law taxed private bills out of existence by levying a tax of one hundred percent on the highest amount of these bills outstanding after March 1, 1863. By the terms of the law of December 16, 1861, however, banks could only issue notes as small as one dollar, and the municipalities were likewise limited in the total amount of their issue; thus a void was left. On April 5, 1864, the state finally acted by providing that its treasury notes could be redeemed for state warrants in denominations of twenty-five and fifty cents as well as one, two, and three dollars. A total face value of $500,000 was permitted for these warrants. It must have been anticipated that such an act would not raise the total debt of the state. But this hope faded when, on the same day, a new state law authorized the reissuance of state treasury notes so exchanged, if the governor felt it necessary. Apparently, the change bills were not well received, because on March 3, 1865, it was directed that $150,000 in state treasury notes could be reissued in lieu of the change bills. Although $146,522 in change warrants were destroyed between the months of January and May 1865, in October, outstanding change warrants still totaled $496,622.[14]

The monetary situation in Mississippi was as severe as elsewhere, and the state was concerned with the issues of the Confederate government as well as its own. On August 6, 1861, the legislature had made Confederate Treasury notes receivable for all sums owed to the state, except the tax passed by the convention for redeeming its paper, and the national notes circulated. As the value of these notes declined, the legislature asked Congress to retire all of its bills and issue new legal tender notes. On June 13, 1863, John G. Humphries, a member of the Winston County Board of Police, noted that cheap money was becoming so plentiful that many people preferred to trade with it rather than with commodities when they could. And to compound problems, Major General S. J. Gholson of the state troops stated that Mississippi's treasury bills were probably being counterfeited and distributed to United States soldiers.[15]

By 1864, all remaining monetary stops in Mississippi had been pulled out and the scramble began. When the new Confederate issue appeared, the old Confederate bills could be converted into bonds. Acting on this, the governor was instructed to dispose of any of the bonds thereby received for state notes, cotton money, or new issue Confederate notes. And after July, the state treasurer could not accept old bills, except those below five dollars, for taxes. On August 6, the county treasurers and other county officials received instructions to dispose of Confederate Treasury notes on the best terms possible and to distribute the proceeds to the destitute. This instruction may have referred to the old issue, but it was not made clear in the law. By November, the state treasurer reported that he had $5,430.75 in specie and $5,120.00 in counterfeit Confederate notes that he was not distributing. The situation by then had obviously deteriorated. In October 1865, the entire indebtedness of the state was estimated at $4,979,324.53, but this debt seems extremely low and may not have included the bonds that had been issued.[16]

Overall, through the use of taxes, bank notes, and Confederate issues, Mississippi brought some order to its own monetary policy. Specie was also used in a few payments, and cotton, a staple commodity, backed another portion of its currency. Perhaps Mississippi's stabilized monetary policy tended to give credit to the majority of the state's issues. But not every state government of the Confederacy was so fortunate.

TENNESSEE

A large debt did not plague Tennessee, but Tennessee did not long maintain a Confederate state government. Even before the war began, a monetary crisis existed in Tennessee. The focus of the controversy seemed to be the earlier so-called conventional or ten percent interest bill. People complained that the bill embarrassed area finances so badly that it forced merchants to collect money to recover funds needed for loans to others. Another group asking for the repeal of the law stated that the "Money crisis is bad enough without such a law."[17] In July 1861, the legislature passed a law stating that the banks of Tennessee must stop the practice of retiring and diminishing their circulation; this action was "detrimental to the public interest" and must be reversed.[18] With apparent lack of money in the state, it would seem logical that the government would be more than willing to issue its own currency, but such was not the case.

Specie payment by the banks had been suspended before 1861. In January 1861, the suspension date was extended until February 8, 1862, but this deadline was repealed on July 1, 1861. Also in January, the Bank of Tennessee was allowed to issue notes in denominations of one, two, and three dollars, at least until November 23 of the same year, but the bank was not permitted to issue change bills.

In the meantime the state, under the leadership of Governor Isham G. Harris, pursued its own monetary course.[19] Tennessee did not formally ally itself with the Confederacy until May 7, 1861, but on the previous day it had provided for funds for its army by passing a $5,000,000 issue of ten year bonds, bearing eight percent interest, and a tax for their eventual redemption. On June 27, the governor received authorization to change $3,000,000 of this amount to treasury notes, with denominations from five to five hundred dollars, bearing an interest rate no greater than six percent. These notes were to be receivable for all debts owed to the state, and new treasury notes could be issued for any amount redeemed. Considering the scarcity of money and the lower interest rate, it would appear that Governor Harris would have immediately printed these notes, but he did not.[20]

Governor Harris did not want a state issuance of notes. Instead, he worked to make the Confederate Treasury note the circulating medium within the state, correctly declaring on June 16, 1861, that the Confederate States must have a uniform currency. Harris privately tried to get the banks in Tennessee to receive and pay out the Confederate notes as money. To Major General Gideon J. Pillow on June 20, 1861, Harris said my "opinion is that they will do all we desire." He further added that the "Bank of Tennessee, and the Planters Bank are doing all in their power to consummate the necessary arrangements."[21] In order to further guarantee the use of Confederate notes, the legislature passed a law requiring all the banks in Tennessee to receive and pay out the notes as money. In addition, on March 14, 1862, the comptroller of the state was directed to pay the state's bond interest with the same Confederate paper.[22] But no matter how much the governor might fight it, events were to dictate a state issuance of notes.

In early 1862, with Nashville in danger of capture, the legislature met at Memphis, where Harris declared that all of the state's military forces were in Confederate hands and that the small militia left was undisciplined and unarmed. Therefore, on March 18, a further $3,000,000 was authorized on terms similar to the 1861 issues. Three days prior to this, the banks doing business within the state had been permitted to remove their assets from the state, but were required to return them after the war; by June 7, 1862, even the banks at Chattanooga were sending their assets south to safety. With these developments, the Confederate state government had to fly before the pursuit of the invading forces of the United States.[23]

It was the mobile Confederate government of Tennessee that finally issued a series of notes, but these were not issued on the terms established in the previous laws. They bore no interest and were only change bills, redeemable in Confederate Treasury notes when presented in amounts of ten dollars or more. The first known type was supposed to have been issued from the town of Cherry Valley, but the surviving bills, all dated January 1863, have this town lined through and Smithville inserted instead. The denominations were twenty-five and fifty cents and one dollar, with a possible two dollar issue. The only other known specimens are one and two dollar bills dated at Kingston in February 1863. Documentation of this paper money is difficult, and only the notes themselves can suggest what was occurring at the time.[24]

In summation, Tennessee sought to make Confederate paper money and bank notes the only circulating medium within the boundary of the state, but when war came to the state a regional currency was required. In order to satisfy this requirement, change bills were finally issued by the exiled government of Tennessee. The war had dictated this drastic change of policy to state officials.

VIRGINIA

Fighting came to Virginia much sooner than to Tennessee, and the state responded more quickly. Virginia was unusually conservative in its monetary policy, but this did not prevent large early issues of paper money. Since Virginia had a number of banks, and the seat of the Confederate government was in Richmond, it had access to other paper money. Even so, Virginia still issued currency through the year 1863. Most of this money was authorized by the secession convention, but one series of small notes came from action of the state's legislature. The lowest denomination ever issued was one dollar, and the state never issued a change bill.

The first four series of state treasury notes came from actions of the secession convention. In ordinances passed on March 14, April 30, June 28, and December 30, 1861, a total of $9,000,000, in the denominations

TENNESSEE

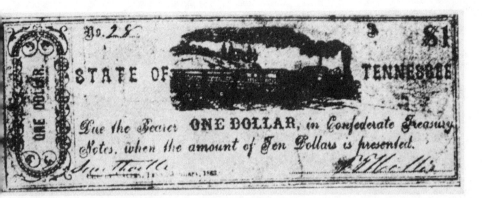

ONE DOLLAR BILL, 1863, SMITHVILLE ISSUE. Tennessee authorized notes but Governor Isham G. Harris chose not to issue them. Small change notes appeared in 1863, after the fall of Nashville. Since all bank funds had been removed from the state, these might have been issued by the state *for* the banks. From Criswell, *Confederate and Southern States Currency.*

Figure 20

ONE DOLLAR BILL, 1863, KINGSTON ISSUE. A rough scene of the State Capitol is flanked by portraits of George Washington (left) and Governor Isham G. Harris (right). Even though Harris and the bank and state funds withdrew to Georgia, various departments remained in scattered towns. If these were state issues and not just done by the state *for* the banks, it is the single use of the dollar sign by a state government. The Cherokee and Choctaw Indian Nations were the only other Confederate areas to use the dollar sign. From Criswell, *Confederate and Southern States Currency.*

Figure 21

ONE DOLLAR BILL, 1862. Governor John Letcher is shown on the left.

Figure 22

ONE HUNDRED DOLLAR TREASURY NOTE, 1861. From Criswell, *Confederate and Southern States Currency.*

Figure 23

of five, ten, twenty, fifty, and one hundred dollars was authorized. As with most of the states, the first issues bore six percent interest, but the bills below twenty dollars had no interest requirement and were merely payable on demand at the state treasury.[25]

On March 31, 1862, the General Assembly of the state passed a law giving the governor authority to issue $1,300,000 in state treasury notes in order to raise money "to arm and equip the militia of the state, and for all defensive and offensive operations of the army and navy."[26] These notes were to be no lower in denomination than five dollars, but on May 14, 1862, this was changed to allow any part of the $1,300,000 sum to be issued as one dollar bills. The state took this authority to heart, and the entire sum was printed as one dollar notes; in fact, the final amount totaled $1,309,200. This should have been more than enough to meet the demand for dollar bills within the state.[27]

But what about the question of change? On March 1, 1861, specie suspension was permitted, and hard money disappeared. Of course, the state reserved the right to obtain coin for notes any time it wished, but excluded the general public. As happened in other Confederate States, shinplasters soon proliferated. By October, the editor of the *Daily Richmond Examiner* estimated that so many shinplasters existed they totaled no less than one-tenth of all the currency in circulation. In November, one soldier, John S. Foster, stated that there was no gold or silver in ciriculation, and all he saw was Virginia shinplasters. This state of affairs demanded action.[28]

The General Assembly on January 24, 1862, required banks to issue notes in the denominations of one and two dollars and forbade them to pay out shinplasters of unauthorized corporations or individuals. Further, on March 29, the state authorized banks to print notes between the values of one and five dollars, including fractional amounts. At the same time the state permitted the city government of Richmond and all the other cities, towns, and counties to print change bills. Ten days prior to this, every shinplaster in circulation had been legalized, and all penalties for issuing them had been removed. But this amnesty did not apply to unauthorized change bills issued after the law was passed or to any parties or persons who did not call in their bills within ninety days. Apparently, this did not work fast enough for some, because on April 16, 1862, Brigadier General John H. Winder, commanding the District of Henrico, issued a general order outlawing shinplasters within his district.[29]

By 1862 Virginia had authorized the last issuance of its notes. When it came time to pay the Confederate war tax in 1862, and to make up subsequent deficiencies in the state treasury, short term interest bearing notes were sold. These were purchased mostly by banks, but some individuals also invested in them. The state issued large amounts of treasury notes early in the war, but none after March 1862, although the authorized notes continued to roll from the presses through 1863. In their place, bonds came to be the main brace of the state's monetary policy.[30]

Virginia, in retrospect, was unique in that it did not issue change bills. It also held a fairly good check on the total volume of outstanding state currency. With both the Confederate Treasury Department and the Army headquartered in Richmond, the city's need for military protection diminished.

SUMMARY

These Eastern states of the Confederacy demonstrated several common features in monetary policy. All four governments required specie for their own use, while prohibiting citizens from securing specie from banks. The central authorities followed essentially this same policy.

Like the central government, the state officials had to find some way to finance their role in the war. Early on they answered this problem by issuing bonds, on which interest had to be paid, to raise money. The example of the Confederate government, however, appeared to inspire the state governments. They soon began printing paper money, currency that was accepted by the citizens of the issuing state. When the central authorities passed the war tax to help the value of their issues, the state governments responded by assuming the obligation for their citizens. They met this extra expense either by selling bonds or by further issuing treasury notes.

All of these states discovered that their paper money was being supplanted by Confederate Treasury notes, and their issues were not being returned to the state treasuries. As a result, the states then prevented the easy retirement of the majority of their notes. Increased monetary demands could be met only by further issuances of state paper money.

[1]*Journal of the Convention of the People of South Carolina* (Columbia, 1862), pp. 121-22, 757; *Charleston Daily Courier* (South Carolina), November 9, 1861; George W. Johnson to wife, Bowling Green, Kentucky, February 15, 1862, [George W. Johnson], "Letters of George W. Johnson," *Register of the Kentucky State Historical Society*, (October 1942); 40(133): 347. Although Kentucky never issued paper money, there is evidence to suggest that some of her sons may have helped in the issuance of small change notes by the state of Tennessee in 1863 (see

section on Tennessee). At the time these bills were issued, Smithville was occupied by the forces of Brigadier General John Hunt Morgan of Kentucky. Colonel William Hollis commanded a Kentucky cavalry regiment under Morgan and the Tennessee notes were signed by a Hollis.

²*Acts of the Seventh Biennial Session of the General Assembly of Alabama* (Montgomery, 1860), pp. 370-71; William R. Smith, *The History and Debate of the Convention of the People of Alabama* (Montgomery, 1861), pp. 38-40.

³Ibid., p. 123; *Acts of the Called Session of the General Assembly of Alabama* (Montgomery, 1861), pp. 9-10; Andrew B. Moore to James J. Donegan, April 9, 1861, Andrew B. Moore Papers, 1860-1861, Alabama State Archives, Montgomery, Alabama; General Statement of the Bank of Selma, January 1, 1861, ibid.

⁴Moore to J. D. Denegre, January 23, 1861; Moore to Donegan, March 16, 1861; H. A. Schroeder to D. B. Graham, October 28, 1861, ibid.; John Gill Shorter to W. P. Chilton, March 31, 1862, John Gill Shorter Papers, 1861-1863, Alabama State Archives.

⁵*Acts of the Called Session*, pp. 16-17; Moore to L. F. Zantzing, August 2, 1861, Moore Papers; Shorter to J. F. Foster, February 1, 1861, Governor Letter Book, 1862-1865, Alabama State Archives.

⁶Donegan to Moore, September 18, 1861, Moore Papers; *Acts of the Called Session, 1862, and of the Second Regular Annual Session of the General Assembly of Alabama* (Montgomery, 1862), pp. 33-35, 50-53; Shorter to J. F. Patterson and Company, November 11, 1862; J. F. Patterson and Company to Shorter, January 19, 1863, Shorter Papers.

⁷*Acts of the Called Session, 1862, and Second Regular Session*, pp. 30-32; *Acts of the Called Session of the General Assembly of Alabama, 1863* (Montgomery, 1863), p. 17; *Acts of the Called Session, 1864, and of the Fourth Regular Session of the General Assembly of Alabama* (Montgomery, 1864), pp. 54-56.

⁸*Acts of the Called Session, 1862, and Second Regular Session*, pp. 68-69.

⁹*Journal of the State Convention and Ordinances and Resolutions adopted in January, 1861* (Jackson, Mississippi, 1861), pp. 126-27.

¹⁰Register of Treasury Notes, Record Group 30, Mississippi State Archives (hereafter cited as MSARG), Jackson, Mississippi; *Laws of the State of Mississippi passed at a Regular Session of the Mississippi Legislature* (Jackson, 1862), pp. 45-46, 244; Proclamation, December 9, 1863, Executive Journal, 1857-1870, Mississippi State Archives; *Laws of the State of Mississippi passed at a Called and Regular Session of the Mississippi Legislature . . . 1863* (Selma, 1864), pp. 215-17; Statement of the Probable Indebtedness of the State of Mississippi, October 25, 1865, MSARG 30.

¹¹*Laws . . . passed at a Regular Session* [1862], pp. 59-66.

¹²Ibid., pp. 64, 247-48; *Laws of . . . a Called and Regular Session . . . 1863*, p. 217.

¹³*Laws . . . passed at a Regular Session* [1862], pp. 286-88; *Laws of the State of*

Mississippi passed at a Called Session of the Mississippi Legislature . . . August, 1864 (Meridian, 1864), p. 22; Statement of the Probable Indebtedness of the State of Mississippi, October 25, 1865.

[14]*Laws of . . . a Called and Regular Session . . . 1863*, p. 77; *Laws . . . passed at a Regular Session* [1862], pp. 278-79; *Laws of the State of Mississippi passed at a Called Session of the Mississippi Legislature . . . March and April, 1864* (Meridian, 1864), pp. 37-38, 51-52; *Laws of the State of Mississippi passed at a Called Session . . . February and March, 1865* (Meridian, 1865), p. 7; Statement of the Probable Indebtedness of the State of Mississippi, October 25, 1865; Report of Notes Destroyed, January 1-May 17, 1865, MSARG 30.

[15]*Laws of the State of Mississippi passed at a Called Session of the Mississippi Legislature . . . July, 1861* (Jackson, 1861), p. 39; *Laws of . . . a Called and Regular Session . . . 1863*, p. 234; John G. Humphries to John J. Pettus, June 13, 1863; S. J. Gholson to Pettus, October 24, 1863, John J. Pettus Papers, 1860-1863, Mississippi State Archives.

[16]*Laws of . . . a Called Session . . . March and April, 1864*, pp. 27, 31; Treasurer's Report, 1864, MSARG 30; Statement of the Probable Indebtedness of the State of Mississippi, October 25, 1865.

[17]J. J. Williams to Isham G. Harris, December 8, 1860, Petition of the Citizens of Blount County, December 10, 1860, Isham G. Harris Papers, 1857-1865, Tennessee State Archives, Nashville, Tennessee.

[18]*Public Acts of the State of Tennessee passed at the Extra Session of the Thirty-Third General Assembly, April, 1861* (Nashville, 1861), p. 51.

[19]*Public Acts of the State of Tennessee passed at the Extra Session of the Thirty-Third General Assembly for the Year 1861* (Nashville, 1861), p. 21; *Public Acts of the . . . Extra Session . . . April, 1861*, p. 51; *Public Acts of the State of Tennessee passed at the First and Second Sessions of the Thirty-Fourth General Assembly* (Nashville, 1862), p. 42.

[20]*Public Acts of the . . . Extra Session . . . April, 1861*, pp. 23-24, 41-42.

[21]Message to the Senate and House of Representatives of Tennessee, June 18, 1861; Harris to Gideon J. Pillow, June 20, 1861; Message to the Senate and House of Representatives of Tennessee, June 18, 1861, Isham G. Harris Letter Book, Tennessee State Archives.

[22]*Public Acts of the . . . Extra Session . . . April, 1861*, p. 50; *Public Acts of the . . . Thirty-Fourth General Assembly*, p. 38.

[23]Harris to the Gentlemen of the Senate and House of Representatives, February 20, 1862, Harris Letter Book; *Public Acts of the . . . Thirty-Fourth General Assembly*, pp. 26, 38; G. C. Torbett to Harris, June 7, 1862, Harris Papers, 1857-1865.

[24]Criswell, *Confederate and Southern States Currency*, pp. 225-26.

[25]Ibid., pp. 282-84.

[26]*Acts of the General Assembly of the State of Virginia, passed in 1861-2* (Richmond, 1862), p. 30.

[27]*Acts of the General Assembly of the State of Virginia, passed at Extra Session, 1862* (Richmond, 1862), p. 4; Register of Notes issued in pursuance of an Act . . . payable on demand to Bearer, and of the denomination of One Dollar, Virginia State Archives, Richmond, Virginia.

[28]*Acts of the General Assembly of the State of Virginia, passed in 1861* (Richmond, 1861), pp. 123-24; *Daily Richmond Examiner*, October 31, 1861; John S. Foster to Aunt Jennie, November 14, 1861, John Foster and Family Correspondence, Archives Division, Louisiana State University Library, Baton Rouge, Louisiana.

[29]*Acts of . . . Virginia, passed in 1861-1*, pp. 82-86; *Daily Richmond Enquirer*, April 23, 1862.

[30]Register of Notes Issued in pursuance of an Act . . . "for the assumption and Payment of the Confederate States War Tax" passed February 21, 1862, Virginia State Archives; Register of Notes Issued in pursuance of an Act . . . "providing for Loans to supply Temporary Deficiencies in the Treasury," passed March 28, 1862, ibid.

Chapter V

CONTRASTS IN EASTERN STATES' PAPER MONEY ISSUES

The three other eastern states—Georgia, North Carolina, and Florida—met the monetary challenge differently. Although most of the Eastern states remained conservative until war expenditures forced greater outpourings of paper currency, Georgia and North Carolina showed very little restraint. Florida, on the other hand, not only began the war with small quantities of paper money, but continued this policy throughout the war. Even with this disciplined approach, Florida still encountered problems. An examination of the monetary policy of these states, therefore, will provide a contrast in their policies.

Georgia and North Carolina did not hesitate to resort to the printing press. Paper money issues were authorized in 1861 and continued until the Confederacy collapsed. In both states, the people apparently collected many of the bills as investments, so they did not circulate to any great extent until produced in large quantities. However, the change bills that were printed did circulate, some for a long time after the war. Florida by contrast was quite conservative; it printed only small amounts of paper money at any one time, and it took the government a relatively long time to exhaust the first series.

GEORGIA

In its first year as a Confederate state, Georgia did not issue paper money. The state sold its bonds to the banks instead which accomplished two things. First, the state treasurer had several different accounts upon which he could draw at any time. Second, besides establishing a bank account, special bank notes were sent to the state treasury and paid out there. In April 1861, the Bank of Columbus in Columbus, Georgia, received $35,000 in six percent bonds. John Jones, the treasurer of Georgia, asked the president of the bank, William H. Young, to dispatch $25,000 in bank notes and to keep the remainder of the amount due on account. The state could then draw upon this account to pay its debts. For example, Georgia sent a specie check to the Tredegar Iron Works in Richmond, Virginia, for supplies purchased from them. Apparently this arrangement proved to be satisfactory for most of the first year.[1]

This state of monetary affairs in Georgia did not continue for long. The first appropriations bill passed by the legislature during the war brought the initial mention of state treasury notes. Like all subsequent authorizations it did not mention the total amount to be printed. The December 14, 1861, act only declared that if the governor found any deficiencies in the treasury and could not pay all the appropriations, he was to issue eight percent bonds maturing in thirty years, or treasury notes, fundable in eight percent stock or specie, payable six months after a treaty of peace was concluded between the two nations. The decision was left to Governor Joseph E. Brown, and he was quite vocal about how he felt the state's interests could best be served.[2]

Brown advised R. R. Cyler, president of the Central Railroad and Banking Company in Savannah, on December 30, 1861, that he intended to raise the money needed for military operations by issuing treasury notes. He intended to use bonds to procure bank money only for the three or four months that might be required to get the state bills printed. Admitting that increased paper would bring about depreciation, he could not see any difference in the final outcome if the extra paper were in the form of state notes or bank bills. His final argument hinged on the proposition that the "true and only question is one of interest." He explained this statement by saying, "shall the State use her own bills without interest . . . or shall she pay the Banks interest for their bills?" Governor Brown answered his own question by stating that he had resolved to look after the interests of Georgia, "and save her the interest . . . if I can."[3]

As it evolved, Brown was a man of his word. In laying the groundwork, Retonion Sheveatt, Georgia's comptroller general, sought information from Confederate Secretary of the Treasury Memminger about how the central government kept a register of its own notes. Treasurer John Jones informed the state banks that any bonds delivered to them would be drawn up for the entire amount loaned instead of by denomination of currency in the loan. Although the comptroller general stated that $5,000,000 was to be registered in this initial issuance, the total actually produced was $2,320,000. This was only the beginning, and as the expenses continued to climb, so did the amount of money printed.[4]

With the Georgia appropriations bill passed on December 13, 1862, came another authorization for an unspecified sum of notes to supply any deficiencies. These bills were to be redeemable in specie or six percent bonds instead of the previous eight percent bonds, and again, neither principal nor interest was payable until six months after a treaty of peace. This may have been done to make the notes less attractive to investors, but by April 1862, only one man, a Dr. George D. Phillips, had asked about the possibilities of investment in these notes. He had, however, been advised against such investment by state officials, because any interest would be lost until after the war, and he would only be betting on the length of the struggle. Nevertheless, some people still held on to large sums, for the amount of notes required in 1863 was $5,268,000, more than twice that of 1862.[5]

By December 1863, the volume of paper money in Georgia had grown fairly large. But the bills were collecting in only a few hands evidenced by the fact that some people were clamoring to be relieved of quantities of these notes. On December 14, 1863, the general assembly of Georgia passed a law allowing the state treasurer to accept these bills and issue certificates of deposit in the sums of $10,000 and $20,000 in lieu of them. These certificates had the same provisions for redemption as the original paper and only served to cut down on the volume—a total of $560,000 had been exchanged by the end of the war.

On December 12, 1863, a new type of treasury bill was authorized. Even though he could have issued these notes or negotiated a loan until taxes were collected, Governor Brown chose the more economical way. These new pieces of paper were to be redeemed at the end of 1864 for Confederate Treasury notes, and when the central authorities changed to a new issue in early 1864, the law was amended on March 17, 1864, making the Georgia paper redeemable in the new Confederate note. If the state bills, however, were not presented within three months of maturity (by December 25, 1864), they could only be received for sums due the state. But by March 9, 1865, this date had been changed to March 25, 1866. Georgia issued the bills in denominations of five, ten, twenty, fifty, one hundred, and five hundred dollars, to a total of $8,895,000.[6]

On November 18, 1864, the Georgia governor once more was empowered by the general assembly to make up any deficiencies in appropriations with treasury notes, and he again followed through with his instructions. By March 1865, a total of $1,700,000 had been issued, all in the denominations of five and fifty dollars. And in May, 1865, $70,000 in ten dollar bills, redeemable for Confederate notes on December 25, 1865, began to roll off the presses, the last paper money to be produced by Georgia. Unlike most of the other states formerly in the Confederacy, Georgia printed no further issues during the period of Reconstruction.[7]

In 1864 the state finally authorized the destruction of state notes. By November, in accordance with the December 25, 1864 deadline, the treasurer was permitted to burn any paper redeemed as well as any other bills found unfit for circulation. When the troops of the United States began to close in on the capital at Milledgeville, and the government had to flee, action by the general assembly permitted the state treasury to remove from the area. In addition, the state treasurer was authorized to burn any amount of the notes he thought proper in order to reduce the great bulk. Because of this blanket authority, there is no way of estimating the amount outstanding at the end of the war.[8]

Besides these monetary problems in Georgia, there was also the question of change. On November 30, 1860, a suspension bill had been passed over the governor's veto. A later requirement stipulated that after January 1, 1862 all suspended banks must issue small change bills in denominations of five, ten, twenty-five, and fifty cents. On October 26, 1861, Georgia legalized shinplasters but they had to be destroyed when redeemed and not reissued. Subsequently, the state authorized change bills for the city of Augusta up to $100,000 and the Western and Atlantic Railroad, up to $200,000. On December 1, 1863, Georgia required the banks to issue a seventy-five cent note in addition to the previously required fractional amounts, as well as one, two, and three dollars.[9]

Apparently this did not fully satisfy the change demand in Georgia. On December 5, 1862, the state entered the arena with notes in values of five, ten, fifteen, twenty, twenty-five, fifty, and seventy-five cents as well as one, two, three, and four dollars. A total of $1,000,000 in these denominations were authorized to be printed. They were to be exchanged for bank, Confederate, or state notes but could be redeemed only for Confederate notes. By the end of 1863, $501,660 of these bills had come from the presses. Further, on December 14, 1863, authorities granted permission for another series of small change bills not to exceed $1,000,000. Although authorized to be issued under the same terms as the others, only denominations of fifty cents, plus one, two, three, and four dollars were printed. It appears that they continued to be printed into 1865. The amount printed in 1864 came to $809,782, with an additional $15,250 produced in April 1865. The total sum of change bills issued then came to $861,532.[10]

Georgia, therefore, provides an example of indiscriminate printing of paper money by a Confederate state. Except for the change notes, no limit was put on each issue as they were authorized. It is to Georgia's credit, however, that some restraint was demonstrated in printing paper money. Even so, a total of $19,716,192 rolled off the presses not including the state's bonds. There is little wonder that Georgia did not need to print more money during Reconstruction.

TABLE 6

GEORGIA TREASURY NOTES AND CHANGE BILLS, 1861-1865*

State Treasury Notes

Dates Issued	Amount of Notes
1862 (April, May, July, August)	$ 2,320,000
1863 (January-September)	5,268,000
1864 (February, April-August)	8,895,000
March, 1865	1,700,000
May, 1865	70,000
Total Treasury Notes Issued	$18,253,000

State Change Bills

1863 (April-October 15)	473,660
October, 1863	73,750
November, 1863	54,250
1864 (Feb., April, May, July, August, Oct.)	809,782
April, 1865	15,250
May, 1865	36,500
Total State Change Bills Issued	1,463,192
Plus Total Treasury Notes	18,253,000
Total Funds Issued by the State of Georgia	$19,716,192

*W. C. Mitchell Ledger, 1843-1863, pp. 432, 443, Georgia State Archives, Atlanta, Georgia.

GEORGIA

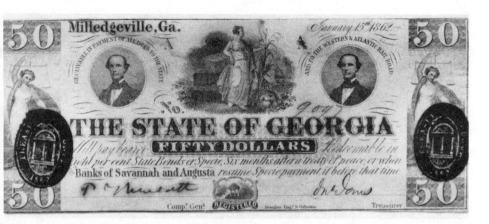

FIFTY DOLLAR NOTE, JANUARY 1862. Issued as a result of the Act of December 1861. The portrait is of Governor Joseph E. Brown.

Figure 24

FIVE DOLLAR BILL, APRIL 1864. Issued as a result of act of December 1863.

Figure 25

NORTH CAROLINA

ONE DOLLAR BILL, JANUARY 1863. Issued under authority of Act of December 1862.

Figure 26

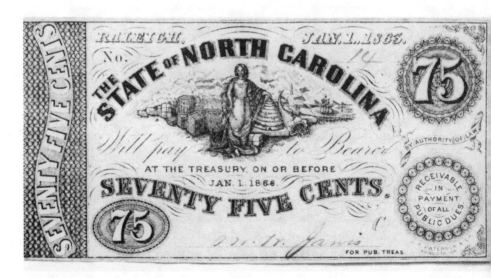

SEVENTY-FIVE CENTS NOTE, JANUARY 1863. Issued under authority of Act of December 1862.

Figure 27

NORTH CAROLINA

North Carolina proved to be an equal offender, having committed itself to a policy of paper money long before Confederate history began. As late as June 30, 1823, the state was still redeeming and destroying the currency it had issued in 1783 and 1785. In the following year, 1824, reports circulated about the destruction of worn and redeemed North Carolina treasury notes issued in 1814 and 1816. It is possible that these treasury notes were not intended as a general circulating medium, but this does not seem likely since some were worn by use.[11]

As soon as North Carolina joined the Confederacy, it provided for paper money, with the legislature voting $3,250,000 in treasury notes on May 11, 1861. Unfortunately, the secession convention did not agree with the legislature, for on June 28, 1861, it passed an ordinance which authorized $200,000 in change bills in values of ten, twenty-five, and fifty cents, redeemable on January 1, 1866, as well as $3,000,000 in six percent bonds, payable in one year. This ordinance, which further abrogated and annulled the May 11, 1861, act of the legislature, also permitted the banks to suspend specie payment, which the legislature had approved on November 24, 1860. It further allowed the banks to print notes of one, two, and two and one-half dollar values.[12]

The secession convention of North Carolina provided that the ordinances it passed could be changed by the legislature. On September 20, 1861, a total of $1,000,000 in state notes in denominations of one and two dollars was authorized, and change bills were issued with five and twenty cent notes added to the list. Apparently, both the May 11 law and the June 28 ordinance were ignored in favor of this issuance. Both of these types of notes appeared with October 1861 dates printed on them. When the secession convention met again, it amended the legislature's act, providing for $3,000,000 in treasury notes of five, ten, twenty, fifty, one hundred, and two hundred dollar amounts, bearing six percent interest. Principal and interest were payable at maturity, and the notes could be exchanged for six percent bonds. Though this ordinance was passed on December 1, 1861, the secession convention amended it on January 25, 1862, to rescind the interest and provided that the remainder of the notes to be issued would be in denominations of five, ten, and twenty dollars. In all, the denominations printed were five, ten, twenty, fifty, and one hundred dollars. Some of the amounts above twenty dollars may have come after the ordinance of February 4, 1862. The final amendment to this ordinance came on February 26, 1862, when the secession convention provided for funding the notes in eight percent bonds or in six percent bonds, the latter being convertible into state treasury notes. This was done in order to achieve acceptance of the bills by the banks.[13]

A February 26, 1862, North Carolina ordinance authorized issuance of an additional $1,500,000, plus $1,000,000 in notes of ten, twenty, twenty-five, and fifty cents, and one and two dollars. These and the other notes could also be reissued by the state treasury anytime they had been paid to the state. Thus a total of $5,500,000 had been authorized, but only the change notes were redeemable on January 1, 1866, and the rest were due one year earlier. In an act of peace keeping, both the September 18, 1861, act, and the December 1, 1861, ordinance, and all issues of notes and bonds were ratified and confirmed. The final ordinance of the secession convention, passed on May 12, 1862, granted an additional $2,000,000 in five, ten, and twenty dollar values as well as $20,000 worth of five and ten cent notes. The total that could be printed amounted to $7,520,000.[14]

North Carolina quickly issued this money. In one month alone, April 1862, the state printed a total of $85,978 in fractional notes and $228,000 in the larger denominations. Soon North Carolina needed even more money. On December 20, 1862, it voted for another $4,500,000 in denominations of one, two, three, five, ten, twenty, and fifty dollars, as well as five, ten, twenty-five, fifty, and seventy-five cent values. All of these notes were payable on January 1, 1866, as were most of the other issues. On December 12, 1863, the state printed an additional $400,000 in twenty-five and fifty cent bills. The final law came on May 28, 1864, and authorized $3,000,000 more, payable two years after the treaty of peace ending the war. The legislature amended this act, however, on December 14, 1864, to make these bills fundable on January 1, 1876, instead of January 1, 1866. When redeemed in 1876, they could only be exchanged for coupon bonds which were not due until January 1, 1896. Obviously the state needed more time to meet its obligations. Although an additional $3,000,000 was authorized, there is no evidence that it was ever issued unless it was printed from old plates. No bill has yet been found dated late enough for this $3,000,000 issue.[15]

The ordinances produced a currency for North Carolina, but there was a continual need for state money for several reasons. The main cause for this condition was that the state attempted to keep close control over all of its economic and monetary affairs. Indeed, the authorities even tried to pay their troops in the Confederate Army with state treasury notes but failed. A committee was appointed to look into this attempt and found there were several explanations for this inability to pay the troops with state money. When the banks in North Carolina refused to accept the state bills, the secession convention passed an ordinance making them fundable in eight percent bonds. This ordinance was designed to make the bills a currency, but it also served to make them command a premium in Richmond, Virginia. When the North Carolina notes were delivered to the state paymaster in Virginia, brokers and speculators immediately converted them. Bonds were then sold for Confederate Treasury notes at par, and a quick profit was made. In this way the larger notes did not readily circulate, and greater and greater quantities were required. The committee also found that, except for purposes of conversion, Virginia merchants tended to reject the North Carolina paper. Eventually, the volume of money issued by the state became quite large.[16]

Confederate paper money soon flooded North Carolina. When it came time to convert old issues of Confederate notes to new ones in 1864, one paymaster alone reported that he had $112,817 on hand by April 1, 1864, and that by August 23, he had received another $2,550. When the banks had refused, by late 1861, to take North Carolina notes, state authorities first debated forcing their acceptance under penalty of law, but this was tabled when funding was considered. Slowly state bills gained intrastate circulation along with Confederate paper. Eventually so much paper circulated that the value began to decline. When that happened, Governor Zebulon B. Vance started his own blockade-running business for the state. A ship was purchased, and cotton was shipped to Europe, sold for pounds sterling, and the proceeds used for purchasing supplies which were then shipped back to North Carolina. Therefore, beginning January 4, 1864, Vance was able to bypass the monetary problems encountered by the state.[17]

North Carolina, overextended monetarily, could save itself only by entering the blockade-running business. The state issued well over $10,000,000 in state treasury notes, and it took many years for these to be liquidated. Probably because of this, North Carolina, like Georgia, never issued a treasury note during the Reconstruction period; however, the issuance of bonds by North Carolina during Reconstruction was large.

FLORIDA

While Georgia and North Carolina exercised little control over their monetary volume, Florida was much more restrained. Its issues were small, and it took time to exhaust each issuance. But like North Carolina,

Florida had conflicts between the legislature and the secession convention over the control of monetary policy. On February 14, 1861, the general assembly of Florida authorized $500,000 in treasury notes, with the stated denominations of one, two, three, four, five, ten, twenty, fifty, and one hundred dollars. The notes were to be legal tender for all payments to the state and were encouraged to circulate as currency. It declared shinplasters illegal, and forced banks to accept Florida notes under penalty of having to remove from the state. The law placed a debt limit of $1,000,000 upon the state, and the total included treasury notes, bonds, and any other liabilities. The secession convention, however, had other ideas. On April 26, 1861, it passed an ordinance which authorized $500,000 in eight percent bonds, payable in ten years, in lieu of the treasury notes voted by the February 14 act of the legislature. Even though the bonds had been printed, John C. McGehee told the secession convention on January 14, 1862, these bonds could not be fully marketed. Obviously, something needed to be done.[18] Apparently the legislature finally acted to correct this situation. The first issue of Florida treasury notes, probably with the same $500,000 limit that had been set previously, appeared with the date of October 10, 1861. These notes bore denominations of one, two, three, five, ten, twenty, fifty, and one hundred dollars, with a possible five hundred dollar bill.

When the Confederate war tax was passed, Florida had to find some means of payment. The first idea, proposed in December 1861, was to use Florida notes to pay its citizens the money owed to them by the central government and return a part of the Confederate appropriation of $300,000 which was due to the state; however, this plan was defeated. Instead a general assembly bill passed on December 16, 1861, provided for an issue of $500,000 in treasury notes which would be exchanged at the banks for Confederate bills. Any bank receiving these Florida notes at par could suspend specie payment. These bills were issued in 1862 and used at that time.[19]

On December 6, 1862, the Florida general assembly forced the governor to issue and use the remaining Florida treasury notes that had already been authorized with at least $200,000 going to the relief of disabled soldiers and their families. The reason for this action may have been the proliferation of Confederate notes. Even in late 1861 the quartermaster general of the state, H. V. Snell, had to use Confederate paper money for purchases in Georgia, because Florida notes did not pass out of the state. But they still had a circulation within the state, and this required even more notes to be printed to meet state debts.[20]

The next issue of paper money in Confederate Florida was approved on December 13, 1862. Originally the $300,000 authorized by this law was to be divided among denominations of one, two, three, five, ten, twenty, fifty, and one hundred dollars, but an amendment made $50,000 of this sum printable in fractional amounts. On November 30, 1863, a further amendment deleted the $50,000 in one hundred dollar bills and changed it to one dollar bills and fractional amounts. When the notes were issued, there were no fifty or one hundred dollar values, and the fractionals were in denominations of ten, twenty-five, and fifty cents.[21]

The needs of the poor in Florida again became a problem, and money was needed for their relief. On December 3, 1863, another $300,000 issue of Florida notes was authorized for the relief of destitute soldiers' families and other indigent individuals. These bills came from the printing presses in 1864 and the highest face value issued was ten dollars. The final issue of notes came when $350,000 was approved on December 7, 1864, to meet the needs of the government. Issuance of these notes continued well into 1865 when the end of the war called a halt to this activity.[22]

Even though suspension of specie payments was not allowed at first, specie still began to disappear. When the Florida government could not issue its own notes in the beginning of the war, it had to borrow bank notes at rates as high as eight percent. Most state revenue came from land sales, and only coin or solvent bank notes could be used for these purchases. But on January 23, 1862, Confederate paper was added to the list. As this and other state resources dried up, it led John C. McGehee to comment on January 14, 1862, that it had become necessary for the state to use credit for money. On December 14, 1861, specie suspension was approved until twelve months after the end of the war, and some action was needed on change bills. Attempts to legalize all shinplasters failed, but certain ones were allowed by the general assembly. For example, it permitted Pensacola on December 17, 1861, to print $25,000 in five, ten, twenty-five, and fifty cent notes. But private change bills were produced without state permission. On December 13, 1862, Florida finally outlawed all shinplasters, and authorized the state issuance of small change notes.[23]

As Confederate paper appeared more often in daily business affairs, legislative attempts were made within Florida to assure its acceptance throughout the state. One proposal recommended a law whereby any creditor who refused either Confederate or Florida notes in payment of a debt would lose all the interest on the loan and could only recover the principal, but this failed to pass the general assembly. Finally, the assembly passed a resolution on December 3, 1863, that if any man exempt from military service refused Confederate bills, he would be pressed into the armed forces immediately. As the war progressed, all paper money declined in value; few Florida notes returned to the state treasury, and Confederate paper was used for all taxes and land sales. In 1864, with the small amount of only $1,103,622.07 outstanding, even Florida notes declined. The governor blamed the Confederate bills for decreasing the value of Florida's notes. To remedy this, he urged the general assembly to make only Florida paper receivable in payment of Florida taxes. A bill providing for half of the state taxes to be paid with state bills was proposed, but it never passed. On December 7, 1864, the legislature empowered the governor to sell all Confederate bonds and Treasury notes on the best possible terms and to use the money for state expenses.[24]

By the end of the war, Florida's entire debt could not have exceeded $1,500,000. In this way Florida was the most controlled of all the Eastern Confederate States and was commendable in its monetary endeavors. Even without a single large issue of bonds, the state still provided for its needy and its military forces, and it did so at far less cost than any of the other states.

SUMMARY

The Eastern states of the Confederacy varied slightly in their approaches to the monetary needs of the war. All except South Carolina and Kentucky issued treasury notes, but depending on military necessity and the degree of control the states exercised over their affairs, the volume of paper required by issuing states varied greatly. Only Florida can be applauded for its efforts at monetary control, while Georgia and North Carolina, both of which tried for greater state control in all of their affairs, had the greatest debts. North Carolina saved itself from gross debts through blockade-running and a large issue of bonds after the war, and Georgia placed a strong reliance on bonds after the war.

The Eastern Confederate States' actions also show what happens with the use of paper money unsecured except for faith in the states themselves. All states either authorized or issued interest-bearing notes at first. As long as these were small in volume, they seemed to be acceptable to many people. When North Carolina's first notes were not backed by bonds, they were usually not acceptable anywhere. After the notes were made convertible into bonds, they became more valuable than Confederate paper money and did not circulate outside of the state; only through overprinting was interstate circulation achieved. The public accepted Mississippi's cotton notes, because they were convertible into cotton. But when states began redeeming their paper money with Confederate bills alone, the monetary needs of the state governments dictated that the volume of notes outstanding must climb. Even Florida had to resort to the printing press more frequently in the latter part of the war as the value of its bills declined. Beginning with the notes authorized on December 13, 1862, Florida's bills provided that public lands of the state were pledged for their eventual redemption. For this reason, perhaps, Florida's paper money declined comparatively little in value.

The Eastern Confederate States also exhibited jealousy between the secession conventions and the state legislatures over control of monetary policy. In several states, these arguments led to the cancellation of early series of notes voted by the legislatures in favor of state issues. But this conflict did not last long. As Georgia's Governor Brown wisely observed, it cost the Confederate state governments less to print their own currency than to borrow bank notes for interest-bearing bonds. This consideration must have been of supreme importance for bond issues grew smaller as the volume of paper money grew larger.

[1]John Jones to G. W. Mercer, April 12, 1861; Jones to William H. Young, April 16, 1861; Jones to J. R. Anderson and Company, May 15, 1861, Treasurer's Letter Book, 1851-1861, Georgia State Archives, Atlanta, Georgia.

[2]*Acts of the General Assembly of the State of Georgia, passed in Milledgeville at an Annual Session . . . 1861* (Milledgeville, 1862), p. 13.

[3]Joseph E. Brown to R. R. Cuyler, December 30, 1861, Executive Letter Book from August 21, 1860 to May 12, 1864, Georgia State Archives.

[4]Retonion Sheveatt to Memminger, December 18, 1861, COR, Letters Received, March 20, 1861-June 18, 1862; Jones to John P. King, December 22, 1861, Treasurer's Letter Book, 1851-1861; Sheveatt to Memminger, December 28, 1861, COR, Letters Received, March 20, 1861-June 18, 1862; Issuance of Treasury Notes, W. C. Mitchell Ledger, 1843-1863, p. 432, Georgia State Archives.

[5]*Acts of the General Assembly of the State of Georgia, passed in Milledgeville at an Annual Session . . . 1862, also Extra Session of 1863* (Milledgeville, 1863), pp. 14-15; Jones to Dr. George D. Phillips, April 11, 1862, Treasurer's Letter Book, 1851-1861; Issuance of Treasury Notes, W. C. Mitchell Ledger, 1843-1863, p. 432.

[6]*Acts of the General Assembly of the State of Georgia, passed in Milledgeville at an Annual Session . . . 1863, also Extra Session of 1864* (Milledgeville, 1864), pp. 13-14, 79, 161; *Acts of the General Assembly of the State of Georgia, passed in Milledgeville at an Annual Session . . . 1864, also Extra Session of 1865, at Macon* (Milledgeville, 1865), pp. 45-46; Treasury Notes Registers, all denominations,

Georgia State Archives; Issuance of Treasury Notes, W. C. Mitchell Ledger, 1843-1863, p. 432.

[7]*Acts of . . . Georgia . . . 1864, . . . 1865*, p. 10; Treasury Notes Registers, all denominations; Issuances of Treasury Notes, W. C. Mitchell Ledger, 1843-1863, p. 432.

[8]*Acts of . . . Georgia . . . 1864, . . . 1865*, pp. 10, 33.

[9]*Acts of the General Assembly of the State of Georgia, passed in Milledgeville at an Annual Session . . . 1860* (Milledgeville, 1861), p. 22; *Acts of . . . Georgia . . . 1861*, pp. 19, 25-28; *Acts of . . . Georgia . . . 1862, . . . 1863*, pp. 15, 18.

[10]Ibid., p. 21; State Change Bills, W. C. Mitchell Ledger, 1843-1863, p. 433; *Acts of . . . Georgia . . . 1863, . . . 1864*, pp. 14-15; Criswell, *Confederate and Southern States Currency*, pp. 147-48; State Change Bills, W. C. Mitchell Ledger, 1843-1863, p. 433.

[11]Report of the Commission to burn Worn and Redeemed Treasury Notes, June 30, 1823, and December 23, 1824, Treasurer and Comptroller Papers, Miscellaneous Group (Currency), North Carolina State Archives.

[12]*Ordinances and Resolutions passed by the State Convention of North Carolina* (Raleigh, 1862), pp. 42-45; *Public Laws of the State of North Carolina passed . . . at its Adjourned Session 1860-1861* (Raleigh, 1861), p. 7.

[13]Ibid., p. 132; Criswell, *Confederate and Southern States Currency*, pp. 192-99; *Ordinances and Resolutions . . . of North Carolina*, pp. 57-62, 79-80, 107, 129-30.

[14]Ibid., pp. 130-32, 173-74.

[15]Reports of the Treasury Department, April 30, 1862, Treasurer and Comptroller Papers, Miscellaneous Group (Currency); Criswell, *Confederate and Southern States Currency*, pp. 210-18; *Public Laws of the State of North Carolina passed . . . at its Adjourned Session 1864-1865* (Raleigh, 1865), pp. 15, 24.

[16]North Carolina General Assembly, 1862-1863 Session, *Report of the Joint Committee . . . to Enquire into the Causes why Soldiers were paid in Confederate Treasury Notes instead of North Carolina Notes* (Raleigh, 1863), pp. 1-14.

[17]W. B. Gulick, certification of amounts received, August 23, 1864, Zebulon B. Vance Papers, 1863-1865, North Carolina State Archives; Ordinance, January 29, 1862, Secretary of State Papers, Constitutional Convention, 1861-1862. Tabled and Postponed Bills, North Carolina State Archives; Sterling Exchange Accounts, 1864-1865, Treasurer and Comptroller Papers, Military Papers, Quartermaster and Blockade Accounts, 1861-1864, North Carolina State Archives.

[18]*Acts and Resolutions adopted by the General Assembly of Florida, at its Tenth Session* (Tallahassee, 1861), pp. 43-46; *Constitution . . . of Florida, Revised and Amended at a Convention begun . . . on the Third Day of January, 1861. Together with the Ordinances adopted by said Convention* (Tallahassee, 1861), p. 36; *Journal of the Convention . . . begun and held . . . in the City of Tallahassee on Tuesday, January 14, 1862* (n.p., n.d.), p. 6.

[19]Criswell, *Confederate and Southern States Currency*, pp. 125-29; A bill to be entitled, "An act to provide for the payment of the War Tax to be assessed upon and

collected from the Citizens of this State," Bills of the House, 1861-1865, Florida State Archives, Tallahassee, Florida; An act to authorize an issue of Treasury Notes to pay the War Tax, ibid.

[20]*Acts and Resolutions adopted by the General Assembly of Florida, at the First Session of its Twelfth Assembly* (Tallahassee, 1862), p. 19; *Journal of the Convention . . . 1862*, p. 75.

[21]An act to provide for an additional issue of Treasury Notes, Bills of the House, 1861-1865; *Acts and Resolutions adopted by the General Assembly of Florida, at its Twelfth Session* (Tallahassee, 1863), p. 23; Criswell, *Confederate and Southern States Currency*, pp. 131-35.

[22]*Acts and Resolutions . . . of Florida . . . Twelfth Session*, p. 19; *Acts and Resolutions adopted by the General Assembly of Florida at its Thirteenth Session* (Tallahassee, 1865), p. 34.

[23]*Acts and Resolutions . . . of Florida . . . Tenth Session*, pp. 86, 230; *Constitution . . . Together with the Ordinances*, p. 60; *Journal of the Convention . . . 1862*, pp. 6, 80; An act to allow the Banks to suspend, An act to allow Pensacola to issue change bills, An act to provide for an additional issue of Treasury Notes, Bills of the House, 1861-1865.

[24]A bill to be entitled, "An act to support the credit of Confederate and State Treasury Notes," ibid.; *Acts and Resolutions . . . of Florida . . . Twelfth Session*, p. 55; *Journal of the Proceedings of the Senate . . . of Florida at the Thirteenth Session* (Tallahassee, 1864), p. 18; A bill to be entitled, "An act to raise the State tax of the State of Florida and to provide an additional issue of Treasury Notes," Bills of the House, 1861-1865; *Acts and Resolutions . . . of Florida . . . Thirteenth Session*, p. 34.

FLORIDA

THREE DOLLAR NOTE, MARCH 1863. The three dollar denomination was
fairly common in these years but is seldom, if ever, used today.

Figure 28

TWENTY-FIVE CENTS NOTE, FEBRUARY 1863. Any note below
the denomination of five dollars was known as a small change note.
Values below one dollar were common among the states, but not with
the central government.

Figure 29

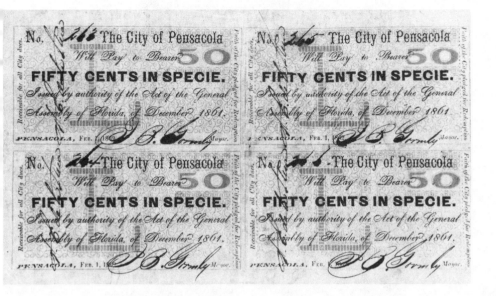

FIFTY CENTS SCRIP OF PENSACOLA, FLORIDA, 1862. Obverse. The city of Pensacola had these change bills printed in Mobile, Alabama. They were dated February 1, 1862. The Confederate city government of Pensacola evacuated the city to establish its government in exile at Greenville, Alabama, shortly before Union forces occupied the city on May 10, 1862. The Confederates left behind $2,276.00 in this scrip for the use of the city under Union control. Thus Confederate Mayor C. H. Gingles signed some of the bills (not shown here), while Union Mayor J. B. Gormly signed others (above). After the war, city treasurer Filo E. de la Rua, whose signature is also on the above bills, accounted for all of the change bills whether used in Greenville or Pensacola. "Statement B accompanying City Treasurer's communication to Board of Aldermen, June 22, 1866," in De La Rua Papers, Box 1, T.T. Wentworth, Jr. Collection, Historic Pensacola Preservation Board. See also Cassidy, *Florida Paper Money*, 156-75. Change bills courtesy of Arnold L. Rosenbleeth of Pensacola.

Figure 30

FIFTY CENTS SCRIP OF PENSACOLA, FLORIDA, 1862.
Reverse. This side of the fifty cents change bill had absolutely
nothing to do with the obverse side. The scarcity of paper compelled the Mobile printer to make use of whatever scraps he
could find. Thus he printed these bills on the blank side of
bank drafts of the Bank of West Florida, Apalachicola,
Florida, that had been used in the 1830s. Courtesy of Arnold
L. Rosenbleeth of Pensacola.

Figure 31

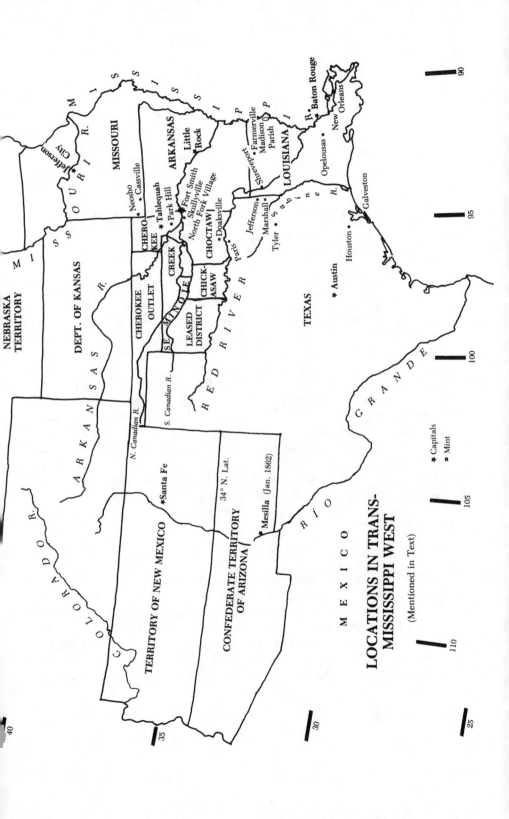

LOCATIONS IN TRANS-
MISSISSIPPI WEST

(Mentioned in Text)

★ Capitals
■ Mint

Chapter VI

THE TRANS-MISSISSIPPI MONETARY SITUATION

The Trans-Mississippi Confederacy faced many of the same problems as the Eastern states but was blessed with one great benefit that the rest of the Confederacy did not enjoy. Because these states were west of the Mississippi River, they had an unobstructed land route to Mexico and a foreign market. Arkansas, Louisiana, and Texas could all make use of this advantage. Missouri could have and probably would have enjoyed the same benefits, but the quick capture of the state by the forces of the United States and the subsequent exile of the Confederate state government made its monetary history unique. Arkansas and Texas relied on treasury warrants; Louisiana on treasury notes; and Missouri on bonds that circulated as currency. These Trans-Mississippi states differed from the Eastern states in that all of them turned from paper money to a reliance upon commodities and specie and thereby steered a different monetary course from that of the Eastern Confederacy.

ARKANSAS

First secession and later the war presented Arkansas with severe problems. Although most of the other states had been able to count upon their banks for paper money, Arkansas had no banks prior to the war. The only money that could be associated with the state and circulated in Arkansas before secession was known as swamp money scrip, authorized on January 6, 1851, by the legislature. This money represented one-quarter section tracts of undeveloped swamp land and was transferable.

Although they continually talked of retiring the scrip, legislative action kept it alive from year to year, and on November 22, 1862, the legislature once more revived the issue. Only specie and the bank notes of other states, particularly Louisiana, circulated in the state prior to 1861.[1]

The Arkansas Secession Convention acted first regarding the state's monetary matters, and on May 11, 1861, it passed two ordinances. The first levied a tax of one-quarter of one percent on the value of all property and appropriated all funds in the treasury, except the school fund, for military purposes. The second voted a $2,000,000 issue of eight percent coupon war bonds with values from five to five hundred dollars and permitted the state treasurer to issue warrants, also bearing eight percent interest, any time he did not have enough funds in the treasury to pay the auditor's warrants. The state treasury warrants were to be dated and numbered and were to be paid according to the date and number; however, these warrants were also receivable for payment of state debts at any time. On June 1, 1861, the convention decided that no more than two-thirds of any tax could be paid in state bonds, their coupons, or treasury warrants. The remainder of the tax had to be paid in coin or overdue coupons. On the same day, June 1, the convention limited the denominations of all treasury warrants to five dollars and above. The way was then open for the legislature to act.[2]

Arkansas treasury warrants did not circulate well at first. North Carolina surmounted this problem by making its notes fundable in bonds, but the Arkansas warrants already carried interest. On November 18, 1861, the legislature circumvented this annoyance with a new law. Any creditor who refused to accept Arkansas treasury warrants or Confederate Treasury notes and bonds could take no further action to collect the money due until two years after the end of the war. The same day the legislature declared that any bank note could circulate within the state, but disallowed shinplasters "or other irresponsible paper."[3] In order to supply the need for small denominations, the legislature on November 18, 1861, repealed the June 1 ordinance fixing five dollars as the smallest value warrant, and authorized non-interest bearing notes of one, two, and three dollars face value. Four days prior to this action, it also repealed the requirement that one-third of all taxes be paid in specie or overdue coupons, and permitted the use of Confederate paper in payment of all sums owed to the state.[4]

Like all the other states, Arkansas also had to face the problem of the Confederate war tax. On November 18, 1861, the legislature proposed to pay the tax by cancelling a portion of the debt which the central authorities owed to Arkansas equal to the amount of the tax payment. This plan was rejected. On March 21, 1862, Arkansas finally decided that the state treasurer should pay the tax with warrants bearing eight percent interest. If the central government refused this offer, the act empowered Governor Henry M. Rector to dispose of these warrants on the best terms possible and to use Confederate bills in settlement of the tax. The legislature appropriated $650,000 for this purpose on March 22, 1862. Rector had to sell these warrants, because the Confederate authorities directed that the tax must be paid either in specie or Confederate Treasury notes.[5]

As Arkansas's needs mounted, the interest-bearing warrants became less and less attractive to state officials. On November 21, 1862, the state deleted this provision from the law and from then on the warrants bore no interest. Slowly but surely Arkansas came to accept Confederate paper, which circulated widely. On December 1, 1862, the collection of any and all taxes, except those due for 1861, was suspended until further notice. In addition, the act permitted fractional notes in denominations of twenty-five and fifty cents, as well as the one, two, three, and five dollars previously authorized, to be paid out *on demand*. This law took effect on December 15, 1862. The final step towards a state currency occurred on October 1, 1864, when the treasurer was empowered to reissue non-interest bills for the amount of principal and interest of deposited interest-bearing warrants.[6]

County scrip and illegal shinplasters circulated in Arkansas, but there still existed a need for fractional notes. None of the state change bills, however, have survived the passage of time. Either Arkansas never issued change bills, or the quantities were so small that they have disappeared. The latter would seem more likely, as every other state that authorized change bills had a large demand for them. Perhaps county scrip and suspension of taxes dried up demand, but this does not appear reasonable. In all probability the twenty-five and fifty cent state change notes did exist. The suspension of taxes would have forced the state to use some form of small change to meet its own requirements.[7]

By September 1863, one man living in southwestern Arkansas commented that only Confederate notes were in circulation in that area. In October 1864, the state passed a law forcing county treasurers to accept Confederate notes as well as state and county paper. Thus Confederate paper money slowly supplanted all other currency within Arkansas. When the time came to convert the old Confederate issues, the state depositor, Edward Cross, informed Governor Harris Flanagin that the paper was being presented daily and that considerable amounts were being funded in bonds.[8] But in 1864, the state of Arkansas slowly moved away from its total reliance on paper money. No Arkansas treasury warrant dated later than 1863 has been found, and state officials began looking for other means of helping their citizens.

Cotton and wool cards were necessary to convert raw products into a form more easily made into fabric, for the people desperately needed clothing. On October 1, 1864, the legislature appropriated a total of $35,000 in specie to pay for cotton and wool cards and medicines to distribute to the families of soldiers. Governor Flanagin, however, also looked into the possibilities of setting up machines to manufacture cotton and wool cards rather than buying them. Governor Henry W. Allen of Louisiana advised him that it would take four months to set up the machines and urged him to purchase them at Memphis, Tennessee, instead. Flanagin went ahead with his plans, even though he ran into problems. The specie appropriation was needed, because Governor Flanagin's agent, H. H. Carter, warned him that the old Treasury note issues would not buy anything in the places he went. Thus Arkansas came to rely more on specie and commodities, while paper money lost value and favor. Efforts to force acceptance of currency worked only for a while.

LOUISIANA

The state of Louisiana retained paper money for a longer period of time than Arkansas, but even Louisiana eventually abandoned it. Perhaps this was due to a portion of the state being located east of the Mississippi River, but by the end of 1862 most of that section had been lost to the United States. Louisiana state authorities found themselves in an enviable position during most of 1861, for the state was blessed with an abundance of specie, and the banks were required to redeem their notes for coin whenever people requested it. The port of New Orleans, a main trade area for decades before 1861, provided a vast amount of wealth for the state, and the notes of the city's banks enjoyed wide circulation and were highly favored by many people. If it were not for the fact that fighting came early to the state, it might have made it through the entire war without issuing paper money.[9]

Louisiana had enough money so that the secession convention could generously transfer its bullion fund and all its customs receipts, a total of $536,787.72, to the Confederate government. Most, if not all of this sum was probably in specie. The reason for this overabundance of specie may be found in the banking laws of the state. Even as late as March 27, 1861, an ordinance of the secession convention required new banks to have two-thirds of their capital in coin before they could begin operations, and the rest must be made up in the first year of business. No bank note lower than ten dollars could be issued, and the total outstanding could not exceed three-fourths of the bank's paid capital. With this ordinance, the secession convention ended its monetary concerns.[10]

The Louisiana legislature also delved into the problems of state finances. On March 20, 1861 the legislature instructed the governor to borrow $300,000 in specie or bank notes from the banks, provided it could be done without interest; the money was to be repaid out of the state's revenues for 1861. The banks soon lent the state the $300,000 with the Citizens Bank at Opelousas and similar institutions joining in the effort. But the situation in early 1861 soon deteriorated. Specie and bank notes were beginning to be withdrawn and times became more difficult. By May, one Kate Stone, complained that her brother, William R. Stone, found it difficult to raise enough money to keep their upper Louisiana plantation open. He finally obtained the money by pledging cotton at a bank in New Orleans. By July it proved difficult even to break a ten dollar bill in the city of New Orleans. To make matters worse, Governor Moore urged the banks in Louisiana to suspend specie payment on September 18, 1861, an action that the legislature legalized on January 20, 1862. The public could no longer obtain specie until twelve months after the war, but the banks could lend coin to both the state and central governments. New Orleans experienced a dearth of silver money by September 22 and no specie at all by November 2.[11]

With suspension of specie payments in Louisiana came a number of remedies for the shortage of change. They pressed shinplasters, omnibus tickets, and other items into service. Rising prices were also noticeable inside and outside of New Orleans. As early as September 28, 1861, people complained about exorbitantly high prices, and by November a bar of soap, which had cost twenty cents before the crisis, was selling for one dollar. On January 20, 1862, the state allowed banks to print bills under the denomination of five dollars, but it did not act again for some time after that.[12]

Also in January 1862, the Louisiana legislature authorized $7,000,000 of eight percent bonds, payable in three to ten years, or non-interest bearing treasury notes. Both of these were to be sold for New Orleans bank notes or Confederate bills. For the most part, the bonds were sold until

ARKANSAS

FIVE DOLLAR TREASURY WARRANT, MARCH 1862. Issued under Acts of 1861. The portrait in the center is of Governor Henry M. Rector. From Criswell, *Confederate and Southern States Currency.*

Figure 32

ONE DOLLAR TREASURY WARRANT, DECEMBER 1861. Arkansas had no state bank just prior to secession. From Criswell, *Confederate and Southern States Currency.*

Figure 33

FIVE DOLLAR BILL. Authorized by Act of October 1862.

Figure 34

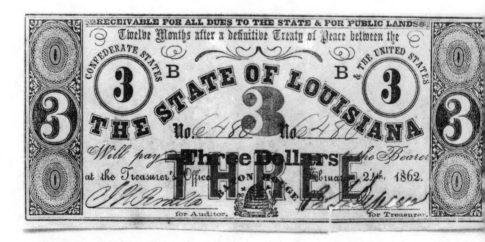

THREE DOLLAR NOTE. Issued under Act of January 1862.

Figure 35

the treasury notes were ready; they were delivered by April 1862, and used immediately. A safe estimate of the total amount of notes issued in this first authorization is $4,000,000. They needed the notes because, on January 23, 1862, the state suspended the collection of all taxes. The same day the legislature made Confederate notes receivable for all amounts owed to the state and local governments.[13]

Louisiana suffered a serious blow with the loss of New Orleans in April 1862. On April 29, 1862, a notice appeared in New Orleans newspapers urging all shops to remain open and receive any ordinary currency. The people who wished to divest themselves of Confederate bills were instructed to take them to the Committee of Public Safety where they would be exchanged for City of New Orleans bills. The committee also prepared a list of corporations and cities that had issued change notes which were considered sound. Memminger saw to it that some of the banks' specie was removed before the city fell, and Governor Moore helped supervise the removal of the rest. Only Confederate paper remained in New Orleans, and Major General Benjamin F. Butler seized the Confederate government accounts. He later dispatched the total confiscated to the Secretary of the Treasury in Washington, D. C.[14]

Louisiana now required more money; all specie was gone, and no taxes were being collected which would have brought funds into the treasury. This state of affairs led to legislative approval of another issue of $20,000,000 in state non-interest treasury notes in denominations from five to one hundred dollars on January 3, 1863. As before, these bills were not redeemable until twelve months after a treaty of peace. While these notes were being issued, the legislature discussed change bills. As of June 20, 1863, unauthorized shinplasters could no longer be issued under penalty of a $1,000 fine for each bill produced. Change bills were permitted, however, for the various parishes, cities and towns, and chartered banks. The first state issuance of change notes and the last state money was approved on February 11, 1864. At that time the legislature allowed $300,000 in twenty-five and fifty cent notes and one dollar bills, and empowered the governor to halt printing before this total was reached if he deemed it best. On February 8, 1864, the legislature also voted for six percent bonds maturing in twenty to forty years to a total of $10,000,000.[15]

Apparently Governor Henry W. Allen hoped to exchange the Louisiana bonds for Confederate Treasury notes in Richmond. In order to facilitate this, Allen sent a man to Richmond on February 22, 1864, but Memminger declined the suggestion. At this point Allen fell back on the sale of cotton for specie. Allen sold Louisiana cotton and tobacco in Texas, and even set up machines to make cotton and wool cards to distribute to the needy. In October 1864, the state also intervened between citizens and merchants to obtain an arrangement whereby people could secure salt for Confederate paper money. By 1865 a man in Shreveport was selling coin to Louisiana authorities for cotton.[16]

Finally, like Arkansas, officials in Louisiana eventually moved towards the sale of commodities for coin, and its use for necessary expenses. Louisiana used Confederate paper money until the end of the war, but special arrangements had to be made in order to get people to accept it. Again, like Arkansas, a general mistrust of paper money occurred during the last part of the war. Louisianians preferred commodities and specie to paper.

TEXAS

Unlike any of the other states, Texas enjoyed direct access to a foreign market — Mexico. This advantage gave Texas a continual flow of hard money. Mexico, with plenty of coin, was but a river away from Texas. The Confederate government and many state governments knew this and used Mexico as a vehicle for obtaining coin. It was only natural that Texas authorities realized their natural advantage and keenly felt that they were in an enviable position. Even so, it was not the people of Texas who made use of this route, but rather the government. Towards the end of the conflict, however, the average citizen became eager for specie and shunned paper money.

Texas began issuing treasury warrants before the Confederacy was conceived, and paid interest on any warrants that could not be redeemed immediately. But on February 9, 1861, the Texas legislature enacted a law making these warrants receivable for money due the state. When the warrants and interest presented exceeded the debt, a new warrant was issued for the remainder. In this way a paper currency was created by allowing warrants to be paid to the state. On April 8, 1861, the state authorized $1,000,000 in eight percent bonds, redeemable in sixteen years. These bonds were to be deposited at banks in New Orleans and were to remain under the control of the state treasurer. At the same time, Texas empowered its governor to borrow $90,000 for seventy-two months at a rate of interest not to exceed ten percent.[17]

Even so, the Texas state treasury had its problems. As of January 1, 1861, most of the specie under state control came from land sales, but by that date treasury warrants could be used for these purchases. By September 24, 1861, the state's treasurer, C. A. Randolph, and comptroller, Clem R. Jones, reported to Governor Edward Clark that they had on hand only $36,000 in state revenue, barely enough to last one month at normal rates. On November 16, 1861, Governor Francis R. Lubbock reported to the legislature that the state had no gold or silver left and urged the issuance of non-interest bearing treasury warrants. And on December 6, 1861, Governor Lubbock received news that the citizens of the state so desperately needed money that they were selling anything they could to speculators from New Orleans.[18]

About this time, the Confederate government entered the monetary picture in Texas. By December 1861, the government sent its agents to Texas to buy cotton for Treasury notes, to sell it in Mexico, and to use the proceeds to buy supplies. But at the same time, Judah P. Benjamin, Confederate Secretary of War, approached Governor Lubbock with a proposal to exchange five percent United States bonds held by Texas for eight percent Confederate States bonds. Louis T. Wigfall, commander of the Texas Brigade, urged Lubbock to accept the offer, stating that by the end of the war the United States would be totally bankrupt, while the bonds of the Confederate States would be sound. On January 9, 1862, Lubbock asked the legislature to accept the proposal, noting that Confederate bonds could be used to purchase arms. The legislature agreed.[19]

On January 11, 1862, the legislature repealed the old February 14, 1860, law providing interest for unpaid treasury warrants. The next day it decided that taxes to pay interest and principal on loans must be paid in specie, but all other debts could be paid in Texas warrants or Confederate notes or bond coupons. In December 1861, the legislature had suspended the collection of private debts until January 1, 1864, but taxes continued. On January 11, 1862, the legislature also directed that county treasurers could disperse money received, but the state treasurer could not reissue Texas warrants.[20]

The people of Texas faced a major problem in being required to pay their taxes in specie. Little specie actually circulated, no matter how much the editor of the *Tri-Weekly Telegraph* in Houston pleaded for it. As early as December 1861, complaints about the growing proliferation of shinplasters began to appear, and by May 16, 1862, they had flooded the market. In June 1863, even outcries against excesses of county scrip were heard. Almost as a reaction to this, on January 8, 1862, the legislature proposed that Texas follow the Confederate example and open trade with Mexico. In this way specie could be obtained. This proved to be so successful that on March 3, 1863, it was directed that people could pay their taxes in paper money, which would be converted to specie at the state treasury from the proceeds of cotton sales.[21]

By 1863, Confederate Treasury notes had become the main medium of exchange in Texas and the standard of value. On March 6, 1863, the state treasurer was allowed to use them for payment of debts. And on March 9, 1863, the state legislature decided that only appropriations for the support of the government and soldiers' dependents were payable in non-interest treasury warrants. Further, it specified that other appropriations could be paid with new issue Confederate notes or treasury warrants redeemable with these bills, and that all unappropriated specie was to remain in the treasury. The only other monetary action undertaken by the legislature came in December 1863, when it delayed the collection of private debts until twelve months after the war, and authorized $2,000,000 in six percent cotton bonds, payable six months after a treaty of peace.[22]

In 1863, Texas also shifted to a policy favoring commodities. At the same time, the value of state treasury warrants declined to fifteen cents on the gold dollar and eventually to two cents. As early as July 1863, the state distributed cotton and wool cards. In March 1864, some people complained about the system used to distribute these cards, preferring that they go to everyone instead of only soldiers and their families. Governor Lubbock stated on May 16, 1863, that the state treasury did not have enough money and wished to have the authority to transfer Confederate bills from one fund to another. On August 15, 1863, the Trans-Mississippi governors concurred that cotton was the only safe and reliable means for procuring supplies for the army and urged that Confederate authorities adopt this policy. Nevertheless, during this period Texas's monetary policies became more successful. When Acting Comptroller James W. Howard reported to the new governor, Pendleton Murrah, on February 29, 1864, the state treasury contained $26,128.69 in specie, $106,073.97 in state warrants, and $221,054.01 in Confederate paper money. Finally, even the people of Texas rejected paper money and demanded only specie, or bartered for what they needed.[23]

Unlike the other Trans-Mississippi states, Texas early relied on cotton and foreign trade. Also unlike the others, taxes were not suspended, although the collection of private debts was set aside. In these ways the state maintained a constant supply of paper money and, through the sale of cotton, specie. Thus the state's monetary situation remained fairly sound, but the withdrawal of interest on the warrants and their lack of immediate convertibility to specie or bonds may have contributed to their drastic decline. Texas issued very few state warrants after 1863, and one may assume that they used Confederate paper money primarily to satisfy state debts. Eventually, Texans shunned paper money, especially that of the central government, and turned to specie or barter.

MISSOURI

The state of Missouri differed significantly from either Texas, the rest of the Trans-Mississippi Confederacy, or the East. It supported the report of the Trans-Mississippi governors on the use of cotton for the army, but before the close of 1861 the Confederate government of Missouri had to flee the state. No other state succumbed so quickly, although it had been the next to last to vote itself out of the Union. Forced to leave the capital at Jefferson City, Governor Claiborne F. Jackson called a special session of the legislature to meet at Neosho on October 21, 1861. The legislature met, but had no quorum until October 28 when it passed the act of secession. Three days later the legislature reconvened at Cassville. There it enacted a law on November 1, which provided for $10,000,000 in state bonds, payable in two, five, and seven years. The law authorized bonds to be issued in denominations of one to five hundred dollars, but only those of five dollars and above carried ten percent interest. It also empowered William Shields, Thomas H. Murray, and Henry W. Lyday to sign the bonds, which were receivable in payment of all money owed to the state.[24]

Shortly after this law passed, the government had to flee the state, but the military forces remained. The new Union state government also authorized an issue of bonds, under the same terms as the Confederate state authorities, but of a smaller total. By 1863, these bonds became the main circulating medium within the state. But this does not imply that Governor Jackson did not issue the Confederate bills, for he went to New Orleans, where he contracted for the bonds to be printed. These bonds in the form of treasury notes could have circulated as such. Soon the money was being printed at the rate of $1,200 per day. Confederate Brigadier General M. Jeff Thompson stated on January 16, 1862, that he had brought $100,000 of the bonds with him and used it to pay the troops of the Missouri State Guard. He noted that he wrote the words "Prior to November 1, 1861," on the bonds in order to show service before that date. He felt if he did not do this, the paper money would be discounted by the merchants of the area.[25]

These bills in denominations of one, two, three, five, ten, and twenty dollars, dated January 1, 1862, were made payable three years after date.

As specified in the act, only the five, ten, and twenty dollar denominations bore ten percent interest, and they were all signed by one of the three commissioners. This money was primitive in appearance, but later Keatinge and Ball of Columbia, South Carolina, printed a much better quality "Missouri Defense Bond." They produced these handsome bills in denominations of one, two, three, four, and four and one-half dollars, as well as three "Requisitions for Missouri Defense Bonds" with values of twenty, fifty, and one hundred dollars. The last three did not bear interest, but were meant to be converted into bonds. This later issue, however, was never signed or used. The reason for this could be found in actions of the Confederate government.[26]

The first distribution of Missouri notes did not occur until late January 1862. By this date, the contract must have already been signed with Keatinge and Ball, but the preparation took longer than that in New Orleans. On December 13, 1861, George G. Vest of Missouri introduced a bill in the Confederate States Provisional Congress which called for a Confederate guarantee of $1,000,000 of Missouri bonds. By the terms of the bill, a commissioner was to be appointed by President Davis to countersign the bonds, thus pledging the faith of the Confederacy to $1,000,000 of the $10,000,000 of Missouri bonds. The bonds were to be used to pay members of the Missouri State Guard for services rendered. But when Robert W. Barnwell of South Carolina reported this bill back on January 24, 1862, he proposed a totally different bill which was passed on the same day. By the terms of this act, the central government loaned Missouri $1,000,000 in Confederate Treasury notes in return for $1,000,000 of its bonds.[27]

But Vest was not yet finished. On January 31, 1862, he introduced another bill to supplement the previous one. On February 6, 1862, that bill returned from committee with their recommendation that it be tabled, but Vest managed to delay the vote on this action. On February 12 Vest submitted another bill to aid Missouri, which went to the Committee on Finance. At the same time Vest reopened debate on his bill of January 31, proposed changing it to read the same as the act passed on January 24, and called for a vote. The act passed and Davis signed it into law on February 15. In this way, Missouri received an additional $1,000,000. Commissioner William Shields carried the full amount, $2,000,000 from Richmond on April 12, 1862.[28]

This concluded the history of Missouri's Confederate monetary policy. The state government remained in exile, issued no further notes or bonds, and the central authorities assumed complete control, including paying

FIFTY DOLLAR TREASURY WARRANT. Authorized by Act of 1862. From Criswell, *Confederate and Southern States Currency.*

Figure 36

FIVE DOLLARS, JUNE 1862. Issued under Act of 1862.

Figure 37

FIVE DOLLARS, JANUARY 1862. Authorized by Act of 1861. Merchants refused to accept these bills until the words "Prior to 1st Novbr. 1861" were added showing service before that date.

Figure 38

REVERSE SIDE OF FIVE DOLLAR BILL. This shows the endorsement on the bill required by merchants.

Figure 39

the troops. How Confederate Missouri paper money would have been redeemed is a mystery, for the state government was completely bankrupt by 1862. Union authorities in Missouri faced much the same situation. But Confederate Missouri did agree to the use of cotton to purchase military supplies. Thus it is reasonable to assume that Missouri would have followed much the same course as the rest of the Trans-Mississippi area had it been able to do so.

SUMMARY

The Trans-Mississippi portion of the Confederacy displayed little initial hesitancy to resort to paper money for credit. Two of the four states involved suspended taxes, while Texas alone suspended the collection of private debts. All of the states showed a desire to use commodities and the specie it could produce. There was also a general reluctance to accept paper money towards the end of the war. Only Texas and Louisiana issued paper money in 1864, but Louisiana used only small change bills, and the amount issued in Texas was minor. Unlike the East, the Trans-Mississippi Confederate States relied more heavily on money of intrinsic value, and none of them displayed abuses of monetary power such as Georgia and North Carolina.

Both the East and the Trans-Mississippi Confederacy shared some basic monetary characteristics. Whenever there was an abundance of other forms of money, such as specie or bank notes, the state governments usually used it in return for bonds. As this source dried up, states began to issue some form of paper money. They eventually eliminated interest on these bills, because it appeared to be an inexpensive way to obtain money. Those states that had commercial areas before secession found their monetary problems less severe at first, but their conditions seriously deteriorated after a few months of war.

As the war continued, increased logistical demands brought greater expenses to the various state governments. Thus state governments continued to print more paper money to meet this demand, and this caused the value of their money to decline. By 1862 more and more states had turned to legislative measures to force the acceptance of Confederate and state paper money. The states may have done so because the central government refused to make its paper money legal tender. Eventually there was so much paper money outstanding that the value of even the best issues began to drop drastically. In the East, the reaction was to use paper or to barter. But in the Trans-Mississippi Confederacy people turned to commodities and specie. Those issues of paper backed by tangibles such as cotton or land tended to hold their value more than those backed only by faith in state governments.

[1]Edward Cross to Memminger, October 3, 1861, CST, Letters Received, 1861-1865; *Acts passed at the Eighth Session of the General Assembly of the State of Arkansas* (Little Rock, 1851), p. 75; *Acts passed at the Fourteenth Session of the General Assembly of the State of Arkansas* (Washington, 1896), p. 15.

[2]*Ordinances of the State Convention, which convened in Little Rock, May 6, 1861* (Little Rock, 1861), pp. 12, 57-58, 69-70, 79-80.

[3]*Acts passed at the Thirteenth or Special Session of the General Assembly of the State of Arkansas* (Little Rock, 1861), pp. 43-46, 70.

[4]Ibid., pp. 19, 78.

[5]Ibid., pp. 41-42; *Acts passed at the Thirteenth or Special Session of the General Assembly of the State of Arkansas* (Little Rock, 1862), pp. 9-11, 15; George W. Randolph to Henry M. Rector, April 19, 1862, Kie Oldham Collection, Arkansas Department of History, Little Rock, Arkansas.

[6]*Acts passed at the Fourteenth Session of the General Assembly of the State of Arkansas*, pp. 14, 35, 59, 74; *Acts passed at the Called Session of the General Assembly of the State of Arkansas* (Washington, 1896), p. 2.

[7]Criswell, *Confederate and Southern States Currency*, pp. 110-20.

[8]Robert C. Park to Harris Flanagin, September 12, 1863; Edward Cross to Flanagin, March 21, 1864, Oldham Collection; *Acts passed at the Called Session . . . Arkansas* [1864], p. 6.

[9]Criswell, *Confederate and Southern States Currency*, pp. 110-20; *Acts passed at the Called Session . . . Arkansas* [1864], p. 18; Henry W. Allen to Flanagin, November 7, 1864; H. H. Carter to Flanagin, November 14, 1864, Oldham Collection.

[10]*Proceedings of the Louisiana State Convention . . . together with the Ordinances passed*, pp. 265, 287.

[11]*Acts passed by the Fifth Legislature of the State of Louisiana, at its Second Session* (Baton Rouge, 1861), p. 190; Citizens Bank to Thomas O. Moore, July, 1861, Letters Received, Executive Department, State of Louisiana, 1860-1865; John Q. Anderson, ed., *Brokenburn: The Journal of Kate Stone, 1861-1868* (Baton Rouge, 1955), p. 19; Solomon, "Diary," pp. 64, 125.

[12]Ibid., p. 125; Anderson, ed., *Brokenburn*, p. 125; Solomon, "Diary," pp. 78, 125; *Acts passed by the Sixth Legislature of . . . Louisiana . . . First Session*, p. 45.

[13]Ibid., pp. 84-86; Record of State Bonds and Treasury Notes, Louisiana State Archives; *Acts passed by the Sixth Legislature of . . . Louisiana . . . First Session*, pp. 79, 82.

[14]*Daily Picayune*, April 29, 1862; *New Orleans Bee*, April 29, 1862; Memminger to Wood and Brothers, June 5, 1862, *Private and Official Correspondence of*

General Benjamin F. Butler, 5 vols. (n.p., 1917), 2:4; James D. Denegre to Moore, April-May, 1862; Moore to State Treasurer, May, 1862, Letters Received, Executive Department, State of Louisiana, 1860-1865; James D. Denegre to Benjamin F. Butler, June 11, 1862, *Correspondence of Butler*, 1:617-18.

[15]*Acts passed by the Twenty-Seventh Legislature of the State of Louisiana, in Extra Session at Opelousas December, 1862, and January, 1863* (Natchitoches, 1864), pp. 29-30; *Acts passed by the Sixth Legislature of the State of Louisiana, at the City of Shreveport on the Fourth of May, 1863* (Shreveport, 1863), p. 5; *Acts passed by the Seventh Legislature of the State of Louisiana, at its First Session, at the City of Shreveport on the Eighteenth Day of January, 1864* (Shreveport, 1864), pp. 11-12, 22, 72.

[16]Allen to Memminger, February 22, 1864, CST, Letters Received, 1861-1865; Memminger to Allen, March 31, 1864; Emory Clapp to Allen, various dates; John M. Sandidge to Allen, October 24, 1864; John J. Hodge to Allen, May 27, 1865, Letters Received, Executive Department, State of Louisiana, 1860-1865.

[17]*Laws of the Eighth Legislature of the State of Texas, Extra Session* (Austin, 1861), pp. 19, 39-40, 48.

[18]Ibid., p. 6; C. A. Randolph and Clem R. Jones to Edward Clark, September 24, 1861, Edward Clark Papers, 1859-1861, Texas State Archives, Austin, Texas; Charles Sheane to Francis R. Lubbock, December 6, 1861, Francis R. Lubbock Papers, 1861-1863, Texas State Archives; James M. Day, ed., *Senate Journal of the Ninth Legislature of the State of Texas* (Austin, 1963), p. 58.

[19]Judah P. Benjamin to George H. Giddings Rich, December 14, 1861; Louis T. Wigfall to Lubbock, December 9, 1861; Lubbock to the House of Representatives and Senate, January 19, 1862, Lubbock Papers, 1861-1863.

[20]*General Laws of the Ninth Legislature of the State of Texas* (Houston, 1862), pp. 5, 32, 37-38.

[21]*Tri-Weekly Telegraph* (Houston, Texas), December 30, 1861, January 13, May 16, 1862; *Tri-Weekly State Gazette*, June 11, 1863; Day, ed., *Senate Journal of the Ninth Legislature of . . . Texas*, p. 225; *General Laws of the Extra Session of the Ninth Legislature of the State of Texas*, p. 8, in H. P. N. Gammel, ed., *The Laws of Texas, 1822-1897*, 20 vols. (Austin, 1898), 5:596.

[22]*Tri-Weekly State Gazette*, October 30, 1863; *General Laws of the Tenth Legislature of the State of Texas*, pp. 18-19; *General Laws of the Extra Session of the Ninth Legislature*, p. 23; *General and Special Laws of the Called Session, Tenth Legislature of the State of Texas*, pp. 10-11; *General Laws of the Tenth Legislature*, pp. 5, 9, in Gammel, ed., *Laws*, 6ll, 659, 663, 672-75, 768-69.

[23]H. J. Richary to James Paul, July 26, 1863, Treasurer's Papers, 1861-1865, Texas State Archives; E. T. Cosley to Pendleton Murrah, March 10, 1864, Pendleton Murrah Papers, 1863-1865; Report of Governor's Conference, August 15, 1863, Lubbock to C. R. Jones, May 6, 1863, Francis R. Lubbock Letter Press Book, Texas State Archives; James W. Howard to Murrah, Murrah Papers, 1863-1865; Robert A. Newell to Sarah A. Newell, late 1864 or early 1865, Robert A. Newell Papers, Archives Division, Louisiana State University Library, Baton

Rouge, Louisiana.

[24]*Journal of the Senate, Extra Session of the Rebel* [Missouri] *Legislature* (Jefferson City, 1865-1866), pp. 1-3, 10, 34-35.

[25]Treasurer's Report, January 1, 1863, *Journal of the House of Representatives of the State of Missouri, at the First Called Session of the Twenty-Second General Assembly* (Jefferson City, 1863), appendix, p. 5; M. Jeff Thompson to Sterling Price, January 1, 1862; M. Jeff Thompson to Claiborne F. Jackson, January 16, 1862, U. S., Department of War, *War of the Rebellion: A Compilation of the Official Records of the Union and Confederate Armies*, 70 vols. (Washington, 1880-1901), Ser. I, 8:727, 735-36.

[26]Criswell, *Confederate and Southern States Currency*, pp. 178-85.

[27]*Confederate Congressional Journals*, 1:565; An act to pledge the Credit of the Confederate States for certain bonds of the State of Missouri, CSC, Legislative Papers, February, 1862-March, 1865; *Confederate Congressional Journals*, 1:700.

[28]Ibid., pp. 735, 762, 804, 831; E. C. Elmore to John H. Reagan, April 12, 1862, CPOD, Letters Sent, March 7, 1861-October 12, 1863.

Chapter VII

THE CHEROKEE SCRIP OF 1862

The Trans-Mississippi Confederacy did not consist of states alone. The Indian nations of the Indian Territory were also its allies. Because their economies were strongly tied to the South, both the Cherokee and the Choctaw issued paper money. The Cherokee acted first when they issued scrip in 1862. On May 2, 1862, the Cherokee Council and National Committee passed an act authorizing the issuance of $20,000 of notes for the Cherokee Nation in denominations of fifty cents, one dollar, two dollars, and five dollars. That the Cherokee needed to print the bills demonstrated the degree to which its economic conditions had degenerated during the early months of the war.[1]

The Cherokee had successfully adapted to the white man's culture long before the beginning of the war in 1861. They possessed a thriving economy aligned with the agriculture of the South, including the use of black slaves. Henry M. Rector, the governor of Arkansas, emphasized this when he contacted Principal Chief John Ross of the Cherokee Nation on January 19, 1861. At that time Rector urged Ross to side with the Confederacy because "your people, in their institutions, productions, latitude, and natural sympathies, are allied to the common brotherhood of slave holding states."[2]

When the South withdrew from the Union, the Cherokee Nation faced several alternatives: it could remain with the United States, join with the Confederate States, or follow a course of strict neutrality. Ross chose the latter path when on May 17, 1861, he issued a proclamation from Park Hill calling upon the Cherokee faithfully to observe the treaties with the United States and to remain neutral. "There has been no declaration of war," Ross stated, "and the conflict may yet be averted by compromise or a peaceful separation."[3]

But Ross's hopes were to be short-lived, for hostilities had commenced with the firing on Fort Sumter in the harbor of Charleston, South Carolina, on April 12, 1861. On August 21, a special convention presided over by Joseph Vann, assistant principal chief of the Cherokee Nation, issued a proclamation which affirmed the nation's neutrality and declared slaves to be property. The members of the convention also declared that there were to be no differences between full-blood and mixed-blood Cherokees — a declaration that proved to be incorrect because differences between them soon surfaced. The full-blood Cherokee, called Pins after their habit of wearing crossed pins in their lapels to identify themselves, came to be strongly pro-Union. The mixed-bloods came to be more solidly for the Confederacy.[4]

The Pins found a spokesman in Ross, while the opposing faction eventually settled on Stand Watie as their leader. Watie finally attained the position of principal chief of the Confederate Cherokee and brigadier general in the Provisional Confederate Army. Gaining a leading position among the Cherokee early in 1861, Watie's followers campaigned for a treaty of alliance with the Confederate States. As a result, they persuaded Ross to ally with the Confederacy, even though the convention had called for a policy of neutrality as Ross wished. Later (August 24, 1861) Ross told Confederate Brigadier General Benjamin McCulloch that he intended to seek a treaty with the new nation and offered a regiment of troops to fight. On September 1, 1861, McCulloch answered Ross, commenting that he had already authorized Watie to organize a force of three hundred men to protect the Cherokee Nation's northern border. This force had been organized even though Ross, in response to an earlier request by McCulloch, had declined to allow those Cherokee with Confederate sympathies to organize as Home Guards.[5]

Why did Ross change his stance? McCulloch informed the Confederate Secretary of War, Judah P. Benjamin, on September 2, 1861, of one possible reason. He maintained that Watie, who belonged "to the true Southern party," was the one "by whose course and influence Ross was induced to join the South."[6] U. S. officials, however, later gave a different version. On August 13, 1862, Brigadier General James G. Blunt, commander of the Department of Kansas, told President Abraham Lincoln that Ross had delayed signing a treaty with the Confederacy in expectation that troops of the United States would arrive and ensure his group's protection. "This hope failing them," Blunt explained, "they were compelled to the policy they adopted as a matter of necessity and self preservation."[7]

On October 7, 1861, the Cherokee Nation and the Confederate States signed a treaty, and two weeks later the National Committee and Council of the Cherokee Nation issued a declaration giving the reasons for this agreement. The Cherokee leaders declared that Cherokee origins were in the South and that their "institutions are similar to those of the Southern States," and that their interests were identical with those of the Confederacy. Further, they reiterated that they were hesitant to break their ties and even tried neutrality. The Confederacy was strong and had established itself in a defensive struggle without denial of personal liberties, whereas the United States was "behaving in an unconstitutional and bestial manner." They complained that "foreign mercenaries and the scum of cities and the inmates of prison were enlisted" and sent south to fight. The final reason given was by far the most telling and prophetic. The Cherokee leaders stated that they feared that the United States would force land allotment on the Cherokee and deny them their slaves.[8]

Almost as soon as the treaty was signed, factionalism divided the Cherokee Nation. The Confederate Provisional Congress ratified the treaty on December 24, 1861, with amendments to which the Cherokee Nation later gave its assent. Earlier, on December 11, 1861, Confederate Colonel Douglas H. Cooper, commander of the Indian Department and later brigadier general, commander of the District of Indian Territory, and Superintendent of Indian Affairs, noted that disaffection was widespread among the Cherokee and that there was a serious need for more white Confederate troops. Soon a secret society of Union Cherokee Indians headed by a Cherokee named One Salmon was formed.[9]

By this time economic conditions within the Cherokee Nation were also declining. In October 1861, prices increased, but they were still not as high as in New Orleans. Different types of money circulated within the nation; they trusted Confederate notes and Louisiana bank bills, but not as much as gold and silver. They mistrusted bank notes of the adjacent state of Missouri, and thus the value of those notes declined daily. Confederate paper also began to circulate, and gold continued to be used sparingly. On October 23, 1861, Andrew R. Nave, a Cherokee merchant, dispatched two hundred dollars in gold, as well as four hundred dollars in Confederate bills, in the course of his business. The little available specie, however, soon began to be withdrawn. Shinplasters proliferated, and by April 1862, they were being sent into the Cherokee Nation from Arkansas. These shinplasters may have been drawn upon Arkansas merchants, or printed elsewhere for local merchants, but in any case, they began to appear.[10]

Such was the monetary situation in early 1862. In order to comply with the terms of the Cherokee Treaty, the Acting Commander of Indian Affairs made a survey of bonds issued by the states now a part of the Confederacy, but held in trust by the United States government for the Cherokee, which he filed with Secretary of War Benjamin on January 17, 1862. The report expressed hope that the states would pay the principal and interest of the bonds to the Confederate States government, which would then collect these sums as trustee and pay the interest to the Cherokee. Apparently the Commander took the survey to determine how much would be paid annually to the Cherokee.[11]

The treaty entitled the Cherokee to a one-time payment of $77,644.36 in fulfillment of the 1846 treaty with the United States, which the Confederacy had assumed, and which would be paid "upon complete ratification of this treaty."[12] Congress voted the money on December 24, 1861, with $265,927.25 of the total sum owed to all treaty Indians payable in gold, an amount rapidly collected. The coin had to be collected and then delivered to Confederate Brigadier General Albert Pike. Confederate authorities purchased $95,000 of this amount in Charleston, South Carolina, with a certificate payable in coin after the blockade was lifted, with interest at eight percent. On January 28, 1862, Pike was at Little Rock, Arkansas, and expected to be at Fort Smith, Arkansas, by at least February 7. He carried with him $265,927.50 in specie, the majority in gold except $65,000 in silver. Pike also carried $172,300 in paper money for the Cherokee. But Pike did not deliver the money immediately. Perhaps he did not do so because in addition to the effects of war, the Cherokee still had to agree to the treaty's amendments before it could be ratified. On March 26, 1862, S. Rindley inquired about the money in order to pay the Cherokee troops. Finally, John Crawford, the Confederate agent for the Cherokee, informed Watie on March 31, 1862, that he had received the money from Pike.[13]

Even though the terms of the treaty did not require the Cherokee to pay for the costs of the war, they still felt a financial pinch. While the gold remained in their treasury, the Cherokee used Confederate paper money. But this did not alleviate the small change plight. The central government printed no bill below the denomination of five dollars in 1861, and did not authorize the 1862 issues until April 17, 1862. Thus the shinplaster nuisance remained.[14]

To correct this situation, the Cherokee National Committee and Council on May 2, 1862, required the Cherokee treasurer to hold $20,000 in Confederate Treasury notes and in lieu of these, to issue bills of the Cherokee Nation in denominations of fifty cents, one, two, and five dollars, which were to be put into circulation. These bills could be redeemed at the Cherokee Treasury with Confederate paper money, when "presented to the amount of Twenty dollars, fifty dollars, One hundred dollars, or above the sum in like denominations."[15] This act made the issuance of individual bills illegal and punishable by a fine of five to two hundred dollars for each offense. Although not specifically authorized by law, a twenty-five cent note was also issued. The act seemed to give the Cherokee treasurer authority to issue other values, if he saw fit, and he may have done so. In any case, the number of twenty-five cent bills produced was small.[16]

The treasury issued the notes in June 1862. These bills were one of only three governmental issues authorized that made use of the United States' dollar sign (the Choctaw and Tennessee also used this sign). Their issuance at that time probably was the result of military events and the political situation, coupled with the arrival of Confederate notes, and not because of any real change in the monetary outlook.

In June 1862, a Union military expedition entered the Cherokee Nation. The Confederate Cherokee attacked the Federals and were defeated. As a result, Colonel John Drew's regiment deserted practically to the last man and joined the forces of the United States, leaving only a small body under the command of Captain Pickens Benji to fight with Watie's regiment. The Pins now rallied and the Confederates were driven back. On July 15 an expedition led by Captain Harris S. Grenno entered Park Hill to take the "surrender of the Cherokees there." He discovered that Ross had just received orders from the Confederate Adjutant and Inspector General, Samuel Cooper, to issue a call for all men between eighteen and thirty-five to enlist in the Confederate army. Grenno stated, however, that his arrival "gives Ross an excuse for not complying with the demand."[17] The Union forces also found that the Cherokee Treasury still had $45,000 in gold and some of the Confederate notes that had been paid to them by Confederate authorities. Grenno made Ross a "prisoner," but paroled him to his house.[18]

Ross's stratagem did not deceive the Confederates for long. Confederate Major General Thomas C. Hindman maintained that Ross was "pretendedly taken prisoner, but, as afterwards appeared, really went over to the enemy with the archives and money of the nation."[19] The Confederates soon began their campaign to reconquer the area, and the Federals withdrew. Ross took the Cherokee Treasury, claimed to have amounted to $65,000 in gold and $150,000 in paper, with him when he left with the Federals. This estimate, however, may have been too high.

Other money also left with the fleeing Pins, for one merchant reported that he took $23.50 in gold with him. On August 8, 1862, Colonel Douglas H. Cooper advised President Davis that within a few days he hoped to retake Tahlequah, the capital, and Park Hill and put the Confederate Cherokee into power. In late August, Cooper accomplished his mission. The Confederate Cherokees removed Ross from office and elected Watie the new principal chief of the Cherokee Nation.[20]

Even with the formation of the new Confederate Cherokee government, the financial and political picture did not improve. Throughout 1862 Union forces prevented the Confederate Cherokee National Council from meeting on various occasions, and money remained extremely scarce. The Cherokee Nation may have received some additional money from the Confederates. When Albert Pike resigned his army commission on March 13, 1863, he deposited $49,980.55 "in Treasury Notes" and $19,263.10 "in gold" with Edward Cross, the Confederate States depositor at Little Rock, Arkansas; additional funds could possibly have been delivered to the Cherokee before this time. Whatever the case, the Cherokee could have taken pride in the fact that they led the way in issuing government change notes, for only North Carolina circulated them before the Cherokee.[21]

On January 22, 1863, Elias Cornelius Boudinot, the Cherokee delegate to the Confederate House of Representatives and nephew of Stand Watie, desired the authority to receive from the Confederate government the money due the Cherokee. He felt that a full treasury would bring new life to the Cherokee Nation, but in this effort, he had a long, hard fight. On June 27, 1863, he cautioned his uncle about a law which had just been passed by the Cherokee concerning the use of treasury funds for refugees. He believed that the commissioners should use warrants or bonds rather than treasury money, or failing that, he urged that army rations and transportation be drawn on until other arrangements could be made with the Confederate government. Apparently, the Cherokee planned to use what little money they had remaining in their treasury. On November 4, 1863, Boudinot borrowed $10,000 on his own responsibility, for the relief of the Cherokee refugees. Finally, on December 18, 1863, Boudinot introduced a bill in the Confederate Congress to appropriate $100,000 for the refugees. By the terms of the act, this was only a loan, to be repaid in gold after the war. Clearly, the Cherokee desperately needed money. Otherwise they would not have made arrangements for this loan, knowing that payment in gold would be required following the war.[22]

Unfortunately, once the Congress voted for the money bill, there was

CHEROKEE NATION ONE DOLLAR NOTE. The nation issued these bills in denominations of twenty-five and fifty cents; and, one, two and five dollars. The Cherokee and Choctaw Nations, and the state of Tennessee, were the only ones in what is today the United States that made use of the dollar sign. Courtesy Oklahoma Historical Society.

Figure 40

JOHN ROSS, PRINCIPAL CHIEF OF CHEROKEE NATION. Ross was the principal chief of the Cherokee when the nation authorized the issuance of notes. In 1862 he retreated with the Union forces and was replaced by Stand Watie. Courtesy Oklahoma Historical Society.

Figure 41

BRIGADIER GENERAL STAND WATIE. Watie led the Confederate Cherokee from 1862 until the end of the war. The Confederate government appointed him a brigadier general. Courtesy Oklahoma Historical Society.

Figure 42

ELIAS CORNELIUS BOUDINOT. The nephew of Stand Watie, Boudinot represented the Cherokee Nation in the Confederate Congress. Courtesy Oklahoma Historical Society.

Figure 43

considerable delay in delivering it to the Cherokee Nation. On January 24, 1864, Boudinot advised using the money wisely, because it would have to be repaid after the war. The money left Richmond under the control of Confederate Indian Agent S. S. Scott in late January 1864. Again, Boudinot advised using it sparingly, because a new issue of Confederate paper money was being debated in Congress, and he felt the Cherokee should demand the best currency available. By April 20, 1864, Scott had returned to Richmond, having traveled as far as Mississippi. Undoubtedly, he had returned in order to obtain the new issue of currency approved by Congress. Two months later Scott was in Meridian, Mississippi, with the entire $100,000 in new issue. On July 25, 1864, he left Arkansas, heading for the Cherokee Nation. The money apparently was delivered in early August 1864. It had taken over six months for the money to reach the Cherokee.[23]

Congress voted for minor funds for the North Carolina Cherokee on May 1, 1864, and January 16, 1865. These funds were the annual interest on $53.33 due to each Cherokee there. On May 6, 1864, Boudinot presented a bill for the relief of the Cherokee Nation, but nothing came of this. Some Confederate money probably circulated in the Cherokee Nation, because when the tax of thirty-three and one-third percent went into effect on the old issues of Confederate money, Boudinot told Watie that he would try to save the Cherokee from this tax. He doubted, however, that he would succeed, and he was right.[24]

Like the rest of the Trans-Mississippi area, the Cherokee eventually placed their reliance upon commodities and cotton. In October 1864, Boudinot advised that with $10,000 or $15,000 he could get cotton cards and medicine for the refugees; there seemed to be a special need for cotton cards. He also stated that he would try to get another $50,000 from Congress. On January 27, 1865, Congress voted cotton for the Cherokee, at the market value in specie, in lieu of their annual annuity which could not be collected. On May 11, 1865, while in Shreveport, Louisiana, Boudinot stated that he was to obtain $3,000 in cotton, specie value, which he would sell to obtain coin. Four days later, on May 15, Brigadier General Douglas H. Cooper issued the necessary orders to transfer the cotton. Since Confederate collapse west of the Mississippi River came shortly thereafter, it is not certain whether the Cherokee received their cotton. If the transfer did not actually take place, it is possible that the Cherokee may have sent people to seize the cotton from government stores before it was destroyed or seized by the United States.[25]

Through these difficulties, the Confederate Cherokee remained true to their cause. On June 24, 1864, the Cherokee troops unanimously declared their intention to reenlist for the duration of the war. They were still fighting when surrender overtook them on June 23, 1865.[26]

Thus the Cherokee Nation was a vital part of the Trans-Mississippi Confederacy, and Cherokee monetary policy had a profound effect on its people. The Cherokee resisted the temptation to print money indiscriminately even though they were in great need of it. Instead they were careful to reserve enough Confederate funds to redeem all of the change bills that they issued. As long as the Cherokee kept their faith in the Confederate bills that backed their change paper, the Cherokee bills would not decline in value. But since Confederate notes depreciated, Cherokee bills likely did also. Ross's withdrawal with the Cherokee Treasury placed a severe monetary handicap on those who remained. Final Cherokee reliance on cotton cards, cotton, and the specie that could be obtained from its sale, demonstrates that the Cherokee Nation largely followed the fiscal pattern of the Trans-Mississippi Confederacy.

The fact that the Cherokee economy was highly organized and operated at the same level as the surrounding Confederate States may be seen in a number of ways. The war affected the Cherokee Nation much as it did the Confederate States: specie disappeared, prices rose, and shinplasters proliferated. That the Cherokee supported the same degree of labor specialization with a money supply that could integrate so well with the Confederacy's monetary system suggests that their economy was highly organized. A tightly controlled government system, with an elected official at the head, also points to this conclusion. When the money was withdrawn from their business community, the Cherokee faced the same panic and search for substitutes common to any government in the same situation.

[1]An act authorizing the issuing of Bills for the purpose of change and prohibiting the issuing and circulating of shinplasters, John Ross Papers, Thomas Gilcrease Institute of American History and Art, Tulsa, Oklahoma, p. 1.

[2]*Official Records, Army*, Ser. I, 1:683.

[3]Ibid., 13:490.

[4]Ibid., 13:499-500.

[5]Ibid., 3:690-91; Benjamin McCulloch to Judah P. Benjamin, September 2, 1861; McCulloch to John Ross, June 12, 1861; Ross to McCulloch, June 17, 1861, ibid., 591-92, 597, 692.

[6]Ibid.

[7]Ibid., 13:566.

[8]Ibid., 13:503-505; Ser. IV, 1:669.

[9]*Confederate Congressional Journals,* 1:611; *Official Records, Army,* Ser. I,8:709; William Weer to Thomas Moonlight, June 13, 1862, ibid., Ser. I, 13:431.

[10]Sam C. Hanby to Andrew R. Nave, October 14, 1861, Nave Papers; George E. White to Nave, October 23, 1861; Ward and Southmayd to Nave, October 23, 1861, Nave Letters, Cherokee Room, Northeastern Oklahoma State University Library; George E. White to Nave, Nave Papers.

[11]S. S. Scott, *Letter of the Acting Commander of Indian Affairs, with Statement, &c., In Regards to Certain Indian Trust Funds* (Richmond, 1862), p. 9.

[12]*Official Records, Army,* Ser. IV, 1:682, 685.

[13]Mathews, ed., *Statutes at Large,* p. 237; Memminger to E. C. Elmore, January 1, 1862, CST, Letters Sent, April 3, 1861-August 2, 1864; Albert Pike to Elias Rector, January 28, 1862, Records of the Wichita Agency, 1861-1862, NARG 75; S. Rindley to Stand Watie, March 26, 1862; John Crawford to Watie, March 31, 1862, Cherokee Nation Papers, Western History Collection, University of Oklahoma Library, Norman, Oklahoma.

[14]*Official Records, Army,* Ser. IV, 1:679; Criswell, *Confederate and Southern States Currency,* pp. 1-34.

[15]An act authorizing the issuing of Bills for the purpose of change and prohibiting the issuing and circulating of shinplasters, p. 1, Ross Papers.

[16]Ibid.; Maurice M. Burgett, "Obsolete Paper Currency of Indian Territory and Oklahoma," *Paper Money* (April 1967), 6(1):3.

[17]Thomas C. Hindman to Samuel Cooper, June 19, 1863; Harris S. Grenno to Weer, July 15, 17, 1862, *Official Records, Army,* Ser. I, 13:40, 161-62, 473.

[18]R. H. Carruth and W. H. Martin to William G. Coffin, July 19, 1862, U. S. House of Representatives, 37th Cong., 3rd Sess., *Executive Documents No. 1;* "Message of the President of the United States" (Washington, 1862), p. 302; Greene to Weer, July 17, 1862, *Official Records, Army,* Ser. I, 13:162.

[19]Thomas C. Hindman to Cooper, June 19, 1863, ibid., 13:40.

[20]Election Pamphlet against William P. Ross, no date, Ross Papers; Andrew R. Nave Day Book, 1862, October 6, 1862, Nave Papers; Douglas H. Cooper to Jefferson Davis, August 8, 1862, *Official Records, Army,* Ser. I, 53:820-21; Hindman to Cooper, June 19, 1863, ibid., 13:43; William Hudson to J. Y. Dashiell, September 15, 1862, ibid., Ser. IV, 1:828.

[21]Edward Cross to Memminger, March 13, 1863, CST, Letters Received, 1861-1865; Criswell, *Confederate and Southern States Currency,* pp. 105-286.

[22]Elias Cornelius Boudinot to Stand Watie, January 22, June 27, November 4, 1863, Cherokee Papers; *Confederate Congressional Journals,* 6:543, 683; An act appropriating one hundred thousand dollars for the use and benefit of the Cherokee Nation, *Official Records, Army,* Ser. IV, 3:40.

[23]Boudinot to Watie, January 24, 27, 1864, Cherokee Papers; Boudinot to Waite, April 24, July 13, 25, 1864, Watie Papers, Cherokee Room, Northeastern Oklahoma State University Library.

[24]*Confederate Congressional Journals*,6:483, 7:19, 489-90; Boudinot to Watie, October 3, 1864, Cherokee Papers.

[25]Boudinot to Watie, October 1, 1864, ibid.; Ramsdall, ed., *Laws*, pp. 24-26; Boudinot to Watie, May 11, 1865, Cherokee Papers; D. H. Cooper to E. Kirby Smith, May 15, 1865, Confederate District of Indian Territory, Letters Sent, May 10-27, 1865, NARG 109.

[26]H. L. Martin to Samuel B. Maxey, June 27, 1864, *Official Records, Army*, Ser. I, 41(Part 2):1013.

Chapter VIII

THE CHOCTAW WARRANTS OF 1863

If the Cherokee were well advanced economically, they were not alone among the Indian nations. All of the Five Civilized Nations—the Cherokee, Choctaw, Chickasaw, Creek, and Seminole—shared this degree of development. Only the Choctaw, however, among the other Indian nations issued paper money within the Confederate sphere of influence. The Cherokee and Choctaw Nations dominated the other three in their relations with the Confederacy. The Chickasaw, Creek, and Seminole fought and worked outside the spotlight. Only the Cherokee and Choctaw initially elected delegates to Congress. The Creek and Seminole finally elected one delegate in 1864, who represented both tribes. At Richmond, the Cherokee representative, Elias Cornelius Boudinot, was the dominate Indian personality. Neither the Chickasaw, Creek, or Seminole Nations, nor the Confederate Territory of Arizona (formed from the southern part of present-day New Mexico and Arizona in 1861) issued currency. They all used the issues of the central government, as well as local shinplasters, and any available specie.

While the Cherokee Nation issued treasury notes backed by Confederate paper money, the Choctaw Nation released treasury warrants redeemable with any funds available in the Choctaw treasury. In this way, the Choctaw Nation was similar to the states of Texas and Arkansas, and, like them, it witnessed the rapid decline in the purchasing power of unsecured paper money. When they reissued these pieces of paper, they corrected this defect. The Choctaw Nation, like the Cherokee Nation, received most of its money from the central government, first from

Federal and later from Confederate authorities. The Five Civilized Nations anticipated large sums of money in settlement of treaties made with the United States, but Washington officials were extremely reluctant to make any settlement. Nevertheless, the Choctaw persisted even in early 1861, and partially succeeded in obtaining some of the money due them.

On March 2, 1861, the United States advanced the Choctaw $500,000 in partial settlement of the treaty made with the United States on June 22, 1855. On March 8, 1861, the Choctaw commissioners in Washington, D. C., applied to collect the amount due in money and bonds. A month later they were still waiting and asked that they be paid in United States stocks, which had a higher resale value than bonds. The government ignored this request, and finally issued $250,000 in bonds, which the Choctaw kept until after the war. By June 12, 1861, the Choctaw treasury had received a United States Treasury Department draft for $112,000, in addition to the $250,000 in bonds, and $3,487.15 in specie. When they added this sum to the $134,512.85 previously given the Choctaw for the purchase of corn, the total came to $500,000.[1]

As these events transpired, the Confederate States in the person of its delegate, Albert Pike, began courting the Choctaw. Pike visited all the Indian nations and tried to negotiate a treaty with each — a task at which he was extremely successful. Because the Choctaw negotiators were absent at the time, arrangements with them were delayed slightly; they were known, however, to be entirely loyal to the principles of the infant Confederacy. The Choctaw Nation signed a treaty with the Confederate States at North Fork Town on July 12, 1861. The terms of this agreement provided that the Choctaw Nation was not to assume any of the costs of the war; and, even though the Choctaw had recently received a shipment of money from the United States government, they adhered strictly to the letter of the treaty. On June 10, 1861, the Choctaw had passed a law which set aside $30,000 for the purchase of munitions to arm the Indian troops, and on June 14, 1861, Principal Chief George Hudson had called upon all able-bodied men to enroll in the militia. But on November 5, 1861, over a month before the Confederate Provisional Congress ratified the treaty, the Choctaw Nation repealed their June 10, 1861, law and placed full responsibility for arming its troops in Confederate hands.[2]

The Confederate Provisional Congress voted on an appropriations bill on December 24, 1861, to pay the treaty Indians the money owed to them under terms of the several Confederate States treaties. A total of $265,927.55 of the funds was to be paid in coin and was quickly procured through purchases from banks. By January 28, 1862, Brigadier General

Albert Pike, the same man who had negotiated the original treaties, was at Little Rock, Arkansas, and was expected at Fort Smith by February 7 at the latest. Pike carried with him over $681,000 in paper money and specie and had requested that another $3,000 be sent ahead to Major Elias Rector, the Confederate Superintendent of Indian Affairs for the area. This last amount was to meet the expenses of recent Indian councils. Included in the money that Pike brought with him was a $50,000 advance payment to the Choctaw. Most of this sum must have been in coin, because Pike noted that "the Treasurer of the Choctaws means to sell the coin his people get, buy Confederate paper, and put the difference in his pocket." Pike felt that such action by the treasurer must be thwarted and urged that the principal chief be advised of the amount paid in coin, and that the treasurer had been paid this amount "in the presence of three Commissioners appointed by myself."[3]

Pike arrived at Fort Smith in early February, but the money did not reach the Choctaw Nation until mid-April 1862. It is possible that the delay occurred because Pike had to await the final ratification of the treaty by the Choctaw Nation and then the appointment of people to receive the funds and transport them to the capital at Doaksville. In mid-April, F. E. Williams transferred the money to Skullyville, and L. L. Libby moved it from there to Doaksville. In all, the men who transported the funds were paid $322. According to the treasurer's report, the total delivered by Williams and paid by Pike was $35,520. Possibly this was only the sum paid in coin with the rest in paper being delivered at some other time. The record indicates that $27,000 was in the hands of E. Loman and T. Folsom, a relative of Choctaw Treasurer H. N. Folsom, as well as $20,260 loaned by the Choctaw treaty delegation. Apparently enough money from the Confederates reached the Choctaw Treasury to purchase munitions, because on May 6, 1862, Sampson Folsom received $50,000 to purchase arms "as per treaty of 1861 and in accordance with an act of the Council in October A. D. 1861."[4] The Choctaw not only needed the money for war matériel, but also to care for various citizens of the nation.

In 1862, there was an unusual shortage of crops due to excessive drought. But Confederate Indian Agent S. S. Scott was convinced that there was little likelihood that the Choctaw would suffer because a large supply of grain was on hand from the previous year. However, sharing supplies with refugee Cherokee living in the Choctaw Nation might have caused hardship; and some families may have suffered because many Choctaw men were in military service. Thus the Council took action. In order to provide for those suffering Choctaw, a bill was proposed in the Choctaw Council on October 18, 1862, to aid indigent families. This legislation passed the Choctaw Senate on October 20, and the next day the House of Representatives amended it to include the blind and sent it back to the Senate where it passed the same day. Principal Chief Samuel Garland signed it into law on October 21, 1862.[5]

By the terms of this act, the Choctaw National Treasury issued $25,000 in the form of treasury warrants, payable in one, two, and three years, in equal installments. These bills were to be receivable for all money due the Choctaw Nation. The warrants were to be given to those who were actually destitute and suffering; it specifically excluded able-bodied male citizens. Those included were "Females, Children, Sick, Crippled, Blind and Wounded"; monthly supplies of food were also to be issued to these same groups. The law required the sheriffs to prepare lists of the people receiving this aid, and these lists were subject to review by the Choctaw Council. In essence this was a welfare act, designed to benefit those in severe need. This law also provided for the only issuance of notes by the Choctaw Nation and gave them status as currency.[6]

The warrants were issued without the names of persons on them, unlike the previous warrants, and were in denominations of fifty cents, one, two and one-half, and five dollars. The fact that no name appeared on the warrants made them readily transferable and served to give them status as a circulating medium. The notes were crude, suggesting that they were designed and printed quickly. It is likely that the majority were issued in early 1863; in fact, one of the few surviving warrants bears the handwritten date of March 1, 1863.

On October 22, 1862, Agent Scott delivered a second payment of $35,520 in Confederate paper money to the Choctaw Nation. The first yearly installment of $8,033.30⅓ was probably set aside from this shipment. These funds must have been the last actually delivered to the Nation, because on October 20, 1863, when the treasury received another $35,520, it cost the Choctaw Nation twenty dollars to travel to Paris, Texas, and return with the money.[7]

On August 6, 1862, the Choctaw and Chickasaw Nations elected Robert M. Jones to the Confederate Congress as their delegate. His total vote of 374 barely beat his closest opponent, Allen Wright, who had 334 votes. But Jones finished well ahead of Peter P. Pitchlynn's total of 137. Undaunted by this defeat, Pitchlynn went on to be elected principal chief before the end of the war, and Wright became treasurer. Wright reached even greater political leadership heights after the war. Jones, however, seems to have done little during his term in Congress and the Cherokee delegate, Elias C. Boudinot, overshadowed him in Indian affairs legislation.[8]

With the Choctaw Nation regularly receiving supplies of Confederate paper money, it soon became its circulating medium and was probably used to redeem the warrants. But the issue of new currency in 1864 by the Confederate government, and the decline in purchasing value of all Confederate paper money, created furor within the Choctaw Nation and was reflected in the other Indian nations as well. In an effort to alleviate this problem, Major General Samuel B. Maxey, commander of the District of Indian Territory and ex-officio Superintendent of Indian Affairs there, asked the Confederate Treasury agent at Houston, Texas, Peter W. Gray, for advice on July 31, 1864. Maxey stated that according to the terms of the several treaties concluded with the Indians, the Indians were to incur none of the actual costs of the war. Further, he felt that the thirty-three and one-third percent tax on the old Confederate issues was merely a way of passing on some of the costs of war to them. But these efforts, and those of Cherokee delegate Boudinot, produced no results. In January 1865, Principal Chief Peter P. Pitchlynn decried the tax as well as the general depreciation of Confederate currency. From Pitchlynn's remarks, the Choctaw were being paid by Confederate authorities as though the new issue paper money was at par with specie. The annuities which were to be paid in coin, were actually paid in paper, with one dollar in paper money being given for what would have been one dollar in coin.[9]

In January 1865, Chief Pitchlynn also detailed his thoughts on the monetary situation to the Choctaw Council. He stated that "few articles can be purchased with Confederate paper and then only at ruinous rates of discount." He continued that most of the items needed by the Choctaw people were of foreign manufacture and required "specie, or those staple commodities which are readily convertible into specie." Pitchlynn wondered if the Choctaw should continue to suffer by receiving Confederate notes at par with specie, particularly since speculators had depreciated the currency with their actions, and even the Confederate government had fixed the conversion rate at twenty dollars in paper to one dollar in gold. Also, Pitchlynn continued, no debtor in any state who had money due him payable in coin "will receive payment in Confederate paper at any discount." Pitchlynn left it to the Choctaw Council to take action, but he gave strong hints about what he favored.[10]

Shortly before this, the Choctaw Nation began to steer a course away from paper money and towards commodities, as did the rest of the Confederate Trans-Mississippi area. On October 11, 1864, the Council appropriated $35,000 from funds in the Choctaw treasury for purchasing cotton and wool cards. They planned to distribute them to the indigent wives of Choctaw soldiers. The law further specified that people who purchased the cotton and wool cards were to be elected by the Choctaw Council; those chosen were Dr. F. J. Bonds and J. M. Nail. On December 1, 1864, they left on their appointed mission, and carried with them $11,500 that had been issued by Choctaw Treasurer Allen Wright and a draft on the Treasurer of the Confederate States for the remaining $23,500. This draft was to be an advance on the interest money due the Choctaw Nation from funds invested in Virginia bonds. In order to cash the draft, the men had to journey to Jefferson, Texas, to speak to Samuel F. Mosely, the Confederate Treasury agent in that city. They also carried with them a letter of introduction from General Maxey. Maxey begged Mosely to do everything within his power to make certain that the draft was cashed so that the men could complete their mission.[11] Presumably they completed their mission successfully.

Monetary affairs in the Choctaw Nation began to deteriorate rapidly by January 1865. On January 19, the Choctaw Council passed a resolution concerning Confederate paper money. Evidently, the council was reacting to comments and suggestions made by Chief Pitchlynn in his January address. The action taken by the council was not as strong as it could have been. The resolution stated that the Confederate currency which the Choctaw Nation was accepting at par with specie was being heavily discounted, causing severe injury to its "financial condition and involving the Nation in heavy losses yearly."[12] But the council only authorized the opening of correspondence with the Confederate Commissioner of Indian Affairs in Richmond, Virginia, in hopes of remedying the monetary deficiencies that had occurred.[13]

Meantime, cotton began to play an even greater role in Choctaw monetary affairs. On January 19, 1865, the council voted funds to allow the transportation of cotton held by refugee Indians in order to sell it and relieve their condition. This trade quickly grew in volume because on April 10, Superintendent of Indian Affairs Cooper, directed a circular letter to the Choctaw officials and people. In this letter he stated that only such quantities of cotton might be exported to Mexico as were absolutely necessary to obtain needed supplies. He further declared that all bales of cotton so exported must be the property of the Choctaw Nation collectively and not of any one individual. Many of the Choctaw citizens had been shipping as much cotton as they could to Mexico.[14]

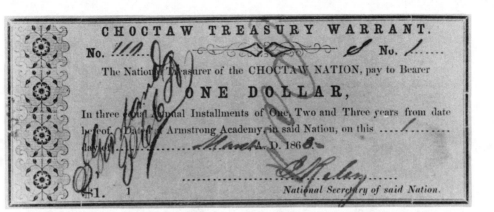

CHOCTAW NATION ONE DOLLAR TREASURY WARRANT. These notes were issued in denominations of fifty cents, one, two and one-half, and five dollars. Like the Cherokee Nation's notes, these bills bore the dollar sign. Courtesy Oklahoma Historical Society.

Figure 44

SAMUEL GARLAND, PRINCIPAL CHIEF OF THE CHOCTAW NATION. Chief Garland in 1862 signed the legislation creating the Choctaw issue of notes. Courtesy Oklahoma Historical Society.

Figure 45

PETER P. PITCHLYNN, PRINCIPAL CHIEF OF THE CHOCTAW
NATION. Peter Pitchlynn guided the Choctaw Nation in the final years
of the war and sought to obtain better terms when the Confederate Congress placed a tax of 33⅓ per cent on all outstanding Confederate
Treasury notes. He also saw to the reissue of the Choctaw Treasury Warrants after the war. Courtesy Oklahoma Historical Society.

Figure 46

This was not the end of cotton trade by the Choctaw. On January 27, 1865, the Confederate Congress, through the actions of Cherokee delegate Boudinot, authorized the Cherokee Nation to receive cotton at its specie value in lieu of annual annuities due them under terms of the treaty. The Congress quickly extended the law to all other Indian nations, and Boudinot carried copies of both laws back to Indian Territory from Richmond. By May 15, 1865, Superintendent of Indian Affairs Cooper was informed of the law, and he gave the necessary orders to carry it into effect. By May 27, Cooper also empowered P. W. Gray, the Confederate Treasury agent at Marshall, Texas, to receive and issue receipts for cotton to be delivered to the Creek and Seminole nations in lieu of their annuities. It is assumed that similar orders were also given to the other nations, and the cotton should have been delivered to the Indians before the Confederate collapse came later that summer.[15]

With the fall of the Confederacy, the Choctaw Nation found itself in extreme financial difficulties. Most of the money held by the nation was Confederate paper which was by then totally worthless. Crops could not be harvested or sold fast enough to satisfy the demands of the people for a medium of exchange. In order to alleviate this problem and pay the debts of the nation, the Choctaw Council decided temporarily to finance itself by resorting to credit or *fiat* currency. On October 17, 1865, the council passed a law authorizing Choctaw Treasurer Allen Wright to issue certificates of deposit, drawing five percent interest, for national warrants returned to him. A sizable number were outstanding and unpaid, probably issued after the end of the war. At the same time the council also authorized Wright to reissue, again with five percent interest, the treasury warrants that had been issued and then redeemed under the terms of the act of October 21, 1862. In this way, the Choctaw issuance of 1863 performed double duty: first, it gave funds to the destitute during the war and served as a minor currency; and second, it served as a national currency after the war. In both roles the issuance was successful.[16]

Thus the Choctaw Nation, like the Cherokee Nation, pursued a monetary policy similar to the rest of the Confederate Trans-Mississippi area. Initially the nation placed heavy reliance upon paper money; it even produced a small regional issue, but eventually the Choctaw shunned paper money and relied more upon commodities and the specie produced by its sale in Mexico. The Choctaw Nation performed one additional service with its money; it created a welfare system that did not breakdown. The Choctaw distributed food, cotton and wool cards, and other necessities to the destitute in the nation, including $25,000 in money. Because the people returned so many of the warrants to the Choctaw Treasury, the system worked exactly as it was designed to function. It is to the credit of the Choctaw Nation that it resisted the temptation to print large quantities of paper money and to give it to the needy. The little money distributed to the destitute appeared to be the quickest way to relieve their wants. The amount of money provided the needy was small and highly controlled, with primary reliance on food and cotton and wool cards. The cards were valuable, because they could be used to prepare raw materials for conversion into cloth. In this way they provided home industry, and for those industrious enough, a source of income, because surplus cloth had a ready market.

The Choctaw Nation, like the Cherokee Nation, received most of its funds from the Confederate government. But sales of commodities and other sources also produced minor income. In this way the Choctaw and Cherokee did not face many of the monetary problems which plagued the states in the Confederacy. In the states most revenue came from taxes, and when these were halted, the states' problems were compounded. Although the Choctaw and Cherokee had to accept Confederate paper money as though it were specie, they still had a fairly steady income. When the value of paper money declined, however, the nations had to locate other means of financing. But the Choctaw and Cherokee issued very little paper money. So its value remained relatively stable; it was easily retired, and these Indian nations avoided the pitfall of overprinting as practiced in most states of the Confederacy.

[1]Statement concerning sale of U. S. bonds, no date but after 1865, Peter P. Pitchlynn to T. Corwekly, March 8, 1861; Choctaw Delegates to Salmon P. Chase, April 6, 1861; Treasurer's Receipt, H. N. Folsom, June 12, 1861; Report of the Committee on the Mission of the Choctaw Delegation, October 23, 1861, Peter P. Pitchlynn Papers, Thomas Gilcrease Institute of American History and Art.

[2]James E. Harrison and others to Edward Clark, April 23, 1861, A Treaty . . . between the Confederate States . . . and the Choctaw Nation [July 12, 1861], Official Records, Army, Ser. IV, 1:323, 445-66; Proclamation, Principal Chief George Hudson, June 14, 1861, ibid., Ser. I, 3:591-92; Resolutions of the Choctaw Nation, November 5, 1861, U. S. Bureau of Indian Affairs, Miscellaneous Documents, 1864-1865, NARG 109.

[3]Mathews, ed., Statutes at Large, p. 237; Pike to Rector, January 28, 1862, Records of the Wichita Agency, 1861-1862.

[4]Choctaw National Auditor's Warrants paid by H. N. Folsom, no date, Treasurer's Report from 1861 to 1862, Sampson Folsom, Receipt, May 6, 1862,

Choctaw Papers, Indian Archives Division, Oklahoma Historical Society, Oklahoma City, Oklahoma.

[5]S. S. Scott to George W. Randolph, October 22, 1862, *Official Records, Army,* Ser. I, 13:890-91; "Senate Journal, October, 1862 Session," Choctaw Papers, p. 251; "House Journal, October, 1862 Session," ibid., pp. 59-60; "Senate Journal, October, 1862 Session," ibid., p. 251.

[6]An act entitled, "An act for the relief of certain families or persons in this Nation," October 21, 1862, Acts and Resolutions of the General Council of the Choctaw Nation, October Session, 1862, ibid.

[7]Burgett, "Obsolete Paper Currency of Indian Territory and Oklahoma," p. 4; Treasurer's Report, 1862-1863, Choctaw Papers.

[8]Certification of election results, Douglas H. Cooper, October 7, 1862, U. S. Bureau of Indian Affairs, Miscellaneous Documents, 1864-1865.

[9]Samuel B. Maxey to Peter W. Gray, July 21, 1864, Pitchlynn Papers; *Message of P. P. Pitchlynn . . . delivered before the Choctaw Council in Extra Session . . . January, 1865* (Fort Towson, Choctaw Nation, n.d.), p. 4.

[10]Ibid., pp. 3-4.

[11]An act entitled, "An act to purchase Cotton and Wool Cards for the use and benefit of the indigent Choctaw Soldiers' Wives &c," Acts and Resolutions of the Choctaw Nation, October, 1864, Choctaw Papers; Samuel B. Maxey to Samuel F. Mosely, Pitchlynn Papers.

[12]Resolution, January 19, 1865, Acts and Resolutions of the Choctaw Nation, 1865, Choctaw Papers.

[13]Ibid.

[14]An act entitled, "An act to appropriate Money to Enable James Thompson to Transport Refugee Cotton &c," ibid.; Circular, Douglas H. Cooper, April 10, 1865, Pitchlynn Papers.

[15]Ramsdell, ed., *Laws,* pp. 24-26; Elias C. Boudinot to Stand Watie, May 11, 1865, Cherokee Papers; D. H. Cooper to E. Kirby Smith, May 15, 1865, Confederate District of Indian Territory, Letters Sent, May 10-27, 1865.

[16]An act entitled, "An act creating interest on National and Treasury Warrants," October 17, 1865, Senate Records, Choctaw Nation, Choctaw Papers.

Chapter IX

SUPREMACY OF PAPER MONEY

When the Confederate States began to organize and prepare for operations, the government faced the problem of monetary policy. Central authorities resorted to paper money and its attendant credit, and it poured from the printing presses in an unending stream. While this was happening, the citizens were left to deal with the large volume of paper money printed by the central government, state governments, private individuals, and corporations. *Fiat* currency, backed by little more than faith in the government, became the order of the day, and it soon established its supremacy. Gresham's Law dictates that bad money will drive good money from circulation. Thus, as Confederate paper money became the standard, first specie, then bank notes, and finally even some state issues disappeared from general circulation.

Banking activities had been going on in the South long before it broke away from the United States, and the ensuing conflict did nothing to diminish business. In addition to the bank notes that provided an early circulating medium, the banks continued to perform their normal functions of loan accounts and checking accounts. The records of the central government show people sending checks to Memminger for bonds; among the banks drawn upon for these funds were the Bank of Virginia and the Bank of the Commonwealth. Another vital function the banks performed was to receive subscriptions to the first Confederate loan and forward them to various officials of the central government. The volume of loans to private citizens varied among the banks of each state, and even though some banks decreased the number of loans they made during the war, they still continued to make some loans.[1]

By far the most recognizable contribution of the banks, however, was

104

their notes. The Bank Convention of the Southern States, held in Atlanta, Georgia, beginning on June 3, 1861, addressed itself to the question of money and made several proposals relating to paper currency. One proposal asked the Confederate Congress to limit the amount of Treasury notes and make them legal tender. The convention also wanted Congress to pass a law making Confederate bonds and currency collateral for banking capital like gold and silver. A resolution that passed the convention allowed banks to accept Confederate paper money on deposit and loan their own notes to the central government.[2]

The banks made generous loans of their bills to Memminger in exchange for Confederate stocks. The *Charleston Daily Courier* observed in August 1861, that the banks "have the highest confidence in the security which the government can give."[3] But the banks also used Confederate bills as backing for their own issue. The governor of Mississippi, John Gill Shorter, noted on February 1, 1862, that the merchants of his state needed an interstate currency. He maintained that this requirement was provided by Confederate paper money as well as the bills of solvent banks. Bank bills had gained out-of-state circulation, Shorter maintained, when "banks of the different States, by an arrangement made with each other, [sought] to adjust their balances by use of Confederate Treasury notes."[4] In addition to Confederate paper money, banks also backed their bills with state bonds and notes as well as limited amounts of specie. Therefore, while the 1861 bank convention did not petition the Confederate Congress to authorize this action, banks were able to work out such arrangements among themselves.[5]

Apparently bank notes of the Confederate states were not the only bank notes circulating in the nation. Records indicate that, in addition, there were bank notes from the following areas: Canada, Massachusetts, Connecticut, Rhode Island, New Jersey, Delaware, New York, Pennsylvania, Maryland, the District of Columbia, Ohio, Indiana, Wisconsin, Michigan, and Nebraska Territory. Because most banks within the Confederacy expanded the amount of their outstanding notes, inflation began to take its toll. Although bank notes experienced substantial inflation, it was decidedly less than the inflation experienced by the paper money issues of the central government. In 1863, when one dollar in gold was selling for twenty dollars in Confederate notes, it cost only three dollars and twenty-five cents in bank notes. The price of bank notes never rose much above this level for the remainder of the war, and they began to command a premium in Confederate paper money. Thus bank notes were considered of more value than Confederate currency. Perhaps this is why

Confederate paper money appeared more and more in commerce, supplanting bank notes. Indications are that the people hoarded bank notes.[6]

Even if bank bills disappeared from circulation in time, the process was not as fast as the rapid evaporation of specie from the commercial life of the states. Well before the close of the first year of the war, as early as the end of September 1861, specie had completely disappeared from general circulation and the business community. With this loss, several remedies were tried to alleviate the shortage of change. Metal tokens made a brief appearance in 1861, but circulated in only a few areas. For the most part, only Alabama, Virginia, Georgia, and South Carolina flirted with token coinage. In 1853, the Mobile Jockey Club issued a token that may have circulated during the war years. Other early tokens, which could have been pressed into service during the emergency, were issued in Selma, Alabama, and Charleston, South Carolina. Charleston had a number of possible contenders for this role, including a penny-size token of brass, copper, and German silver (the latter was an alloy of copper, zinc, and nickel which had a white, silver-like appearance). These tokens were made in 1846 and stamped on them was the name of slave auctioneer W. W. Wilbur. One authority states that they definitely circulated during the early part of the war. In 1859, the Marshall House token appeared in Virginia and circulated as the equivalent of one cent in Richmond, until at least the early part of 1862.[7]

By far the best known of all Confederate tokens was called the "Wealth of the South." Struck in Cincinnati, Ohio, it was shipped to the South through Louisville, Kentucky, and Nashville, Tennessee. Supposedly it was for distribution throughout the Southern states, but large quantities were seized and never placed in circulation. Worn specimens are still found today, however. These tokens are usually associated with the state of South Carolina and may have been used within the city of Charleston.[8]

The study of tokens in the Confederacy is difficult. Not only is there little documentation, but the pieces themselves are scarce. Also, a large number of fantasy tokens created after the war to sell to collectors have appeared. In 1878 a Confederate silver token and a "quarter" were reported to have been discovered, but the conclusion was reached at the time that these were of postwar manufacture. Other bogus Confederate tokens created after the war have complicated the story. An attempt to produce a national token system for the Confederacy never gained much congressional support. Therefore, only a few tokens can be authenticated as definitely Confederate.[9]

Thus metal tokens were not widespread in the Confederacy and did not solve the change shortage even for a brief period. Because of the small denominations involved, postage stamps were often used in lieu of change. At first, even United States stamps were accepted. In July 1861, James Gardner, the editor of the Augusta, Georgia, *Constitutionalist*, offered to accept United States stamps in payment of subscriptions to his tabloid. Postmasters also occasionally gave postage stamps instead of coin in change. In April 1861, the postmaster at Madison, Louisiana, finding that he had no stamps, printed his own shinplasters with a value of three cents each and gave these instead of change. And on December 31, 1861, A. G. Mayers, the postmaster at Fort Smith, Arkansas, complained because he had not received any two cent stamps. He stated that these were "greatly needed to make change."[10]

In time, specie became so scarce that there was not even enough to pay for postage. On November 27, 1861, Confederate Postmaster General John H. Reagan reported this situation to Congress and urged passage of a law which would allow individual postmasters to receive Treasury notes for stamps. Since the smallest denomination of a bill at the time was five dollars, Reagan felt that change should be arranged between postmaster and customer. Congress soon voted the requested authority. Apparently the most common solution was to purchase the precise number of stamps for a bill, and to use the stamps as change for other purchases. But postage stamps were only accepted as a substitute for specie at certain times and rejected at others. In May 1862, postage stamps were unacceptable, but by January 1863, the demand for them was great. In 1864 the Post Office Department printed 500,000 twenty cent stamps to meet the demand for small change. At first they were freely accepted, but the demand eventually died down. Perhaps this was because the stamps deteriorated as they passed from person to person.[11]

Although coupons from government bonds as well as the bonds themselves served as substitutes for money, by far the best known replacement for change, and the biggest nuisance, was shinplasters. These small paper items always had a limited area of circulation, never straying far from where they originated, but the quantity issued created problems. By November 1861, shinplasters circulated as change only in Virginia, but soon not even Texas was far enough removed to be immune from them. In December 1861, one Texas newspaper editor decried shinplasters as a major nuisance. He stated that twenty merchants had already told him that they would not accept them and that even the best paper shinplasters were selling at a twenty percent discount. The following May, this same editor reported that shinplasters were at flood levels, and a number of firms that had issued them had folded. He openly suggested that many people had printed shinplasters in order to obtain government money with which to speculate. Seven months later, he advocated the removal from circulation of all notes, except those of the Confederacy. On June 11, 1863, another Texas newspaper editor urged the redemption of all county scrip. Many Confederate states sought to control the situation by replacing shinplasters with state change bills, or as in the case of Richmond, Virginia, the issue of city notes, but these efforts came too late.[12]

Change was not the only monetary problem faced by both central and state governments early in the war. For the most part, small change bills were considered to be any denomination below five dollars. Most of the shinplasters bore face values below one dollar and were merely for purposes of change. This left a void between one and five dollars. To further complicate the situation, the Confederacy and many other states did not print paper money below the value of five dollars until late 1862. Some banks, however, were authorized to issue these denominations early in the conflict, and these bills must have been used in the meantime. Since the number produced must have been small, hardships and demand were created. In July 1861, one Confederate official asked to be supplied with $50,000 in the "smallest possible denomination notes."[13] A Georgia state official made reference to the fact that the smallest bills he could get from the banks were the twenty dollar denominations because both banks and citizens had withdrawn the smaller bills from circulation, causing a great void. In June 1861, a North Carolina bank teller and a Confederate Navy paymaster at Charleston, South Carolina, pleaded with the central government to have $100,000 in bills of large denominations exchanged for small ones. As bills of lesser value became more readily available, requests for them declined. By November 1862, the cashier of the Bank of South Carolina verified that he had received a shipment of $12,000 in Confederate two dollar bills. The next month the Branch Bank of Columbia, South Carolina, asked the Confederate Treasury officials for the immediate shipment of one and two dollar bills. By 1863, this crisis had passed.[14]

When Confederate notes first appeared, they were on a par with gold and continued so, at least in many of the interior portions of the country, well into 1862. Early in Confederate history, foreign visitors to Richmond freely spent specie as well as Confederate paper money, but this situation did not continue. While Confederate paper money declined in value and prices soared, people sought the causes of their plight. At an early date, they blamed speculators. On June 15, 1861, the editor of the *Daily Rich-*

mond Examiner complained about the speculators, and the protests grew louder with time. In December 1861, a Texas trader, identified only as "S. M.," defended himself against charges of extortion, by maintaining that the price of coffee had gone from thirteen cents to twenty cents a pound because of shortages due to speculators buying up the crop. In late October 1862, a Baptist preacher in Richmond could not find it in his heart to pray for speculators and extortioners, and the next month a church newspaper attacked extortioners, claiming "extortion is moral treason."[15]

With the war's continuation, public indignation grew against speculators. Soldiers in the field also decried them and the conditions which they felt the speculators had created. Some even feared that the Confederacy would lose the war because of their currency manipulations. By October 1862, prejudice against extortioners was so strong in Richmond that John B. Jones opined that there would be much violence during the winter months. Two months later, Jones's fears escalated to the point that he speculated monetary policies would bring about governmental bankruptcy within a year or so. Not only did the cost of goods increase, but all values rose: stock prices skyrocketed and land costs had reached astronomical limits by the middle of 1863. In the interior of the country, the inflationary pinch was not quite as severe at first, but prejudice against speculators was evident. An example can be found on August 5, 1863, when a Columbia, South Carolina church newspaper, the *Confederate Baptist*, reported on the price of flour in the port city of Charleston. The newspaper wryly stated: "we are almost afraid to mention the price, lest some extortioner, in the interior, should take courage at it, and advance the prices of his wheat."[16]

A few people complained about the actions of corrupt officials in addition to the speculators. John B. Jones reported in June 1863, that all civilians seemed to have gone wild with speculation; he also noted that official corruption was widespread. In October 1863, Jones recorded an incident where a Mr. Moffitt, an agent of the Confederate Commissionary General, was buying beef on his own at government prices from sixteen to twenty cents per pound, which he then sold to butchers at forty-five to fifty-five cents per pound. In the United States, an excess of money existed as a result of the war and thus speculation prevailed. Officials of the Washington government conspired with naval contractors and army suppliers to syphon off as much of this money as possible, and the same situation existed in the Confederacy. In both countries clerks filled out blank vouchers which suppliers then forged. It is a documented fact that Confederate Quartermaster's checks were forged. Thus both governments unquestionably encountered widespread corrupt practices throughout the war.[17]

While the general public in the Confederacy blamed speculators and extortioners for rising prices, some people were slowly starting to examine other possibilities. After the war one man summed up their conclusions: "It has often been charged that speculators ruined the currency. But, to give the children of the devil their due—we can scarcely think but that the currency made the speculators."[18] Early in Confederate monetary history, a proposal had been made to back Confederate paper money with cotton and tobacco, promising substantial commodities for its redemption and probably making it preferable to specie, but nothing came of it. In time knowledgeable people decided that too much paper money was outstanding, with shinplasters and non-current banking paper receiving the first blast of indignation. But by 1862, even Confederate notes were added to the list when a Texas editor urged his readers to convert excess paper money into bonds. Voluntary public conversion of notes to bonds, however, did not even begin to remove the surplus paper money circulating in the business community.[19]

In 1863 the cry began for taxation as the only way to reduce excess currency. The people and the press clamored for this remedy, and on March 16, 1863, the *Daily Richmond Enquirer* cried, "For God's sake tax us."[20] On March 23, the Confederate Congress gave the public its answer when it authorized the issuance of $50,000,000 per month in Treasury notes without any pledge for their redemption. By November 1863, far more currency circulated in the Confederacy than was ever needed for the normal transaction of business. Only by reducing this volume could paper money be kept from depreciating further. Even President Davis admitted that by December 1863, there was more than three times the amount of paper money in circulation than was required to support the business affairs of the country. In November 1863, at least one Confederate official had come around to the taxation solution: he proposed a $600,000,000 levy, payable in paper, commodities, or slaves. The government, he argued, could use commodities and slaves tendered for the tax, and the paper money received could be retired from circulation. But Congress did not consider this plan, and on November 1, 1863, Robert Garlick Hill Kean, head of the Bureau of War, reflected the growing sentiment when he observed that the "currency is *hopelessly bankrupt*."[21]

The original governmental idea of keeping the level of currency at manageable limits called for the conversion of Confederate Treasury

CONFEDERATE TOKENS

W. W. WILBUR TOKEN, 1864. Obverse. This Charleston, South Carolina, token named for the slave auctioneer, W. W. Wilbur, circulated during the early part of the Civil War. The token was slightly larger than a modern quarter. Courtesy American Numismatic Society.

Figure 47

W. W. WILBUR TOKEN, 1846. Reverse. Courtesy American Numismatic Society.

Figure 48

MARSHALL HOUSE TOKEN. Obverse. This coin circulated in Richmond, Virginia, as the equivalent of one cent, 1859-62. Courtesy American Numismatic Society.

Figure 49

MARSHALL HOUSE TOKEN, 1859-62. Reverse. Courtesy American Numismatic Society. For an interesting account of the Marshall House—Alexandria, Va., which issued this coin —and the killing of Union Col. Elmer E. Ellsworth by Inn-keeper James Jackson on May 24, 1861, see Davis, *The Civil War: First Blood*, 64-69.

Figure 50

THE WEALTH OF THE SOUTH TOKEN, 1860. Reverse. This side expressed the Confederate determination: "NO SUBMISSION TO THE NORTH." Courtesy American Numismatic Society.

Figure 52

THE WEALTH OF THE SOUTH TOKEN, 1860. Obverse. This was the best known of all Confederate tokens. Courtesy American Numismatic Society.

Figure 51

BEAUREGARD "DIME," 1861. Reverse. This side gives the day and year for the beginning of the First Battle of Bull Run (Manassas) but missing is the month [July] 21, 1861. Courtesy American Numismatic Society.

Figure 54

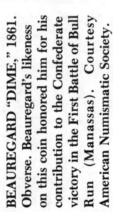

BEAUREGARD "DIME," 1861. Obverse. Beauregard's likeness on this coin honored him for his contribution to the Confederate victory in the First Battle of Bull Run (Manassas). Courtesy American Numismatic Society.

Figure 53

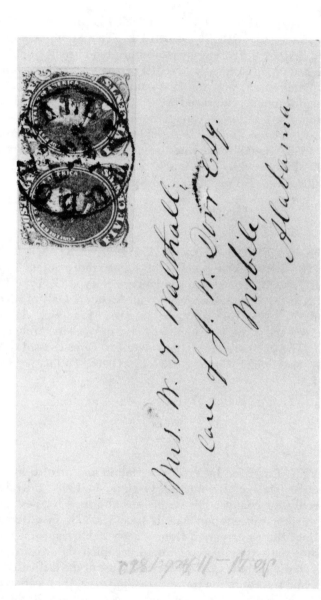

THE FIRST CONFEDERATE POSTAGE STAMP, FIVE CENTS – GREEN. This envelope has two of the five-cents green stamps, the first Government-issued Confederate postage stamp. The stamps went on sale October 16, 1861. In contrast to the policy adopted for U. S. stamps, this stamp featured a living president, C. S. A. President Jefferson Davis. Hoyer & Ludwig of Richmond, Virginia, printed the stamp, the first printed by lithography. See Dietz, *Catalog*, 123-26; Dietz, *Postal Service*, 89-113.

Figure 55

CONFEDERATE POSTAGE STAMPS ALSO SERVED AS SMALL CHANGE

THE FIRST "AMERICAN" (U. S. AREA) STAMP PRODUCED ABROAD, FIVE CENTS — PALE GREENISH BLUE. This stamp claimed many firsts: the first engraved and printed abroad, the first produced typographically, the first plate subjected to change of denomination, and the first captured on a Confederate blockade-runner. Engraved by J. Joubert and printed by Thomas De La Rue & Company, Ltd., London, England, the earliest cancellation date is September (?), 1862. After July 1, 1862, when postage rates increased to ten cents, pairs of this stamp were used. Thus pairs are much commoner than singles. See Dietz, *Catalog,* 134-36; Dietz, *Postal Service,* 156-82.

Figure 56

THE FIRST RECESS-ENGRAVED CONFEDERATE POSTAGE STAMP, TEN CENTS — BLUE. Two types of this stamp were printed: Type I and Type II. The stamp shown here is Type II. Type I is known as the "Frame-Line" type and Archer & Daly of Richmond, Virginia, first printed it in 1863. Frederick Halpin engraved the Type II which was also printed by Archer & Daly. The earliest cancellation date for Type II is May 1, 1863. See Dietz, *Catalog,* 137-42; Dietz, *Postal Service,* 191-230.

Figure 57

TWENTY CENTS — GREEN. Engraved by Frederick Halpin and printed by Archer & Daly of Richmond, Virginia, in 1863. Intended primarily for change, this stamp was also used for postage. The earliest cancellation date is June 1, 1863. In different printings the color varied from a deep rich green to a dull bluish-green. After Federal troops occupied the Mississippi River, it divided the Confederacy. Because of the difficulty in supplying stamps to the trans-Mississippi area, that section of the Confederacy was soon without ten cents stamps. But with a large supply of twenties on hand, Texas postmasters began bisecting the twenties and using the halves in place of ten cents stamps. Other states quickly followed suit. The twenties were bisected either diagonally or horizontally and, although not officially sanctioned, the halves were accepted as a matter of expediency. See Dietz, *Catalog,* 143-44; Dietz, *Postal Service,* 252-61.

Figure 58

MERCHANT SCRIP – SHINPLASTERS
LOUISIANA

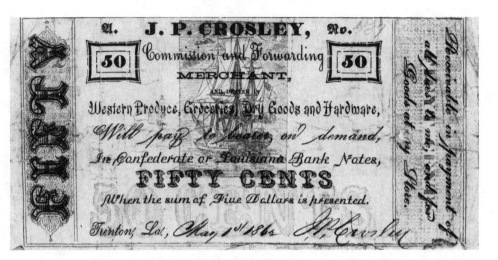

FIFTY CENTS SCRIP, MAY 1, 1862. Issued by J. P. Crosley, merchant, of Trenton, Louisiana.

Figure 59

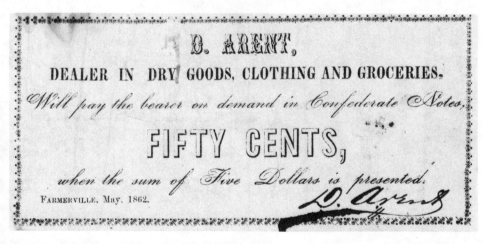

FIFTY CENTS SCRIP, MAY, 1862. Issued by D. Arent, merchant, of Farmerville, Louisiana.

Figure 60

As small change disappeared from circulation, businesses issued their own currency. These examples of Louisiana scrip courtesy of the Department of Archives and Manuscripts, Louisiana State University, Baton Rouge.

ONE DOLLAR NOTE, BANK OF AUGUSTA, GEORGIA, 1861.

Figure 61

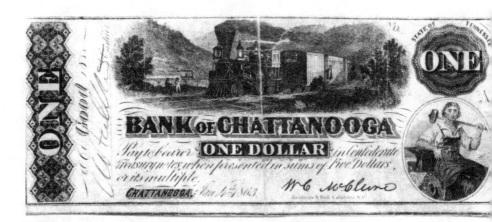

ONE DOLLAR NOTE, BANK OF CHATTANOOGA, TENNESSEE, 1863.

Figure 62

It was believed that bank notes would be the normal circulating paper money in the Confederacy, but the war drove many of these notes into hiding. After the war, the United States Congress taxed them out of existence.

notes into eight percent bonds with interest payable in specie. Thus any excess notes would be invested in interest-bearing bonds. As Jefferson Davis observed later, the success of this plan depended on the Confederacy being able to pay in specie, but specie became more expensive and difficult to secure as time passed. What Davis did not say was that the plan also required a limited issuance of paper money, but the government set no limit on that. Nevertheless, the Confederate monetary system did succeed for a while, and it had its supporters. When the Confederacy began, it was generally thought reprehensible by the public for any person to refuse the national currency in payment, and in this way patriotism and the pressure of public opinion dictated its early acceptance. On January 13, 1862, a Texan had claimed that silver was not money, but was needed only for change and should not be hoarded. The general population, however, neither shared this opinion nor heeded his advice. On April 22, 1862, another person attempted to calm people's fears about paper money by maintaining that there was no reason why it should not be a good domestic currency. He questioned why people should fear that the government would abuse this privilege and overprint paper money. Further, he observed that even if it did, other governments had debased coins by reducing the amount of precious metal in them, or by substituting non-precious metals.[22]

As the volume of paper money increased, its purchasing power declined. In Richmond, with its swelling population, numerous visitors, and limited supplies, prices climbed higher and faster than elsewhere. Nevertheless, ways existed for cutting costs. Gardens were planted, and prices were lower for those who could shop at the government commissary. In December 1863, a barrel of flour cost $115 on the street, but could be purchased for forty dollars in the commissary. In May 1863, a meal of corn bread, boiled fish, and two hard-boiled eggs could be purchased for one Confederate dollar in Petersburg, Virginia. But as many soon discovered, whenever Federal forces approached an area, Confederate paper became worthless and was often refused in payment of bills. By December 1863, many people felt that Confederate paper money would eventually collapse, and that no amount of reform could save it. Every person and all property in the Confederacy had been pledged to pay the paper money, observed John B. Jones, and since the same persons and property would have to be pledged to redeem new paper money there was no reason to suppose that new paper money would not also depreciate. Only independence could help the value of Confederate Treasury notes, Jones noted, for there would be no redemption if the Confederacy failed. Only people's faith in eventual victory kept the system from collapsing earlier.[23] By the close of 1863, the Confederacy had been inundated by a flood of paper money. The population had accepted the situation through patriotism and faith that the nation would finally triumph. The plan adopted by the Confederacy might have worked, but only if the paper issues had been kept relatively small in volume and if specie could have been obtained at a reasonable cost to pay interest on the bonds. Neither of these conditions prevailed, however, and official corruption provided still another minor cause for undermining Confederate credit. At first, speculators and extortioners were generally blamed for rising prices, but soon many began to blame the excess of paper money. Confederate paper money became identified with the Confederate debt, and many began to despair that it would never be paid in its entirety. Even by mid-1863, it had become obvious to many that something had to be done to bring order to the chaotic Confederate monetary situation. Plans had been suggested earlier, but it was up to Confederate authorities to act. The cry grew to reduce the volume of paper money. After much delay, the Confederate government commenced monetary reform in 1864.

[1]Ralph Sorrell to Memminger, November 1, 1862; John D. Kirkland to Memminger, November 13, 1862, CST, Letters Received, 1861-1865; Thomas R. Moring to Memminger, February 8, 1862, COR, Letters Received, March 20, 1861-June 18, 1862; Anderson, ed., *Brokenburn*, p. 19.

[2]*Daily Richmond Examiner*, June 10, 1861.

[3]*Charleston Daily Courier*, August 27, 1861.

[4]John Gill Shorter to J. F. Foster, February 1, 1862, Shorter Papers, 1861-1863.

[5]Various bank reports, CST, Miscellaneous Office Records, June 5, 1861-March 8, 1863, NARG 365.

[6]"Schedule of Bank Notes," undated, ibid.; Schwab, *The Confederate States of America,*, p. 133.

[7]Joseph N. T. Levick and Edward Groh, "Names of Firms on Tokens issued during the Civil War. Names of Firms on Tokens other than War Series and issued from 1789-1890," American Numismatic Society Museum Library (New York); George and Melvin Field, *Token Collector's Pages* (Boston, 1972), pp. 22-26, 39, 50; Watie Raymond, *The Standard Catalogue of United States Coins and Tokens* (New York, 1941), p. 186; Russell Rulau, "1860 and 1861 Civil War Cents," *Calcoin News* (Winter, 1962), 16(1):10.

[8]E. B. G. of Cincinnati, " 'No Submission' Token," *American Journal of Numismatics* (July, 1878), 13(1):16; George and Melvin Field, "The Wealth of the South Mulings," *Numismatic Scrapbook Magazine* (September, 1958), 24(9):1786.

[9]"Editorial," *American Journal of Numismatics and Bulletin of American*

Numismatics and Archaeological Society (January, 1878), 12(3):80.

¹⁰J. B. Campbell to James Gardner, July 5, 1861, Executive Letter Book from August 21, 1860 to May 12, 1864, Georgia State Archives; *Daily Picayune*, April 11, 1861; A. G. Mayers to the Chief Clerk of the Finance Department of the Post Office Department, December 31, 1861, Records of the Fort Smith Post Office, 1858-1862, Arkansas and Red River Superintendency, Captured Miscellaneous Records, 1861-1862, NARG 75.

¹¹Report of the Postmaster General, November 27, 1861, Record of Letters and other Communications from the Post Office Department, Confederate Collection, Library of Congress; F. A. Nast, "History of Confederate Stamps," *Confederate Veteran* (March, 1894), 2(3):78; Schwab, *The Confederate States of America*, p. 163.

¹²Thomas C. Reynolds to Jefferson Davis, January 18, 1864, Rowland, ed., *Davis, Constitutionalist*, 6:151; Report of the Postmaster General, November 27, 1861, Record of Letters and Other Communications from the Post Office Department; John S. Foster to Aunt Jennie, November 14, 1861, John Foster and Family Correspondence; *Tri-Weekly Telegraph*, December 30, 1861, May 16, December 10, 1862; *Tri-Weekly State Gazette*, June 11, 1863; *Daily Richmond Enquirer*, April 16, 1862.

¹³John C. Booth to A. J. Guirot, COC, Letters Received, April 15, 1861-January 10, 1862.

¹⁴George W. Rains to the Confederate States Treasurer [1861]; George W. Mordecai to Memminger, June 4, 1862; George H. Ritchie to E. C. Elmore, June 4, 1862; W. C. King to E. C. Elmore, November 3, 1862; J. S. Clark to T. Grier Erey, November 13, 1862; M. L. Brown to Memminger, December 3, 1862, CST, Letters Received, 1861-1865.

¹⁵Thomas C. DeLeon, *Four Years in Rebel Capitals: An Inside View of Life in the Southern Confederacy, from Birth to Death* (Mobile, 1890), p. 231; *Daily Richmond Examiner*, June 15, 1861; *Tri-Weekly Telegraph*, December 30, 1861; *The Confederate Baptist* (Columbia, South Carolina), October 15, November 12, 1862.

¹⁶Bell I. Wiley, *The Life of Johnny Reb: The Common Soldier of the Confederacy* (New York, 1943), p. 135; Jones, *Diary*, 1:164, 200; *The Confederate Baptist*, June 3, August 5, 1863.

¹⁷Jones, *Diary*, 1:350, 2:70; Henry S. Olcott, "The War's Carnival of Fraud," *The Annals of the War written by Leading Participants North and South* (Philadelphia, 1879), pp. 707, 709; Memminger to Lewis Cruger, August 27, 1863, COC, Correspondence, 1861 and 1863.

¹⁸DeLeon, *Four Years in Rebel Capitals*, p. 235.

¹⁹*Daily Richmond Examiner*, July 12, October 31, 1861; *Tri-Weekly Telegraph*, December 10, 1862.

²⁰*Daily Richmond Enquirer*, February 17, March 8, 16, 1863.

²¹Fitzgerald Ross, *Cities and Camps of the Confederate States* (Urbana, 1958),

p. 160; *Daily Richmond Enquirer,* November 11, 1863; Jefferson Davis, *A Short History of the Confederate States of America* (New York, 1890), p. 123; Edward Younger, ed., *Inside the Confederate Government: The Diary of Robert Garlick Hill Kean, Head of the Bureau of War* (New York, 1957), pp. 116, 118.

²²Davis, *Short History,* p. 122; Edward A. Pollard, *The Second Year of the War* (New York, 1864), p. 288; *Tri-Weekly Telegraph,* January 13, 1862; *Charleston Daily Courier,* April 11, 1862.

²³Chesnut, *Diary from Dixie,* p. 329; R. M. Collins, *Chapters from the Unwritten History of the War between the States* (St. Louis, 1893), p. 121; Cornelia McDonald, *A Diary with Reminiscences of the War and Refugee Life in the Shenandoah Valley, 1860-1865* (Nashville, 1934), p.104; Betsy Fleet and John D. P. Fuller, eds., *Green Mount — A Virginia Plantation Family during the Civil War* (Lexington, 1965), p. 250; Jones, *Diary,* 2:113-15.

Chapter X

THE DEMISE OF PAPER MONEY

The year 1864 opened with the people of the Confederate States inundated by a flood of paper money. Change bills, state issuances, shinplasters, bank paper, and Confederate Treasury notes had combined to create monetary chaos. Much more paper currency was afloat than could ever be absorbed by the Confederate economy for many years, even if the nation had been able to build factories and other industries instantly. This would have been the only way that the economy could have absorbed the surplus paper money, but the South was not ready to industrialize. It had been simple for the governments, banks, and merchants to print promises to pay, and they had eagerly resorted to this course of action as an inexpensive way of financing the war. Now this situation needed immediate correction if any semblance of order and stability were to be brought to a currency rapidly depreciating in value.

By the beginning of 1864, most people in authority acknowledged that the surplus of paper money was the primary cause of inflation. With each increase of paper money, all outstanding issues decreased in purchasing power. President Davis maintained that the volume of paper money had to be reduced to carry on the business activity of the country. In February 1864, the Confederate Congress acted by attempting to force the redemption of as much of the old money issues as possible. The Congress declared that the old notes could be exchanged for bonds, without loss of value, if they were presented before April 1, 1864, east of the Mississippi River, or before July 1, west of the river. Notes above the value of five dollars presented after that date, could only be exchanged for new issue notes with a thirty-three and one-third percent tax imposed. Thus three dollars in old bills would be worth two dollars in new bills. One newspaper felt that the success of the new issue would depend upon the people's willingness to convert their old bills at a discount. If they refused, which was the general consensus before April 1, 1864, then the new issue paper money would remain in the Confederate Treasury because it was not to be used except to replace the old issues of paper money, and the old notes would continue to circulate at a discount worked out during each transaction.[1]

The new issue paper money excited high hopes of what it would accomplish. One editor expected that over $700,000,000 would eventually be withdrawn from circulation. President Davis claimed that by July 1, 1864, over $300,000,000 had been funded. Everyone hoped that prices would soon go down, but unfortunately only notes above five dollars were affected. Lower denominations were at par with the new issue. Some prices rose prior to April 1864, because of uncertainty about the effects of the law. People began saving all five dollar bills they received prior to April 1, 1864, and used the larger values to pay their debts. East of the Mississippi River, a trade sprang up after April 1, in buying up unfunded notes above the denomination of five dollars and sending them west of the river to be funded. While some areas reported a decline in prices after April 1, such was not the case in Richmond. In April sugar and molasses increased in price, and by April 23, the *Daily Richmond Enquirer* called for living with the situation instead of trying to reform it. The *Richmond Dispatch* reflected bitter feelings and expressed resentment that Congress debated financial legislation while the war was raging, and the Congress itself was making emergency plans to flee. By June 10, the new issue was still to be found only in the towns of Virginia and had not reached the interior areas. The plan to reduce the excess of currency had failed to restore the chaotic monetary conditions to a healthly situation. Although some prices had fallen, such declines were local and did not follow the general pattern of continuing inflation.[2]

The army and the currency were the two principal questions on people's minds by 1864. The Confederacy met the monetary problem in different ways in the various areas. In the interior portions, a system of barter developed, and a disdain of Confederate paper money manifested itself. Compared to the United States, there was virtually no industry in these areas to absorb the excess of paper money, and the quantity was therefore overwhelming. The Trans-Mississippi Confederacy developed a growing reliance on commodities, the specie produced by the sale of these goods in Mexico, and an aversion to Confederate bills. As early as October 1863, many people in Texas and northwestern Louisiana refused to accept

Confederate money, and those who would accept it charged high prices. In June 1864, a person told about paying off debts in Tyler, Texas, with old issue paper money and finding creditors hesitant to accept it. People were eagerly seeking to liquidate their debts with the old issue. By April 1865, no one in Texas would accept Confederate bills. For a year or more before the end of the war the state had been for all practical purposes on a gold basis.[3]

But the East was not so fortunate, for it had only paper money. There, the monetary situation deteriorated to the point that the *Confederate Baptist* wanted its readers to pay their ministers in provisions instead of money. For those who had specie, life turned out to be much more enjoyable and not nearly as difficult as for those who lacked it. Persons with only Confederate paper money encountered many monetary problems in daily living. This was the case with Mrs. Mary Boykin Chesnut who had lived in Richmond, Virginia, and various places in South Carolina during the war. In May 1864, Mrs. Chesnut, then in Camden, South Carolina, showed her faith in the Confederacy by purchasing Confederate bonds from a private party for articles of gold she had scraped together. But eventually she developed a willingness to dispose of Confederate paper money for whatever could be obtained. In August 1864, Mrs. Chesnut, then in Columbia, South Carolina, inadvertently paid one hundred dollars too much to a merchant. When the merchant called her attention to this oversight, she merely laughed and said, "Who steals my purse steals trash — if it contains Confederate bills."[4] By February 25, 1865, she referred to the notes as waste paper, and the next month she confided, "I hager in yarn for the millionth part of a thread! When they ask for Confederate money, I never stop to chaffer."[5] Even Confederate bonds fell out of favor. On October 11, 1864, an artillery officer who perceived how the war would end referred to bonds as poor securities. Thus the average citizen was beginning to lose faith in a Confederate victory. And with this loss of morale, the value of Confederate paper money declined further.[6]

Midway during the war, another type of paper money was growing more in favor with the people of the Confederacy. This was the legal tender Treasury notes, or "greenbacks," issued by the United States. By the second year of the war, Edward A. Pollard, editor of the *Richmond Examiner*, reported that a lively trade had developed in greenbacks which were sold by brokers at one dollar for four Confederate dollars. Millions of dollars in state bonds and bank notes were sent to the United States in order to secure greenbacks. These United States notes eventually found their way into general circulation throughout the Confederacy and were willingly accepted by the public. Moreover, the central authorities did nothing to stop this practice and even appeared to condone it by making use of the currency themselves. Indeed, on April 19, 1865, Forrest's Cavalry was paid in greenbacks at the rate of one United States dollar to fifteen Confederate dollars. Thus any money, even that of the enemy, grew to be preferable to Confederate paper money.[7]

With prices skyrocketing, the central government and its officials began to feel the inflationary pinch. On March 15, 1864, Mrs. Chesnut reported that the President's wife, Varina Howell Banks Davis, could no longer live within their income and had to give up their carriage and horses. When the new issue paper money appeared and did nothing to reduce prices, some other remedy had to be found to give credit to Confederate paper money and buoy up its purchasing power. The central government turned its attention to gold, since it seemed to be coveted by everyone. In a move that would be duplicated by many governments in years to come, the authorities attempted to manipulate gold in an abortive effort to increase the value of Confederate paper money.[8]

Why should the Confederacy not try to manipulate gold? In January 1864, the editor of a newspaper had attempted to point out to the public that gold was only merchandise like any other commodity. He stated that commerce should be transacted in paper currency, and he called for full confidence in Confederate notes. On January 17, 1865, Representative Humphrey Marshall of Kentucky presented a plan to the House of Representatives for increasing the value of the central government's money. Under terms of his suggestions, he believed that all cotton, tobacco, and gold in the Confederacy should be seized and become the property of the government. Marshall stated that these items would then be used for the public good and would be paid for with Confederate Treasury notes which would be legal tender. Congress never acted on this proposal. Another member of Congress advocated in private a different idea which a person who had overheard the plan later recalled.[9]

This unnamed Congressman—near the end of the Confederacy's existence when a gold dollar was selling for over one hundred Confederate dollars—offered a simple solution to this complex problem. He reasoned that gold was an inconvenient currency and only a few people wanted it for anything other than a monetary basis. Therefore, Congress had only to declare all Treasury notes redeemable at par in gold to solve its monetary problems. As long as the notes were theoretically exchangeable for gold, few people would want to exchange them. The Confederate Treasury would have enough gold to meet this small demand, and the rest of the people would be satisfied in the belief that they could convert their paper money to gold any time they wished. Accordingly, the government could issue any amount of paper money required to meet its expenses, and there would be full confidence, low prices, and a strong currency. In this way the Confederacy "shall have created the untold wealth which our currency represents."[10]

But the new Secretary of the Treasury, George A. Trenholm, was a little more practical than this. His solution, the one that was followed by the central authorities, was an attempted manipulation of the money market through the buying and selling of gold. On December 31, 1864, he took his first plunge and sold gold. Initially his efforts were rewarded by a decline of thirty-three percent in the price of gold, but John B. Jones felt this would not last. By January 6, 1865, Jones reported that the price of gold had fallen to thirty dollars Confederate for one dollar of gold, but five days later it had doubled this value. Trenholm again acted by selling cotton and tobacco to the United States for gold and pounds sterling bills which he used for buying outstanding Treasury notes. His efforts were once again rewarded as gold dropped from eighty Confederate dollars for one gold dollar to a rate of fifty to one. Jones added, however, "the flood will soon overwhelm all opposition, sweeping every obstacle away."[11] Six days later, on January 27, 1865, Jones reported a broker had informed him that he had an order from the government to sell gold at thirty-five Confederate dollars for one dollar in gold, but this was not the market price at the time. When the last official sale of Confederate notes occurred in May 1865, the rate had climbed to $1,200 for one gold dollar.[12]

TABLE 7

GOLD PRICES IN CONFEDERATE BILLS, JANUARY 1, 1861 TO MAY 12, 1865*

1861	Cost of $1.00 gold in Confederate Bills
January 1 to May 1	1.05
October 1	1.10
October 15	1.12
November 15	1.15
December 1	1.20

	1862	Cost of $1.00 gold in Confederate Bills
February 1		1.25
February 15		1.40
March 1		1.50
March 15		1.65
April 1		1.75
April 15		1.80
May 1		1.90
May 15		1.95
June 15		2.00
August 1		2.20
September 1		2.50
	1863	
February 1		3.00
February 15		3.10
March 1		3.25
March 15		5.00
May 15		6.00
June 1		6.50
June 15		7.50
July 1		8.00
July 15		10.00
August 15		15.00
November 15		15.50
December 15		21.00
	1864	
March 1		26.00
April 1		19.00
May 1		20.00
August 15		21.00
September 15		23.00
October 15		25.00
November 15		28.00
December 1		32.00
December 31		51.00

1865	Cost of $1.00 gold in Confederate Bills
January 1	60.00
February 1	50.00
April 1	70.00
April 15	80.00
April 20	100.00
April 26	200.00
April 30	800.00
May 1	1,200.00

*John C. Schwab, *The Confederate States of America: A Financial and Industrial History of the South during the Civil War* (New York, 1901), p. 375.

The final result of all of Trenholm's financial manipulations was that he temporarily reduced the market conversion rate and thus strengthened the Confederate dollar. But the result was not lasting, and Congress had to pass laws to permit the confiscation of coin for the needs of the central government. As another indication of the desperate condition of the Confederate Treasury, on March 13, 1865, a resolution was passed allowing Trenholm to accept public contributions of money, jewels, gold and silver plate, and public securities. Trenholm issued a notice to this effect on March 15. The proclamation appeared in the Richmond newspapers on March 25, but it is doubtful if many contributions were received. On March 9, 1865, the final estimate of appropriations for expenses for the calendar year 1865 was made by the Treasury Department; it totaled $1,141,642,148.28. Any successes Trenholm had enjoyed were obviously short-lived.[13]

The Confederate Treasury never contained a large amount of coin. Most of it had been shipped overseas earlier for foreign purchases and other operations. In addition, a sizeable quantity of specie was spent in the final months trying to bolster the value of the Confederate dollar. In this same period before Richmond was evacuated on April 2, 1865, silver coin sold at the rate of sixty Confederate dollars for one silver dollar. While the fleeing government rested in Danville, Virginia, silver sales were resumed at the rate of seventy dollars to one. Interestingly, there have been continual rumors of a large cache of buried Confederate gold.

Ironically, there had been very little gold to begin with, and there was even less when the government was forced to flee Richmond. But the story of the flight presents several possibilities for rumors of buried Confederate gold. Whether Confederate authorities buried any gold or not is pure speculation, but if they did it may have been the gold removed from the banks in Richmond.[14]

Shortly after Confederate officials fled Richmond, Secretary of the Treasury Trenholm resigned due to ill health and went his own way. Postmaster General John H. Reagan assumed his duties. Years later, Reagan recalled that when he received the Confederate Treasury, it amounted to $600,000 or $700,000 in Treasury notes, about $85,000 in gold coin and bullion, approximately $35,000 in silver coin, and some $36,000 in silver bullion. Altogether, Reagan estimated he assumed control of approximately $156,000 in gold and silver coin and bullion. Another individual estimated the total of Confederate specie at about $200,000, and still others placed the total slightly higher. Richmond banks also sent about $300,000, mostly in gold, *in the care of their own officials.* Nearly all contemporary authorities make reference to this fact, emphasizing that the specie of the Richmond banks merely accompanied the fleeing Confederate authorities, and that officials of the Richmond banks were also present to oversee the security of their gold.[15]

According to other estimates, Reagan's report of the value of the precious metals carried by the retreating government was extremely low. The final acting Treasurer of the Confederate States, Micajah H. Clark, reported that a total value of $327,000 was carried from Danville, Virginia, on April 6, 1865. By April 12, President Davis was at Greensboro, North Carolina, where he met with General Joseph E. Johnston. There they used $39,000 of the treasure to pay Johnston's troops, and another $35,000 was dispatched with President Davis when he left. Payments and salaries ate away this $35,000 until a final distribution was made in Florida. The records show that this shipment consisted mainly of gold sovereigns from Great Britain. The main Confederate treasure train later caught up with Davis at Washington, Georgia.[16]

It was at Washington that the final distribution of Confederate funds was made. President Davis instructed Reagan to close the business of the Post Office Department and Treasury Department and leave the city. Reagan said that he complied and departed the day after Davis had taken his leave of the city, but not before he had delivered the funds from the Richmond banks to their agents; estimates place the amount of specie involved at this point between $200,000 and $300,000. This final distribution of specie from the Confederate Treasury was not made by Reagan but by acting Treasurer Clark. He reported that John C. Breckinridge accepted $1,000 for transmission to the Confederate Trans-Mississippi Department; James A. Semple carried $86,000 for delivery to some foreign port; and Reagan received $3,500 for his services. The remaining $162,500 had already been used for pay and provisions, or was distributed at the time to those who remained. About $40,000 in silver bullion was also turned over to the Commissary Department to feed paroled soldiers and stragglers who passed through the area. Therefore, the only amount of specie that could have been buried, giving rise to the numerous legends, was the $86,000 paid to Semple.[17]

The only large sum of money remaining undistributed at Washington, Georgia, was the specie from the Richmond banks. The officers of the banks sought the help of Federal authorities in returning the coin to Richmond. While the shipment was heading north, the men of Vaughan's Brigade, one of the escorts, heard about it, and believing that it was the property of the Confederate government which had been seized by the United States, decided to help themselves to it as a reward for their faithful service. They captured the train and made off with as much of the coin as they could carry, but some of it was eventually recovered. According to various people who later wrote about the incident, some individuals later used this money to start businesses in Missouri, California, Texas, a banking house in Kansas, and at least one bank in the city of Richmond itself. The remaining $100,000, some of which had been recovered from the culprits, went to the District of Columbia where it remained in Federal hands. The Richmond banks made repeated but unsuccessful efforts to secure its return in later years.[18]

This only accounts, however, for the funds held within the Confederacy. What happened to the funds that were overseas at the time of the collapse? Could they have composed a large hidden treasure? Judah P. Benjamin told S. L. Barlow on November 28, 1881, that all Confederate funds in Europe had been exhausted before the end came. Indeed, Benjamin maintained that it was only due to a last minute sale of cotton that Confederate officials in Europe were able to meet the final payment of coupons due on bonds sold previously in Europe. The only Confederate items that United States authorities found to seize in Europe were supplies, machinery, and several vessels. But there were other foreign areas where funds had been sent. Some money had been delivered to Canada, and this money seems to have been distributed to destitute ex-Confederates. One woman in the Shenandoah Valley in Virginia reported that she received one hundred dollars in October 1865, that she later learned had been in Confederate hands in Canada when the end came. The Confederate fiscal agent at Havana, Cuba, Charles Helms, reported that he had $30,000 in gold at the time of the collapse of the Confederate government, and that he took these funds to Canada where he personally used them to send Confederate soldiers to college. Helms maintained that the money was not his and that the Confederacy owed its soldiers their pay; therefore, he established a type of veterans' benefits. Most of the soldiers helped were escaped prisoners from the United States prisoner-of-war camp on Johnson's Island in Lake Erie. From this it would seem that most, if not all, of the overseas funds were used to help the destitute. Perhaps the $86,000 sent with Semple was included in the money distributed in this way.[19]

In the final months of the Confederacy's life its people drew away from paper money and grew to rely more on specie and commodities. Eventually, the central authorities joined in this general movement. The Trans-Mississippi area led the way, due to the easy access it had to Mexico, a foreign market. Texas, by far the most advantageously located state, was virtually on a gold basis for at least a year before the collapse of the Confederacy. Any money became preferable to the overprinted Confederate currency. The people willingly accepted the enemy's paper money more readily than the paper money of their own government. As citizens shunned the worthless bills, specie came out of hiding to a greater extent than at any other time during the war. As it did, Confederate Treasury notes became less acceptable.

Confederate authorities tried desperately to make paper currency work and hold some value. In 1864, an effort was made to reduce the amount of paper money outstanding. This effort forced conversion of paper money into bonds and the issuing of a new paper dollar, with a conversion rate of two dollars new for three dollars old. This effort failed to accomplish its purpose, however, and it even seemed to be a repudiation of part of the Confederate debt. As the war ground on, the people in the East continued to hope for ultimate victory, but eventually hope faded. Then, paper money became so worthless in their minds that they were willing to give any amount of it away to obtain what they needed. In late 1864 and early 1865, the central authorities used Confederate gold to improve the purchasing power of the paper dollar, but this also failed. Finally, Confederate officials made one last, but unsuccessful, effort to obtain coin, just as governmental collapse was at hand. The remaining coin in the Confederate Treasury, by then, was used to pay salaries, buy emergency supplies, and as in the case of the funds overseas, help the needy after the war. Thus, paper money that had been tied to faith in government and belief in eventual independence faded with their demise. As the war dragged on and hope in ultimate victory faded, Confederate morale declined, and the overprinting of the currency, backed by little or nothing of intrinsic value, resulted in runaway inflation which helped further to decrease morale.

[1]Ross, *Cities and Camps of the Confederate States*, p. 160; Davis, *Short History*, p. 123; *Daily Richmond Enquirer*, March 23, 1864.
[2]Ibid., April 4, 1864; Davis, *Short History*, p. 123; *Daily Richmond Enquirer*, March 28, 1864; Eliza M. Smith to family, February 23, 1864; Eliza M. Smith to daughters, March 10, 1864; Daniel E. Huger Smith and others, eds., *Mason Smith Family Letters, 1860-1868* (Columbia, 1950), pp. 82, 86; *Daily Richmond Enquirer*, April 19, 1864; *The Confederate Baptist*, May 25, 1864; *Daily Richmond Examiner*, April 16, 23, 1864; *Richmond Dispatch* as quoted in *Montgomery Daily Advertiser*, May 29, 1864; *Daily Richmond Enquirer*, June 10, 1864.
[3]*Daily Richmond Examiner*, January 6, 1864; DeLeon, *Four Years in Rebel Capitals*, pp. 234-35; Edward A. Pollard, *The War in America, 1863-1864* (London, 1865), pp. 244-45; *Tri-Weekly State Gazette*, October 26, 1863; Anderson, ed., *Brokenburn*, pp. 194, 288, 333; *New York Evening Post*, November 10, 1894.
[4]*The Confederate Baptist*, March 4, 1864; Edward L. Wells to Lawrence Wells, April 21, 1864, Smith and others, eds., *Smith Family Letters*, p. 89; Chesnut, *Diary from Dixie*, pp. 403, 431.
[5]Ibid., pp. 487, 499.
[6]John Hampden Chamberlayne to Hartwell Macom Chamberlayne, October 11, 1864, C. G. Chamberlayne, introduction and notes, *Ham Chamberlayne — Virginian: Letters and Papers of an Artillery Officer in the War for Southern Independence, 1861-1865* (Richmond, 1932), p. 277.
[7]Pollard, *The Second Year of the War*, p. 288; Schwab, *The Confederate States of America*, p. 161; Circular, H. Q. Forrest's Cavalry, *Official Records, Army*, Ser. I, 49(Part 2):1254.
[8]Chesnut, *Diary from Dixie*, p. 395.
[9]*Daily Richmond Examiner*, January 8, 1864, January 18, 1865.
[10]George Cary Eggleston, *A Rebel's Recollections* (Cambridge, 1875), pp. 99-100.
[11]Jones, *Diary*, 2:373, 378, 383, 393-94.
[12]Ibid., p. 400; DeLeon, *Four Years in Rebel Capitals*, p. 375.
[13]*Daily Richmond Examiner*, March 21, 1865; Estimates of Appropriations . . . January 1 to December 31, 1865; Estimates of Appropriations, January, 1863 to February, 1865.
[14]M. H. Clark, "Departure of President Davis and Cabinet from Richmond, Va.,

and the Last Days of the Confederate Treasury and what became of Its Specie," in Ben LeBree, ed., *The Confederate Soldier in the Civil War* (Paterson, [1959]), p. 318.

[15]Reagan to Davis, February 18, 1878, Rowland, ed., *Davis: Constitutionalist*, 8:113; John F. Wheless to Davis, February 10, 1882, ibid., 9:147.

[16]A. J. Hanna, *Flight into Oblivion* (Bloomington, 1959), pp. 90-91, 115-16.

[17]John H. Reagan, *Memoirs with Special Reference to Secession and the Civil War* (New York and Washington, 1906), pp. 212-13; Hanna, *Flight into Oblivion*, pp. 90-93; Clark, "Departure of President Davis," p. 321.

[18]Lewis Shepherd, "The Confederate Treasure Train," *Confederate Veteran* (June, 1917), 25(6):257-58; D. H. Maury to Davis, January 18, 1882, Rowland, ed., *Davis: Constitutionalist*, 9:144.

[19]Daniel Grinnan, "Disposition of Confederate Funds," *Confederate Veteran* (September, 1929), 38(9):328-29; McDonald, *Diary*, p. 270.

NORTHERN BANK NOTE

FIVE DOLLARS NOTE, THE EGG HARBOR BANK, EGG HARBOR CIT
NEW JERSEY.

Figure 63

Even the notes of Northern banks circulated in the Confederacy. Like th
Southern counterparts, Congress also taxed these notes out of existence after
war, leaving United States bills victorious.

$20 NOTE. At the top is an example of a chemicography reverse that was supposed to be used in 1864 but was captured. Below is the actual design that appeared on the 1864 Confederate bill's reverse when the chemicography reverse was not available.

Most of the 1861 issue of Confederate notes bore no design on the reverse side. In 1863 the Confederacy commissioned S. Straker and Sons of London, England, to design the reverses for the 1864 issue of notes. The firm employed the process known as chemigraphy by which engravings and etchings were made with chemicals. The shipments, however, fell into the hands of the United States.

Figure 64

NON TAXABLE CERTIFICATES

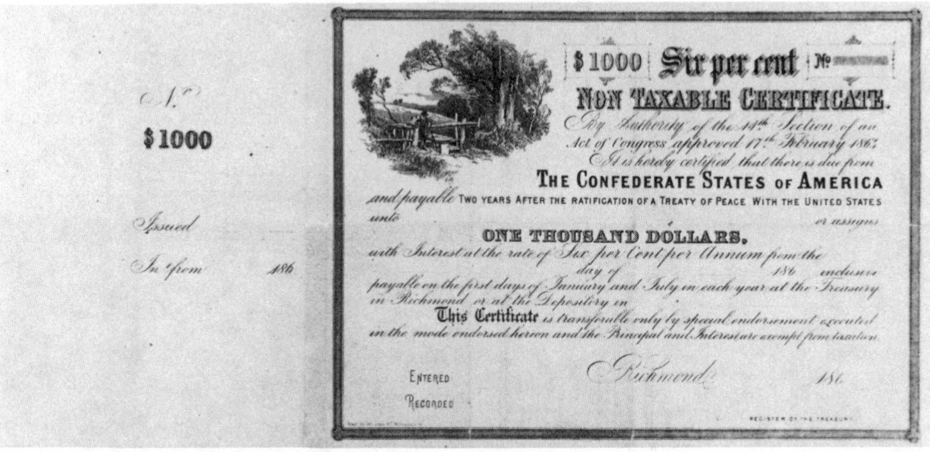

No.
$1000
Issued
In from 186

$1000 Six per cent No.
NON TAXABLE CERTIFICATE.
By Authority of the 14th Section of an Act of Congress approved 17th February 1864
It is hereby certified that there is due from
THE CONFEDERATE STATES OF AMERICA
and payable TWO YEARS AFTER THE RATIFICATION OF A TREATY OF PEACE WITH THE UNITED STATES
unto or assigns
ONE THOUSAND DOLLARS,
with Interest at the rate of Six per Cent per Annum from the day of 186 inclusive
payable on the first days of January and July in each year at the Treasury in Richmond or at the Depository in
This Certificate is transferable only by special endorsement executed in the mode endorsed hereon and the Principal and Interest are exempt from taxation
Richmond 186
ENTERED
RECORDED
REGISTER OF THE TREASURY

$1000 NON TAXABLE CERTIFICATE. This certificate with its registration stub (left) had not been issued.

Figure 65

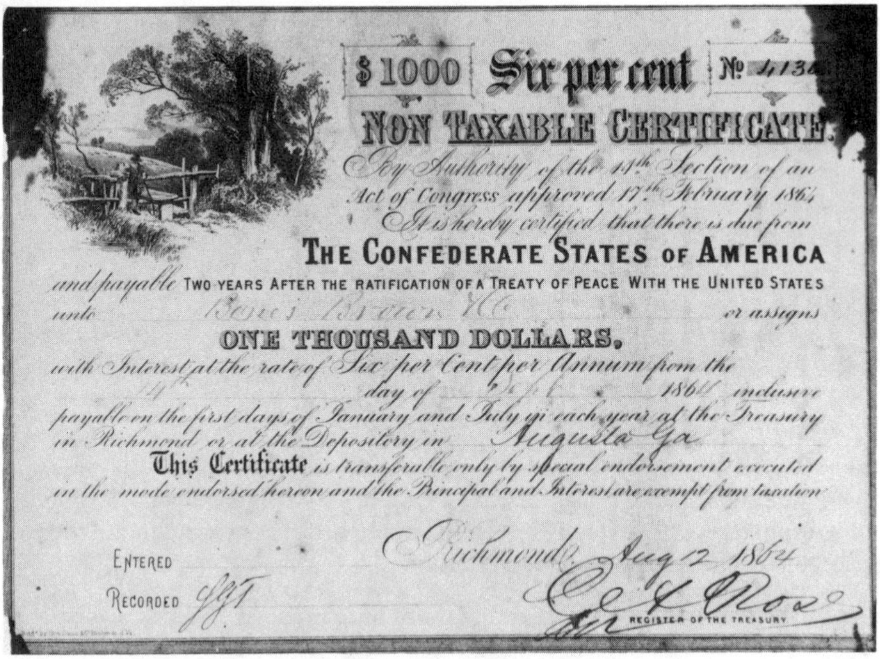

$1000 Six per cent No. 4138
NON TAXABLE CERTIFICATE.
By Authority of the 14th Section of an Act of Congress approved 17th February 1864
It is hereby certified that there is due from
THE CONFEDERATE STATES OF AMERICA
and payable TWO YEARS AFTER THE RATIFICATION OF A TREATY OF PEACE WITH THE UNITED STATES
unto Bones Brown & Co or assigns
ONE THOUSAND DOLLARS,
with Interest at the rate of Six per Cent per Annum from the 14th day of Sept 1864 inclusive
payable on the first days of January and July in each year at the Treasury in Richmond or at the Depository in Augusta Ga
This Certificate is transferable only by special endorsement executed in the mode endorsed hereon and the Principal and Interest are exempt from taxation
Richmond Aug 12 1864
ENTERED
RECORDED
REGISTER OF THE TREASURY

$1000 NON TAXABLE CERTIFICATE. This certificate with its registration stub removed had been issued.

Figure 66

These certificates were issued to satisfy the public debt. They could be issued to any "public creditor" who incurred the debt after February 1864, and who chose to accept them. They bore six per cent interest, were redeemable two years after the war (like Treasury notes) and were exempt from any taxes on both principal and interest. In this way, they eliminated the need for more notes and were as secure as registered bonds.

Chapter XI

AN EPILOGUE
ON MONETARY POLICY

When the Confederate States organized, its officials and people assumed that coinage and bank notes would make up the bulk of the circulating medium, the same as in the United States. The Confederate Provisional Congress authorized interest-bearing Treasury notes early, but the notes were not intended for wide circulation or as the primary medium of exchange. They resembled miniature denomination bonds which could be used to pay debts owed the central government, except for export duty on cotton. Secretary of the Treasury Memminger began early preparations for a Confederate coin, in response to dictates of the Provisional Congress, and several trial strikes were made of one design. If these coins had been minted, they would have been, according to law, legal tender for payment of debts up to a limit of ten dollars; the United States had previously set its limit at five dollars. But before ideas for a coinage system could be fully formulated, war began and plans for coins had to be shelved until after the conflict. The central government needed the bullion it had to purchase supplies overseas because its paper money was not acceptable there. When the bullion arrived overseas, it was converted into coin of the realm at that country's mint.

With the coming of war the central authorities searched for some other circulating medium as well as a way to pay off its debts at minimum cost to the government. Non-interest bearing Treasury notes appeared to be the ideal solution to both problems. They could be produced inexpensively; no interest need be paid; they could be used as money by the public; the principal on them was not payable until after a treaty of peace; and,

127

best of all, they could be used to pay government debts and exchanged for specie and bank notes. This last consideration, exchange for specie and bank notes, was at the core of all central and state government issues; the authorities wanted to exchange their paper money, or in effect be loaned a different medium of exchange. These bills were, therefore, merely promises to pay at some future date. Until the Confederate bills could be printed, bank notes had to be used, and the banks loaned their notes to the central government in return for interest-bearing Treasury notes, plus the promise of the eventual return of the bank bills or new Confederate paper money bearing no interest. Because the central government produced the new non-interest bearing issue in the usual denominations of bank notes, they were meant to be integrated with the system then in existence. But the rapid disappearance of hard money placed a severe test on these plans. The ultimate superiority of bank paper money also complicated the situation, because the people hoarded it.

Memminger, through a series of early maneuvers, brought about the total domination of Confederate paper money in the monetary life of the community. Private arrangements saw to it that the banks accepted this currency and paid it out at par with specie in the first year of the war. When the banks of New Orleans held out, Memminger used all the leverage he could muster to force their compliance with his wishes. He pressured Governor Thomas O. Moore of Louisiana to get the banks in that state to accept this arrangement. Before the end of September 1861, all banks throughout the Confederacy had complied.

The public displayed little reluctance to accept Confederate bills at first. Moved by patriotism, citizens felt it was reprehensible not to accept their national currency, and many of the state legislatures prodded the few who would not accept the notes in payment of debts. Memminger had the answer for this small segment of the population. Bypass them in making government purchases, or require them to wait until after the war for payment.

By 1862 the central government's paper money virtually served as legal tender, and because of this, a congressional statute legalizing it as such was never enacted. This was a blessing for some creditors who could afford to wait until after the war to collect their debts, but many debtors were begging for the opportunity to pay off their debts with the plentiful, low value paper money in circulation. Legal tender status would have accomplished this end. It would also have made it compulsory to accept these notes from the government; the central authorities soon saw the results of not making Confederate paper money legal tender.

The central government also failed in controlling state issuances of paper money. Confederate bills circulated widely throughout the Confederate States, and existed side by side with the various state notes. Although the state bills circulated in limited areas, the quantity printed reduced the value of all paper money. The central government should have prevented this, but it took no action.

The various states of the Confederacy issued their own currency in order to meet their obligations at low cost, much the same as the central government. Georgia copied the Confederate Treasury Department's system for keeping records of its issues. Like other small issues, these bills did not circulate outside the state boundaries. Even the most conservative state governments, however, saw the value of their notes decline; Florida considered the modest decline of its notes a sympathetic reaction to the collapse in value of Confederate Treasury notes. Perhaps the public began to lose faith in the ability of the state governments ever to redeem their outstanding paper money and bonds. It would require years after the end of the war for the states to pay off their many unsecured debts, if they could pay them off at all.

Bank bills, however, enjoyed wide circulation. This was because the banks made use of Confederate paper money — the national currency — as well as bonds issued by the central government as collateral for their own notes. At first this may have been required to provide interstate circulation. However, eventually bank paper money was seen as a better medium of exchange than any of the central or state government issuances, and this may have helped to sustain demand for bank bills in later years. The purchasing power of bank bills declined only slightly during the war.

The disappearance of coins brought about a number of emergency monetary measures. Tokens were used in lieu of change in some areas, but they disappeared in a short time. Attempts at a national token coinage system never passed Congress, although that body briefly considered the idea. Postage stamps were used for change, but their demand as such varied over the years. One obvious reason for this was that stamps deteriorated when frequently passed from person to person. A number of non-governmental solutions emerged locally, including the use of five-cent omnibus tickets in the city of New Orleans. But by far the most widely practiced remedy was the issuance of shinplasters by merchants, corporations, and others. These pieces of paper soon became a real nuisance, because many firms issued them in large quantities and later went out of business. Some firms were accused of printing shinplasters so that they could obtain government money for speculative purposes. By 1862, the states of the Confederacy generally outlawed shinplasters and printed change bills of their own. The states, however, did permit certain municipalities and some businesses to print change notes, and required banks to print these same denominations. Some of the shinplasters were withdrawn, but probably not all of them. The people appeared to prefer any type of so-called money, rather than the inconvenience of barter.

To compound the monetary problems faced by the Confederacy; prolongation of the war, rising costs, hoarding of specie, and replacement of bank bills in circulation with governmental issuances, all combined to drive prices up and to force the central authorities to issue more paper money. It was a vicious cycle, because additional paper money increased the public's mistrust of it. The Confederacy soon found itself in the grip of out-of-control hyperinflation. In March 1863, the Confederate Congress authorized the printing of $50,000,000 in Treasury notes *per month* to meet expenses, with nothing of intrinsic value pledged for the redemption of the bills. If this situation was not corrected, the result would be the collapse of the Confederate monetary system.

Reluctantly more and more Confederate citizens in the East turned to barter, while in the West they turned to commodities and specie, as a substitute for Confederate paper money. Those who could not do so were forced to pay as much paper money as was demanded to obtain the necessities of life. Regardless of the price of goods, most people eagerly disposed of their Confederate paper money. It soon became apparent that too much currency was in circulation for the needs of the nation's economy, thus forcing the central government to act. People clamored for removal of excess currency, but the tax levied on it in 1864 by the central authorities shook people's confidence in paper money. The government enacted a law which cancelled all previous paper money issues and sought to force their redemption in bonds by taxing unconverted notes. Those notes not presented for bonds before the cutoff date could only be exchanged for a new issue of bills at the rate of three dollars old for two dollars new. In this way Confederate officials expected to remove most excess currency from circulation and thus bring down prices. Instead, prices stabilized for a while and then continued to rise. It would have been far better if the old issues had continued to circulate and had a tax been levied on them to be paid in old issue bills.

The plan failed for several reasons. Many people saw it as repudiation of part of the Confederate debt, for the currency had become synonymous with debt. If the tax could be levied once, the people felt there would be nothing to prevent it from happening again. The Indian nations also disliked the tax because they viewed it as an attempt to make them bear some of the costs of the war, which was expressly forbidden by the terms of the treaties they had ratified. This tended to increase the general public mistrust of the government and its currency and to decrease morale.

The plan had other shortcomings. Only bills above the value of five dollars were affected; there was, however, a large quantity of outstanding bills below this denomination. Of all the interest-bearing notes issued by the government, not one was below the face value of fifty dollars, and this may have been of consideration to the Confederate Congress. Additionally, since different deadlines existed for redemption of the notes east and west of the Mississippi River, some people started buying unredeemed bills east of the river and shipping them west of it to be redeemed at full value for bonds. Because the new issue was exchanged for old issues, a shortage of the new bills developed, and people held on to the old bills and continued to use them. In acknowledgment of this, the central authorities prolonged the time for redemption until July 1865. The public reacted to the time extension by increasing the value of the old notes and devaluing the new, so that they were both at the same level.

The Trans-Mississippi Confederacy led the way in valuing specie and commodities more than paper money. But the East lacked the means for obtaining specie, because it did not have easy access to foreign markets. Only North Carolina was an exception to this general rule when it entered the blockade-running business. This may have been why North Carolina did not need to issue state treasury notes in late 1864 or early 1865 as did so many of the other states in the East. In the meantime, the Confederate government saw the value of its bills declining lower and lower, even after the passage of the 1864 law for which there had been such high hopes. By December 1864, it was obvious that this condition had to be remedied. At the time, the new Secretary of the Treasury, George A. Trenholm, decided that the only way to relieve the dire monetary situation was to drive down the price of gold. In December Trenholm began to sell gold from the Confederate Treasury on the open market for Treasury notes in an effort to increase the value of Confederate paper money. He successfully decreased the conversion rate, but the result was short-lived. As a result he had to return to the market place, but the results were always the same: a temporary decline followed by a rapid rise in the price of gold. Soon even Trenholm realized that his attempt had failed to give lasting relief.

By March 1865, because Confederate paper money had never been made legal tender, many people would not accept it in payment of needed supplies, even if the supplies were for the army upon which the survival of the nation depended. At this time the central authorities began their scramble for coin. Specie from the banks of New Orleans was appropriated, donations solicited, and the states were required to loan gold and silver to the central government. If the previous metals were not forthcoming by April 1, 1865, a twenty-five percent tax payable only in kind would be levied on all coin and bullion under the control of citizens of the Confederacy. Nowhere can the repudiation of former Confederate monetary policy be seen better than in this action by Confederate officials. Paper money had been king, and until it totally inundated the economy, it had worked. First the public began to shun it and finally, in reaction, so did the central government. Thus barter, commodities, and specie became the accepted exchange among the people of the Confederacy, and in the end, the central authorities had no choice but to follow suit.

The monetary practices of the Confederacy undoubtedly helped to undermine Confederate morale. While the people's faith in the central government showed some strengthening during the first two years of the war and minor strengthening in late 1864, prices did not decline accordingly. The only time when a slight decline in prices occurred, which was only a local phenomenon, came with the new paper money issue first introduced in early 1864. Even then its effects on the economy were uncertain. In early 1865 the value of Confederate Treasury notes reached an all time low, and morale declined accordingly. Thus morale and paper money seemed to go hand in hand, with Treasury notes leading the way.

Confederate monetary policy provides an opportunity to study the failure of several monetary theories. One such concept is that governments would not abuse the privilege of issuing paper money by use of printing presses. Even before the printing press was invented, governments increased the amount of money in circulation by reducing the amount of precious metals in their coins, or by replacing all of them with base metals. The invention of paper money merely made it easier to accomplish this end. The Confederacy began with every intention of having a limited and orderly paper currency. As Confederate internal and external expenses continued to rise, however, the central authorities were not loath to overprint paper money. Like many other governments past and present, the Confederacy gave little thought about how a large amount of currency could be retired or absorbed by the economy. Near the collapse of the Confederacy, the government printed a five hundred dollar bill for general circulation, the highest denomination ever printed in a non-interest bearing Confederate Treasury note. As prices increased there was a need for larger denomination bills. Such has always been the case with inflated economies.

Throughout the history of Confederate monetary policy repeated attempts were made to relegate gold and silver to the status of commodities with no place in the monetary picture except as bullion. Central authorities long considered paper money the only official circulating medium in the Confederacy. Confederate officials considered gold and silver as barbaric relics. Later theories expanded on this by declaring that precious metals were of no use as money because the supply could not be expanded to meet the needs of the economy, something with which Confederate officials would have been in accord. Thus Confederate authorities resorted to paper money backed by small quantities of gold and silver which were unavailable to the public. In substance, Confederate officials would have agreed that it is the faith of people in a government that creates money. As in other governments, Confederate authorities believed they could always sell gold to regulate their currency. They attempted this in late 1864 and early 1865, but this attempt failed just as their earlier attempt to reduce the volume of outstanding paper money had failed. The citizens were not allowed to obtain specie from banks, but the governments could and did. In 1865, when the Confederacy was in its final hours, it allowed the public to purchase precious metals from the Confederate Treasury at market prices.

It might be profitable to compare Confederate monetary policy with what later became known as Keynesian monetary economics, named for the British economist John Maynard Keynes. During the course of its monetary history, the Confederacy attempted to establish the supremacy of paper money, tried to relegate specie to a minor role within the country, flirted with a token coinage system, and attempted to regulate the volume of currency in circulation. In this way, the Confederacy was among the first governments to put into practice many of the elements germane to Keynesian monetary economics. The Confederacy, however, never made its paper money legal tender, a point which Keynes later advocated. Nevertheless, Confederate paper money soon established itself as virtually legal tender. Keynes felt that gold had no place in monetary policy, that paper currency was best, because it was elastic and could be expanded or contracted to meet the needs of the economy, and that the faith of the people in the government was the main ingredient in determining what was money and its value. *Fiat* currency then — money created by the will of the government, backed solely by people's faith in that governing body, and being acceptable for all debts through the threat of legal recriminations — was the answer to any monetary problem. Many countries in recent decades have followed Keynesian monetary economic thinking in formulating their monetary policies; the Confederacy implemented many of these ideas long before Keynes espoused them.

What would have happened to Confederate monetary policy if the Confederacy had achieved independence? It appears reasonable that a coinage system would have been introduced, with coin being legal tender for payment of debts up to a total of ten dollars. Coinage would have been on European rather than United States standards. The weight and fineness of the coins would have been those of either France or Great Britain. This would have facilitated a growing trade with Europe. The term "dollar" would have remained. In the independent Confederate States, taxes would have been high in order to pay off the national debt and to retire the paper money that had been printed during the war. There may have been a further issue of bonds to allow more time to repay all debts. Because of the general reluctance of authorities to make Treasury notes legal tender, it is possible that they would have been retired in time. Bank notes probably would have been candidates for paper money in an independent Confederacy, but the central government could have decided on a new issue of notes, again repudiating some of the debt and making the notes legal tender.

If Memminger had been the Secretary of the Treasury in an independent Confederate States, some other conclusions can be drawn. The amount of coinage in circulation would have been extremely small, bullion would have been kept in bars as it was in England, and the coinage standards may have conformed to England's. Because of Memminger's attachment to Great Britain, it may also be assumed that he may have favored a central bank, such as the Bank of England, with all paper money coming from the central bank alone. In this way, a national paper currency would have been created.

At the end of the war, the resources of the Confederate States were virtually exhausted. The money to rebuild the independent Confederacy and to pay off the war debt would have come from its citizens and from foreign investors, but this would have required the development of new industries. Some manufacturing began in the Confederacy during the war and would have continued after the conflict ended. Some foreign investors would have been found, but not if the national debt had been repudiated. If the independent Confederacy could not have attracted investors quickly enough, then the country would have been forced to liquidate some of its debt, and this action would have frightened many potential investors.

If the Confederacy had established its independence early in the war, its monetary problems would have been simpler. But if that event did not come until late 1864, the problems in attempting to reestablish monetary order would have been astronomical. It is not impossible to conceive that the new nation might have carried its financial burden well into the twentieth century. As in the United States, some of the total amount of paper money issued during the war may still have been circulating in the 1980's. But independence did not happen, and the entire Confederate debt was repudiated by the Fourteenth Amendment to the United States Constitution.

The lesson to be learned from Confederate monetary policy is that *fiat* currency can work, that gold and silver can be withdrawn from circulation and denied to the citizens, but both policies cannot go on indefinitely. As the volume of paper money grows and prices rise, people become dissatisfied. Eventually some event occurs that helps to undermine public confidence in government, and abuses of the money supply serves to magnify this mistrust. Once this has happened, the monetary collapse of the government is only a matter of time. It was not paper money itself that contributed to the Confederacy's fall, but the abuses of it, caused by the length of the war and the accompanying enormity of public expenses. The general population of the Confederacy despaired that the huge public debt would ever be fully paid with anything of intrinsic value. The public considered the idea of repudiation from at least 1864 until the collapse of the Confederacy.

TABLE 8

CONFEDERATE FUNDED DEBT, JANUARY 1, 1864*

Bonds and Stock

Act of February 28, 1861	8%	$ 15,000,000
Act of May 16, 1861	8%	8,774,900
Act of August 19, 1861	8%	100,000,000
Act of April 12, 1862	8%	3,612,300
Act of February 20, 1863	8%	95,785,000
Act of February 20, 1863	7%	63,615,750
Act of March 25, 1863	6%	2,831,700
Act of April 30, 1863 (Cotton Interest Coupon)	6%	8,252,000
Total of Stocks and Bonds		$ 297,871,650

Notes:

"The Call Certificates issued under the Acts of December 24, 1861, and March 23, 1863, respectively, it is deemed proper, on account of their peculiar character, to exclude from a statement showing the funded debt. It is not possible, from the material available to this office [the Confederate Register's Office], to ascertain what amount of them, if any, has assumed the character of permanent bonds, or been so converted."

Call Certificates bore interest, but like their business world counterparts, were designed for easy conversion into another medium such as bonds or, for the most part, Treasury notes.

*Official report of the Treasurer's Office, January 22, 1864, CST, Miscellaneous Office Records, June 5, 1861-March 8, 1865, NARG 365.

TABLE 9

CONFEDERATE FUNDED DEBT, 1861-1865*

Bonds & Stocks by Act of	Interest	Value
February 28, 1861	8%	$ 14,990,000
May 16, 1861	8%	9,086,600
August 19, 1861	8%	99,564,250
April 12, 1862	8%	3,222,550
February 20, 1863	8%	96,580,900
February 20, 1863	7%	66,941,900
March 23, 1863	6%	21,018,400
March 23, 1863 (Bonds)	4%	22,300
April 30, 1863 (Cotton Interest Coupon)	6%	8,372,000
February 17, 1864 (Stocks)	6%	32,040,000
February 17, 1864 (30 year Bonds)	6%	145,755,000
February 17, 1864 (20 year Bonds)	6%	6,000,000
February 17, 1864 (Non-Taxable Cert.)	6%	38,045,000
February 17, 1864 (Registered Bonds)	4%	10,783,900
February 17, 1864 (Bonds)	4%	16,263,500
June 13, 1864 (Bonds)	8%	2,164,000
June 14, 1864 (Bonds)	4%	4,000,000
Total Funded Debt		$ 565,877,600

*Raphael P. Thian, *Register of the Confederate Debt* (Boston, 1972), pp. 179-90. Although call certificates bore interest, they represented surplus treasury notes deposited at the treasury by private companies or individuals.

137

TABLE 10

CONFEDERATE NATIONAL DEBT, 1865*

Type of Debt	Amount
Funded Debt	$ 565,877,600.00
£3,000,000 Foreign Loan, at $4.85/£	14,550,000.00
Old Issue of Notes, outstanding on April 30, 1864, less one-third as per 1864 law	571,078,284.34
New Issue of Notes, as of April 1865	456,142,990.50
Total Debt	$1,607,648,874.84

Note: The conversion rate used for the British pound is the value at whick the gold sovereign passed as current coin within Confederate territory. The actual conversion should not have exceeded this.

Under the terms of the 1864 currency law, all outstanding Treasury bills issued before 1864 and not funded by April 1, 1864, were reduced by a tax of 33⅓ % (up to 100 % after January 1, 1865). The Trans-Mississippi was given until July 1, 1864, to redeem, and all notes below five dollars were exempt from the 33⅓ % tax. Because the Treasury Department figures do not provide a breakdown of the amount of small change bills outstanding under the Acts of October 13, 1862, and March 23, 1863, the same percentage shown for the April 17, 1862, one and two dollar notes, have been used in these calculations. On December 29, 1864, the date for the final exchange before imposition of the 100 % tax, it was extended until July 1, 1865. The total shown for old issue notes represents the estimated amount outstanding on April 30, 1864, less those bills below five dollars, reduced by one-third.

The figures given above do not include those bills reduced by the 100 % tax, the unconverted eight percent call certificates of 1861 and 1862 which became bonds, cotton certificates, non-interest notes used to meet the 1864 payment on the February 28, 1861, loan, the actual total of new issue Treasury notes released in 1864 and 1865, or any other fiscal paper. The true national debt of the Confederate States of America must have been about $1,750,000,000.

*Author's calculations; Matthews, *Statutes at Large*, pp. 62-63, 193-94; Ramsdell, *Laws of the Last Confederate Congress*, pp. 12-13.

CONFEDERATE CALL CERTIFICATE

FIFTY THOUSAND DOLLARS CALL CERTIFICATE.

A Call Certificate was a receipt for an amount of Treasury notes deposited with the Treasury Department. The Certificate drew interest and could be quickly redeemed for the same amount of notes that had been deposited. In this way, the investor received interest on what might otherwise have been idle cash reserves.

Figure 67

FOREIGN LOAN BOND

SEVEN PER CENT COTTON LOAN BOND. In 1863 the Confederacy authorized an overseas loan to reduce the need for bullion shipments. These loans were payable in pounds, francs, or cotton valued at six pence sterling per pound.

Figure 68

BIBLIOGRAPHY

Abbreviations used in Footnotes

COC   Confederate Office of the Comptroller
COR   Confederate Office of the Register
CPOD   Confederate Post Office Department
CSC   Confederate States Congress
CST   Confederate Secretary of the Treasury
MSARG Mississippi State Archives Record Group
NARG   National Archives Record Group

Manuscripts

ALABAMA

Montgomery
  State Archives
    Letter Book, 1862-1865.
    Andrew B. Moore Papers, 1860-1861.
    John Gill Shorter Papers, 1861-1863.
    Thomas N. Watts Papers, 1863-1865.

ARKANSAS

Little Rock
  Department of History
    Kie Oldham Collection.

FLORIDA

Pensacola
Historic Pensacola Preservation Board.
"Statement B accompanying City Treasurer's Communication to Board of Aldermen, June 22, 1866," File 1861-67, in Filo de la Rua Papers, Box 1, T. T. Wentworth, Jr. Collection.

Tallahassee
State Archives
Bills of the House, 1861-1865.
Bills of the House and Senate, 1861-1890s.

GEORGIA

Atlanta
State Archives
Joseph E. Brown Letter Book, 1861-1865.
Executive Letter Book from August 21, 1860 to May 12, 1864.
W. C. Mitchell Ledger, 1843-1863.
Treasurer's Letter Book, 1851-1861.
Treasury Notes Registers, all denominations.

LOUISIANA

Baton Rouge
State Archives
Letters Received, Executive Department, State of Louisiana, 1860-1865.
Record of State Bonds and Treasury Notes.
Statement of Bank Deposits by the Auditor of Public Accounts for the Free Banks.
State University Library
Archives Division
John Foster and Family Correspondence.
Christian D. Koch and Family Correspondence.
Robert A. Newell Papers.

Louisiana Room
    Clara Solomon, "Diary of a New Orleans Girl, 1861-1862."
New Orleans
Tulane University Library
    Davis Papers

                        MISSISSIPPI

Jackson
State Archives
        Executive Journal, 1857-1870.
        John J. Pettus Papers, 1860-1863.
    Record Group (MSARG) 30
        Register of Treasury Notes.
        Report of Notes Destroyed, January 1-May 17, 1865.
        Report of the Sheriff of Itawamba County, 1864.
        Statement of Probable Indebtedness of the State of Mississippi,
            October 25, 1865.
        Treasurer's Report, 1864.

                         NEW YORK

New York
American Numismatic Society Museum Library
        Levick, Joseph N. L., and Edward Groh, "Names of Firms on
            Tokens issued during the Civil War. Names of Firms on
            Tokens other than War Series and issued from 1789-
            1890."

                     NORTH CAROLINA

Raleigh
State Archives
        Henry T. Clark Papers, 1861-1863.
        Henry T. Clark Letter Book, 1861-1862.
        John W. Ellis Papers, 1859-1861.
        Secretary of State Papers, Constitutional Convention, 1861-
            1862, Tabled and Postponed Bills.

Treasurer and Comptroller Papers, Miscellaneous Group (Currency).
Treasurer and Comptroller Papers, Military Papers, Quartermaster and Blockade Accounts, 1861-1864.
Zebulon B. Vance Papers, 1863-1865.

OKLAHOMA

Norman
  University of Oklahoma Library
    Western History Collection
      Cherokee Nation Papers.

Oklahoma City
  Historical Society
    Indian Archives Division
      Cherokee Papers.
      Choctaw Papers

Tahlequah
  Northeastern State University Library
    Cherokee Room
      Nave Correspondence.
      Nave Papers.
      Stand Watie Papers.

Tulsa
  Thomas Gilcrease Institute of American History and Art
      Peter P. Pitchlynn Papers.
      John Ross Papers.

TENNESSEE

Nashville
  State Archives
      Isham G. Harris Papers, 1861-1862.
      Isham G. Harris Letter Book.

TEXAS

Austin
  State Archives
    Francis R. Lubbock Papers, 1861-1863.
    Francis R. Lubbock Letter Press Book.
    Pendleton Murrah Papers, 1863-1865.
    Treasurer's Papers, 1861-1865.

VIRGINIA

Richmond
  Confederate Museum
    Confederate Office of the Register, Letters Received, March
      20, 1861-June 18, 1862.
  State Archives
    A List of Payment into the Treasury of Treasury Notes.
    Register of Notes issued in pursuance of an Act . . . "for the
      assumption and Payment of the Confederate States War
      Tax," passed February 21, 1862.
    Register of Notes issued in pursuance of an Act . . . payable on
      demand to Bearer, and of the denomination of One
      Dollar.
    Register of Notes issued in pursuance of an Act . . . "providing
      for Loans to supply Temporary Deficiencies in the
      Treasury," passed March 28, 1862.

WASHINGTON, D. C.

Library of Congress
  Confederate Collection
    Confederate Office of the Comptroller, Letters Received,
      April 15, 1861-January 10, 1862.
    Confederate Post Office Department, Letters Sent, March 7,
      1861-October 12, 1863.
    _____, Record of Letters and other Communications from the
      Post Office Department.

National Archives

Record Group (NARG) 75
Arkansas and Red River Superintendency, Captured Miscellaneous Records, 1861-1862.
Records of the Wichita Agency, 1861-1862.

Record Group (NARG) 109
Confederate District of Indian Territory, Letters Sent, May 10-27, 1865.
Confederate States Congress, Legislative Papers, February 1862-March 1865.
_____, Memorials and Petitions, 1861-1865.
Confederate Secretary of the Treasury (CST), Letters Received from James D. B. DeBow, February 5, 1862-January 20, 1865.
_____, Letters Sent, April 3, 1861-August 2, 1864.
_____, Letters Sent to Custom Collectors and Depositories, March 21, 1861-March 31, 1865.
Confederate States Treasurer, Letters Received, February 1861-December 1862.
Confederate Officer of the Comptroller, Correspondence, 1861 and 1863.
_____, Records of the Custom Service, August 1847-March 1865.
Confederate Office of the Register (COR), Letters Sent, March 18, 1861-April 1, 1865.
Gray Box.
United States Bureau of Indian Affairs, Miscellaneous Documents, 1864-1865.

Record Group (NARG) 365
Confederate Secretary of the Treasury (CST), Estimates of Appropriations, January 1863-February 1865.
_____, Letters Received, 1861-1865.
_____, Letters Sent, March 1, 1861-October 12, 1861.
_____, Letters Sent, April 3, 1861-June 25, 1861.
_____, Miscellaneous Office Records, February 1861-March 1865.
_____, Regulations and Circulars of the Treasury Department, March 1861-July 1864.

_____, Resolutions and Acts of Congress and the State
Legislatures, February 1861-March 1865.
_____, Telegrams Sent, February 23, 1861-July 30, 1864.
Confederate States Treasurer, Miscellaneous Office Records,
June 5, 1861-March 8, 1865.
Confederate Office of the Comptroller, Letters Sent, March
23, 1861-December 16, 1861.
_____, Records of the Custom Service, 1861-1865.
Confederate Treasury Note Bureau, Miscellaneous Records,
August 1861-March 1865.

Newspapers

Bee, New Orleans, Louisiana, 1861-1862.
The Confederate Baptist, Columbia, South Carolina, 1862-1865.
Daily Advertiser, Montgomery, Alabama, 1861-1865.
Daily Courier, Charleston, South Carolina, 1861-1865.
Daily Enquirer, Richmond, Virginia, 1861-1865.
Daily Examiner, Richmond, Virginia, 1861-1865.
The Daily Picayune, New Orleans, Louisiana, 1861-1862.
Evening Post, New York, New York, selected issues.
The Tri-Weekly State Gazette, Austin, Texas, 1861-1865.
Tri-Weekly Telegraph, Houston, Texas, 1861-1865.

Federal and State Documents

*Acts and Resolutions adopted by the General Assembly of Florida, at its
Tenth Session*. Tallahassee: Dyke and Carlisle, 1861.
*Acts and Resolutions adopted by the General Asembly of Florida, at the
First Session of its Twelfth Assembly*. Tallahassee: Dyke and
Carlisle, 1862.
*Acts and Resolutions adopted by the General Assembly of Florida, at its
Twelfth Session*. Tallahassee: Dyke and Sparhawk, 1863.
*Acts and Resolutions adopted by the General Assembly of Florida, at its
Thirteenth Session*. Tallahassee: Office of the *Floridian* and
Journal, 1865.
Acts of the Called Session of the General Assembly of Alabama. Mont-
gomery: Shorter and Reid, 1861.

Acts of the Called Session, 1862, and of the Second Regular Annual Session of the General Assembly of Alabama. Montgomery: Montgomery Advertiser Book and Job Office, 1862.

Acts of the Called Session of the General Assembly of Alabama 1863. Montgomery: Montgomery Advertiser Book and Job Office, 1863.

Acts of the Called Session, 1864, of the General Assembly of Alabama 1864. Montgomery: Saffold and Figures, 1864.

Acts of the Called Session, 1864, and of the Fourth Regular Session of the General Assembly of Alabama. Montgomery: Saffold and Figures, 1864.

Act of the General Assembly of the State of Georgia passed in Milledgeville at an Annual Session . . . 1860. Milledgeville: Boughton, Nisbet, and Barnes, 1861.

Acts of the General Assembly of the State of Georgia, passed in Milledgeville at an Annual Session . . . 1861. Milledgeville: Boughton, Nisbet, and Barnes, 1862.

Acts of the General Assembly of the State of Georgia, passed in Milledgeville at an Annual Session . . . 1862, also Extra Session of 1863. Milledgeville: Boughton, Nisbet, and Barnes, 1863.

Acts of the General Assembly of the State of Georgia, passed in Milledgeville at an Annual Session . . . 1863, also Extra Session of 1864. Milledgeville: Boughton, Nisbet, and Barnes, 1864.

Acts of the General Assembly of the State of Georgia, passed in Milledgeville at an Annual Session . . . 1864, also Extra Session of 1865, at Macon. Milledgeville: Boughton, Nisbet, and Barnes, 1865.

Acts of the General Assembly of the State of Virginia, passed in 1861. Richmond: William F. Ritchie, 1861.

Acts of the General Assembly of the State of Virginia, passed in 1861-2. Richmond: William F. Ritchie, 1862.

Acts of the General Assembly of the State of Virginia, passed at Extra Session, 1862. Richmond: William F. Ritchie, 1862.

Acts of the Seventh Biennial Session of the General Assembly of Alabama. Montgomery: Shorter and Reid, 1860.

Acts passed at the Called Session of the General Assembly of the State of Arkansas. Washington: Statute Law Book Company, 1896.

Acts passed at the Eighth Session of the General Assembly of the State of Arkansas. Little Rock: Arkansas Banner Office, 1851.

Acts passed at the Fourteenth Session of the General Assembly of the State of Arkansas. Washington: Statute Law Book Company, 1896.

Acts passed at the Thirteenth or Special Session of the General Assembly of the State of Arkansas. Little Rock: Johnson and Yerkes, 1861.

Acts passed at the Thirteenth or Special Session of the General Assembly of the State of Arkansas. Little Rock: Johnson and Yerkes, 1862.

Acts passed by the Fifth Legislature of the State of Louisiana, at its Second Session. Baton Rouge: J. M. Taylor, 1861.

Acts passed by the Seventh Legislature of the State of Louisiana, at its First Session, at the City of Shreveport on the Eighteenth Day of January, 1864. Shreveport: *News* Office, 1864.

Acts passed by the Sixth Legislature of the State of Louisiana, at the City of Shreveport on the Fourth of May, 1863. Shreveport: Caddo *Gazette* Office, 1863.

Acts passed by the Twenty-Seventh Legislature of the State of Louisiana, in Extra Session at Opelousas December 1862, and January 1863. Natchitoches: *Times* Office, 1864.

Constitution . . . of Florida, Revised and Amended at a Convention . . . on the Third Day of January, 1861. Together with the Ordinances adopted by Said Convention. Tallahassee: Dyke and Carlisle, 1861.

Day, James W., ed. *Senate Journal of the Ninth Legislature of the State of Texas.* Austin: Texas State Library, 1963.

Gammel, H. P. N., ed. *The Laws of Texas, 1822-1897.* 20 vols. Austin: Gammel Book Company, 1898.

General Laws of the Ninth Legislature of the State of Texas. Houston: E. H. Cushing, 1862.

Journal of the Convention . . . begun and held . . . in the City of Tallahassee on Tuesday, January 14, 1862. n.p.: n.d.

Journal of the Convention of the People of South Carolina. Columbia: R. W. Gibbs, 1862.

Journal of the House of Representatives of the State of Missouri at the First Called Session of the Twenty-Second General Assembly. Jefferson City: n.p., 1863.

Journal of the Proceedings of the Senate . . . of Florida at the Thirteenth Session. Tallahassee: Office of the Florida *Sentinel*, 1864.

Journal of the Senate, Extra Session of the Rebel [Missouri] *Legislature.* Jefferson City: Emory S. Foster, 1865-1866.

Journal of the State Convention and Ordinances and Resolutions adopted in [March] 1861. Jackson, Mississippi: E. Barksdale State Printers, 1861.

Laws of the Eighth Legislature of the State of Texas, Extra Session. Austin: John Marshall and Company, 1861.

Laws of the Ninth Legislature of the State of Texas. Houston: E. H. Cushing, 1862.

Laws of the State of Mississippi passed at a Called Session of the Mississippi Legislature . . . July 1861. Jackson: E. Barksdale, 1861.

Laws of the State of Mississippi passed at a Regular Session of the Mississippi Legislature. Jackson: Cooper and Kimball, 1862.

Laws of the State of Mississippi passed at a Called and Regular Session of the Mississippi Legislature . . . 1863. Selma, Alabama: Cooper and Kimball, 1864.

Laws of the State of Mississippi passed at a Called Session of the Mississippi Legislature . . . August, 1864. Meridian: J. J. Shannon and Company, 1864.

Laws of the State of Mississippi passed at a Called Session of the Mississippi Legislature . . . March and April 1864. Meridian: J. J. Shannon and Company, 1864.

Laws of the State of Mississippi passed at a Called Session of the Mississippi Legislature . . . February and March 1865. Meridian: J. J. Shannon and Company, 1865.

Mathews, James M., ed. *The Statutes at Large of the Provisional Government of the Confederate States of America.* Richmond: R. M. Smith, 1864.

Message of P. P. Pitchlynn . . . delivered before the Choctaw Council in Extra Session . . . January 1865. Fort Towson, Choctaw Nation: Government Printing Office, n.d.

North Carolina General Assembly, 1862-1863 Session. *Report of the Joint Committee . . . to Enquire into the Causes why Soldiers were paid in Confederate Treasury Notes instead of North Carolina Notes.* Raleigh: W. W. Holden, 1863.

Ordinances and Resolutions passed by the State Convention of North Carolina. Raleigh: John W. Syme, 1862.

Ordinances of the State Convention which convened in Little Rock May 6, 1861. Little Rock: Johnson and Yerkes, 1861.

Proceedings of the Louisiana State Convention . . . together with the Ordinances passed. New Orleans: J. O. Nixon, 1861.

Public Acts of the State of Tennessee passed at the Extra Session of the Thirty-Third General Assembly, April 1861. Nashville: J. O. Griffith and Company, 1861.

Public Acts of the State of Tennessee passed at the Extra Session of the

Thirty-Third General Assembly for the Year 1861. Nashville: E. G. Eastman and Company, 1861.

Public Acts of the State of Tennessee passed at the First and Second Sessions of the Thirty-Fourth General Assembly. Nashville: Griffith, Camp, and Company, 1862.

Public Laws of the State of North Carolina passed . . . at its Adjourned Session 1860-1861. Raleigh: John Spelman, 1861.

Public Laws of the State of North Carolina passed . . . at its Adjourned Session of 1863. Raleigh: W. W. Holden, 1863.

Public Laws of the State of North Carolina passed . . . at its Adjourned Session 1864-1865. Raleigh: Cannon and Holden, 1865.

Ramsdell, Charles W., ed. *Laws and Joint Resolutions of the Last Session of the Confederate Congress*. Durham: Duke University Press, 1941.

Scott, S. S. *Letter of the Acting Commander of Indian Affairs, with Statement, &c., In regards to Certain Indian Trust Funds*. Richmond: Ritchie and Dunnacrent Printers, 1862.

Smith, William R. *The History and Debates of the Convention of the People of Alabama*. Montgomery: White, Pfister, and Company, 1861.

United States Department of the Navy. *Official Records of the Union and Confederate Navies in the War of the Rebellion*. 31 vols. Washington: Government Printing Office, 1894-1922.

United States Department of War. *War of the Rebellion: A Compilation of the Official Records of the Union and Confederate Armies*. 70 vols. in 128 books. Washington: Government Printing Office, 1880-1901.

United States House of Representatives, 37th Congress, 3rd Session. *Executive Documents No. 1*. "Message of the President of the United States." Washington: Government Printing Office, 1862.

United States Senate, 37th Congress, 3rd Session. *Executive Documents No. 1*. "Report of the Secretary of the Treasury . . . for the Year ending June 30, 1862." Washington: Government Printing Office, 1863.

United States Senate, 58th Congress, 2nd Session. *Journals of the Congress of the Confederate States of America*. 7 vols. Washington: Government Printing Office, 1905.

Diaries, Memoirs, and Papers

Anderson, John Q., ed. *Brokenburn: The Journal of Kate Stone, 1861-1868*. Baton Rouge: Louisiana State University Press, 1955.

Annals of the War written by Leading Participants North and South. Philadelphia: Times Publishing Company, 1879.

Anonymous. *"Cato" on Constitutional "Money" and Legal Tender*. Charleston: Evans and Cogswell, 1862.

Chamberlayne, C. G., intro. *Ham Chamberlayne — Virginian: Letters and Papers of an Artillery Officer in the War for Southern Independence*. Richmond: Dietz Printing Company, 1932.

Chesnut, Mary Boykin. *A Diary from Dixie*. Edited by Ben Ames Williams. Boston: Houghton Mifflin Company, 1949.

Collins, R. M. *Chapters from the Unwritten History of the War between the States*. St. Louis: Nixon-Jones Printing Company, 1893.

Davis, Jefferson. *A Short History of the Confederate States of America*. New York: Belford Company, Publishers, 1890.

Davis, Varina. *Jefferson Davis; Ex-President of the Confederate States of America: A Memoir by His Wife . . .* 2 vols. New York: Belford Company, [1890].

DeLeon, Thomas C. *Four Years in Rebel Capitals: An Inside View of Life in the Southern Confederacy, from Birth to Death*. Mobile: Gossip Printing Company, 1890.

Eggleston, George Cary. *A Rebel's Recollections*. Cambridge: Riverside Press, 1875.

Fleet, Betsy, and Fuller, John D. B., eds. *Green Mount: A Virginia Plantation Family during the Civil War*. Lexington: University of Kentucky Press, 1965.

E. B. G. of Cincinnati. " 'No Submission' Token." *American Journal of Numismatics* (July 1878); 13(1):16.

Johnson, Robert U., and Buel, Clarence D., eds. *Battles and Leaders of the Civil War*. 4 vols. New York: Century Company, 1887.

Jones, John B. *A Rebel War Clerk's Diary at the Confederate States Capital*. 2 vols. Philadelphia: J. B. Lippincott and Company, 1866.

LeBree, Ben, ed. *The Confederate Soldier in the Civil War*. Paterson, New Jersey: Pageant Books, Inc., [1959].

McDonald, Cornelia. *A Diary with Reminiscences of the War and Refugee Life in the Shenandoah Valley, 1860-1865*. Annotated and supplemented by Hunter McDonald. Nashville: Cullom and Ghertner Company, 1934.

Moore, Frank, ed. *The Rebellion Record: A Diary of American Events.* 11 vols. Supplement. New York: G. P. Putnam and others, 1861-1868.

Patrick, Rembert W., ed. *The Opinions of the Confederate Attorneys General, 1861-1865.* Buffalo: Dennis and Company, Inc., 1950.

Pollard, Edward A. *The Lost Cause: A New Southern History of the War of the Confederates.* New York: E. B. Treat and Company, 1867.

_____. *The Second Year of the War.* New York: Charles B. Richardson, 1864.

_____. *The War in America, 1863-1864.* London: Saunders, Otley, and Company, 1865.

Private and Official Correspondence of General Benjamin F. Butler. 5 vols. n.p.: Plimpton Press, 1906.

Reagan, John H. *Memoirs with Special Reference to Secession and the Civil War.* Edited by Walter F. McCaleb. New York and Washington: Newle Publishing Company, 1917.

Richardson, James D., ed. *A Compilation of the Messages and Papers of the Confederacy including the Diplomatic Correspondence, 1861-1865.* 2 vols. Nashville: United States Publishing Company, 1905.

Ross, Fitzgerald. *Cities and Camps of the Confederate States.* Edited by Richard B. Harwell. Urbana: University of Illinois Press, 1958.

Rowland, Dunbar, ed. *Jefferson Davis, Constitutionalist: His Letters, Papers, and Speeches.* 10 vols. Jackson, Mississippi: State Department of Archives and History, 1923.

Smith, Daniel E. Huger, *et al.*, eds. *Mason Smith Family Letters, 1860-1868.* Columbia: University of South Carolina Press, 1950.

Taylor, F. Jay, ed. *Reluctant Rebel, The Secret Diary of Robert Patrick, 1861-1865.* Baton Rouge: Louisiana State University Press, 1959.

Tyler, Lyon S. *The Letters and Times of the Tylers.* 2 vols. Richmond: Whittel and Shepperson, 1885.

Younger, Edward, ed. *Inside the Confederate Government, The Diary of Robert Garlick Hill Kean, Head of the Bureau of War.* New York: Oxford University Press, 1957.

Articles and Books

Adams, Edgar H. "Civil War Tokens of Tennessee." *The Numismatist* (April 1915); 28(4):140-43.

Adreano, Ralph Louis. "A Theory of Confederate Finance." *Civil War History* (December 1956); 2(4):21-28.

Burgett, Maurice M. "Obsolete Paper Currency of Indian Territory and Oklahoma." *Paper Money* (April 1967); 6(1):3-10.

Capers, Henry D. *The Life and Times of C. G. Memminger*. Richmond: Everett Waddey Company, 1893.

Cassidy, Daniel G. *The Illustrated History of Florida Paper Money*. Jacksonville: Published by Daniel G. Cassidy, 1980.

Clark, M. H. "Departure of President Davis and Cabinet from Richmond, Va., and the Last Days of the Confederate Treasury and what became of Its Specie." In Ben LaBree, ed., *The Confederate Soldier in the Civil War*. Paterson, New Jersey: Pageant Books, Incorporated [1959].

Criswell, Grover C., Jr. *Criswell's Currency Series: Confederate and Southern States Bonds*. St. Petersburg Beach, Florida: Criswell's Publications, 1961.

_____. *Criswell's Currency Series: Confederate and Southern States Currency*. [Iola, Wisconsin]: Krause Publishing Company, 1964.

Curto, J. J., and Swarty, Max M. "Tentative List of Sutler Tokens and Scrip." *The Numismatist* (September and December 1946) 59(9):1027-35; (12):1415-19.

Davis, William C. *First Blood: Fort Sumter to Bull Run*. Civil War Series, vol. 2. Alexandria, Virginia: Time-Life Books, 1983.

Dictionary of American Biography. 22 vols. and three supplements. New York: Charles Scribner's Sons, 1922-1973.

Dietz, Arthur. *The Postal Service of The Confederate States of America*. Richmond, Virginia: Press of the Dietz Printing Company, 1929.

Dietz Press, Inc. *Dietz Catalog & Hand-Book (Specialized) of the Postage Stamps and Envelopes of the Confederate States of America*. . . . Richmond, Virginia: The Dietz Press, Inc., 1945.

"Editorial." *American Journal of Numismatics and Bulletin of American Numismatics and Archaeological Society* (January 1878); 12(3):80.

Field, George and Melvin. *Token Collectors Pages*. Boston: Quarterman Publications, 1972.

_____. "The Wealth of the South Mulings." *Numismatic Scrapbook Magazine* (September 1958); 24(9):1785-86.

Grinnan, Daniel. "Disposition of Confederate Funds." *Confederate Veteran* (September 1929); 38(9):328-29.

Hanna, A. J. *Flight into Oblivion.* Bloomington: Indiana University Press, 1959.

Hawk, Emory Q. *Economic History of the South.* New York: Prentice-Hall, Inc., 1934.

[Johnson, George W.] "Letters of George W. Johnson." *Register of the Kentucky State Historical Society* (October 1942); 40(133): 330-51.

Lerner, Eugene M. "Monetary and Fiscal Programs of the Confederate Government." *Journal of Political Economy* (December 1954); 62(6):506-22.

_____. "Money, Prices, and Wages in the Confederacy." *Journal of Political Economy* (February 1955); 63(1):20-40.

Nast, F. A. "History of Confederate Stamps." *Confederate Veteran* (March 1894); 2(3):77-78.

"Proceedings of the Confederate Congress." *Southern Historical Society Papers* (1923-1959); 44-52.

Raymond, Wayte. *The Standard Catalogue of United States Coins and Tokens.* New York: Wayte Raymond, Inc., 1941.

Reinfield, Fred. *The Story of Civil War Money.* New York: Sterling Publishing Company, 1959.

Rulau, Russell. "1860 and 1861 Civil War Cents." *Calcoin News* (Winter 1962); 16(1):10.

Schwab, John C. "Prices in the Confederate States, 1861-1865." *Political Science Quarterly* (June 1899); 14(2):281-304.

_____. *The Confederate States of America, 1861-1865: A Financial and Industrial History of the South during the Civil War.* New York: Charles Scribner's Sons, 1901.

Shepherd, Lewis. "The Confederate Treasure Train." *Confederate Veteran* (June 1917); 25(6)257-59.

Taxay, Don. *Comprehensive Catalogue and Encyclopedia of United States Coins.* Omaha: Scott Publishing Company, 1971.

Thian, Raphael P. *Register of the Confederate Debt.* Boston: Quarterman Publications, Inc., 1972.

Todd, Richard C. *Confederate Finance.* Athens: University of Georgia Press, 1954.

Upham, Samuel C. "Counterfeit Confederate Circulation." *Confederate Veteran* (March 1900); 8(3)102-103.

Wiley, Bell I. *The Life of Johnny Reb: The Common Soldier of the Confederacy.* New York: Bobbs-Merrill Company, 1943.

_____. *The Road to Appomattox.* Memphis: Memphis State College Press, 1956.

INDEX

Alabama: 14, 27, 31, 44-45, Figs. 16-17.
  Greenville, Fig. 30
  Mobile, 2, 24, 44, Figs. 30-31;
    Jockey Club, 106;
    Mobile Point (see Fort Morgan), 26;
    Southern Bank of, 44;
    tokens in, 3, 106;
  Montgomery, 2, Fig. 13;
    Bank of, 28, 43;
    Northern Bank of Huntsville, 43-44;
  Selma, 106;
    Commercial Bank of Alabama, 28;
    banks in, 43;
Allen, Henry W., 73, 75.
Archer & Daly, Figs. 57-58.
Arent, D., Fig. 60.
Arizona, Confederate Territory of (see New Mexico), 95.
Arkansas: 1, 5, 26, 70, 72-73, 76, 85, 87, 91, 95, Figs. 32-33.
  banks in, 2, 70;
  Little Rock, 67-68, 88, 90, 97, 112, 146;
  swamp money scrip, 70-71;
  Fort Smith, 88, 97, 107.

Baily & Company, 12.
Baker, Bolling, Fig. 10
Barlow, S. L., 123.
Barnwell, Robert W., 17, 33-34, 80.
barter, 81, 139, 132.
Bayne, Maj. Thomas L., 32.
Beane, Connie J., xi.
Benjamin, Judah P., 14, 77, 86, 88, 123, Fig. 9.

Benji, Capt. Pickens, 89.
Bennett, Thomas, 3.
blockade-running, 7-8, 31, 63, 66, 88, 131.
Blunt, Brig. Gen. James G., 86.
bonds: 6, 8, 10, 24, 27-28, 30-32, 43, 45-49, 52, 56-58, 62-64, 66-67, 70-71, 73-81, 88, 90, 96, 100, 104-107, 110-12, 115, 117, 123-24, 127, 129-31, 134, 136-38, Figs. 1, 3-4, 65-66;
  denominations, 44, 71, 79;
  "Missouri Defense," 80;
  "Requisition for Missouri Defense," 80;
Bonds, Dr. F. J., 100.
Boudinot, Elias Cornelius, 90-91, 95, 99, 101, Fig. 43.
Bragg, Thomas, Fig. 9.
Breckinridge, John C., 123.
Brown, Joseph E., 57-58, 67, Fig. 24
bullion, 3, 5, 8, 11-12, 15-18, 22, 29, 73, 122-23, 127, 132-34.
Butler, Maj. Gen. Benjamin F., 75.

Caldwell, Green W., 15.
California, 123.
Canada, 105, 123-24.
Carter, H. H., 73.
Certificates: 4, 10, 28.
  Call, 136, 138, Fig. 67;
  Confederate Stock, Figs. 1-2;
  Corporate, Fig. 2;
  U. S. Stock, 96;
  $1,000 Non Taxable, Figs. 65-66.
Chesnut, Mary Boykin, 117-18.
Clain-Stefenelli, Vladimir, xi.
Clark, Edward, 77.
Clark, Henry T., 15-16.

Clark, Micajah H., 122-23.
Clay, Clement C., 14.
Clitherall, Alexander B., Fig. 10.
Connecticut, 105.
coinage (coins): x, 2-3, 5, 11-13, 15-17,
    22, 28, 30-33, 35, 44, 51, 59, 61-62,
    65, 74, 76, 91, 96-97, 99, 107, 121,
    123-24, 127, 129, 132, 134, Figs. 5-
    6, 7-8.
    Cavalier, 14-15;
    copper tokens, 5-8, 14, 106;
    counterfeit, 12;
    English sovereigns, 13-14, 122, 138;
    gold, 6-7, 14-15, 22, 32-33, 78, 87,
        105, 108, 122;
    foreign, 13;
    French Napoleons, 13;
    metal tokens: 106, 132;
        Beauregard "Dime," Figs. 53-54;
        "Marshall House," 106, Figs.
        49-50;
        "Wealth of the South," 106, Figs.
        51-52;
        "W. W. Wilbur," 106, Figs. 47-
        48;
    Mexican-Spanish doubloons, 13;
    silver, 6, 13-14, 18, 22, 25, 30, 74,
        87, 105, 111, 122;
    tokens, 3, 18-19, 129, 133.
Conrad, Charles M., 31.
Cooper, Col. Douglas H., 87, 90-91.
Cooper, Samuel, 89, 100-101.
Cotton: 2, 5, 30, 48, 67, 73-79, 81-82,
    91-92, 100-101, 110, 118-19, 123,
    127, Figs. 18, 68.
    cards, 73, 76, 78, 91-92, 100-102;
    certificates, 138;
    exports, 7-8, 32, 63;
    planters, 24, 27, 46;
    speculation on, 1;

Counterfeit money, 12, 34-35, 48.
Coupons, 28, 33, 71, 123, 137.
Crawford, John, 88.
Crosley, J. P., Fig. 59.
Cross, Edward, 72, 90.
Cruger, Lewis, 34.
Cuba, Havana, 124.
Customs collectors, 29;
    in New Orleans, 32, 73.
Cyler, R. R., 57.

Davis, George, 13, 30-31.
Davis, Jefferson:
    President, 17, 25, 27, 80, 110-
        11, 115-16, 118, 122, Fig. 55;
    offers reward for Samuel C. Upham,
        34.
Davis, Varina Howell Banks, 118.
DeBow, James D. B., 30.
Delaware, 105.
Denegre, J. D., 25.
District of Columbia, 105, 123.
Donegan, James J., 43-44.
Drew, Col. John, 89.

Ellis, John W., 15.
Ellsworth, Col. Elmer E., Fig. 50.
Elmore, Edward C., Fig. 10.
Elmore, William A., 11-12, 14-18.
England: Liverpool, 32;
    Bank of Englamd, 35, 134;
    London, Fig. 64.

factors, 1-2.
First Battle of Bull Run (see Manassas),
    Figs. 53-54.
Fisher, LeRoy H., xi.
Flanagin, Harris, 72-73.

Florida: 4, 42, 56, 63-67, 122, 129,
Figs. 28-29.
Bank of West Florida, Apalachicola,
Fig. 31;
fifty cents scrip, Figs. 30-31;
Pensacola, 24, 26, 65.
Folsom, H. N., 97.
Folsom, Sampson, 97.
Folsom, T., 97.
Forrest [Nathan Bedford] Cavalry, 118.
Fort Morgan (see Mobile Point), Ala.,
26.
Foster, John S., 51.
Fraser & Company, John, 31;
Fraser, Trenholm & Company, 31.
Gallier & Esterbrook, 12.
Gardner, James, 107.
Garland, Augustus H., 26.
Garland, Samuel, 98, Fig. 45.
Gartrell, Lucius J., 26.
Georgia: 5, 14, 18, 42-43, 56-60, 63-64,
66-67, 81, 108, 129, Figs. 21, 24-25.
Atlanta, 105;
Augusta, 17, 29-30, 44, 59, 107, Figs.
11, 61;
Augusta *Constitutionalist*, 107;
Bank of Columbus, 57;
Central Railroad & Banking Com-
pany of, 57;
Dahlonega mint, 3, 11, 14-19, 22;
Milledgeville, 59.
Savannah, 17, 29, 57;
Washington, 122-23.
Gholson, Maj. Gen. S. J., 48.
Gibbon, John H., 15-16.
Gingles, C. H., Fig. 30.
gold, x, 2, 5-7, 14-15, 17-18, 22, 29-30,
32-33, 35,43, 46, 51, 77-78, 87-90,
105, 108, 117-19, 121-22, 124, 131-
33, 135.

Gormly, J. F., Fig. 30.
Gray, Peter W., 99, 101.
Grenno, Capt. Harris S., 89.
Gresham's Law, 104.
Guirot, Anthony J., 11, 15, 17, 29, 3

Hackett, Neil J., xi.
Haplin, Frederick, Figs. 57-58.
Handy, John, 29.
Harris, Isham G., 49, Figs. 20-21.
Haynes, Landon C., 26.
Helms, Charles, 124.
Hindman, Maj. Gen. Thomas C., 89
Howard, James H., xi.
Howard, James W., 78.
Hoyer & Ludwig, Fig. 55.
Hudson, George, 96.
Humphries, John G., 47.

Illustrated Newspaper (see Frank Les
lie), 34.
Indiana, 105.
Indian(s): nations, x, 6-7, 85, 99, 131
Cherokee, 5-7, 85-92, 95-96, 101-
102, 131, Figs. 21, 40-44;
called Pins, 86, 89-90;
in Choctaw Nation, 97;
Council & National Committee,
85, 87, 90, 97;
District of Indian Territory, 85,
87, 99, 101;
Home Guard, 86;
Park Hill, 85, 89-90;
scrip, 85-87, 90-92, 102;
Tahlequah, 90;
Union (U. S.), 87, 89;
use of slaves, 85-87.
Chickasaw, 95-96, 98, 101, 131;

Choctaw, 2, 5-7, 85, 95-102, 131,
Figs. 21, 40, 44-46.
Council, 97-101;
Doaksville, 97;
scrip, 85, 89, 102;
Skullyville, 97;
warrants, 95, 98-99, 101, Figs.
44, 46.
Creek, 95-96, 101, 131.
North Fork Town [Village] in, 96;
Seminole, 95-96, 101, 131.
Investors, 134-35, Fig. 1.

Jackson, Andrew, 1.
Jackson, Claiborne F., 79.
Jackson, James, Fig. 30.
Johns, John, 57.
Johnson, George W., 43.
Johnson, Robert W., 26.
Johnson's Island (see Lake Erie), 124.
Johnston, Gen. Joseph E., 33, 122.
Jones, Clem R., 77.
Jones, John B., 26, 32, 109, 111, 119.
Jones, Robert M., 98-99.
Joubert, J., Fig. 56.

Kansas, 123;
Department of, 86.
Kean, Robert Garlick Hill, 110.
Keatinge & Ball (see Columbia, S. C.),
80.
Kellogg, George, 16.
Kenner, Duncan F., 11, 14.
Kentucky, 6, 13, 42-43, 66, 118;
Louisville, 106.
Keynes, John Maynard (Keynesian
monetary economics), 133-34.

Lake Erie (see Johnson's Island), 124.
Leadbetter, J. D., 25-26.

Lee, Gen. Robert E., 27.
legal tender, x, 4, 6, 8, 26-27, 30, 47,
64, 81, 105, 117, 127-28, 132-34;
Leslie, Frank (see Illustrated Newspaper), 34.
Letcher, John, Fig. 22.
Libby, L. L., 97.
Lincoln, Abraham, 86.
loans: 24, 28-29, 104;
foreclosures of, 1-2;
foreign, 32, 138, Fig. 68.
Loman, E., 97.
Louisiana: 11, 13-15, 25, 27, 30-31, 70-
71, 73-76, 81, 87, 116, 128, Figs. 34-
35, 59-60.
banks in, 1;
Farmerville, Fig. 60;
Madison, 107;
New Orleans, 2, 73-74, 77, 79-80;
banks in, 5, 17, 25, 31-32, 74, 76,
128, 132;
Citizens Bank, 25;
Committee of Public Safety, 75;
fall of, 17-18, 29, 31, 75;
mint at, 3, 11-12, 14-17, 22-24;
prices in, 87.
Opelousas, Citizens Bank at, 74.
Shreveport, 76, 91.
Lovett, Robert Jr., 12-13.
Lubbock, Francis R., 77-78.
Lyday, Henry W., 79.
Lyon, Francis S., 31.

Mahnken, Norbert R., xi.
Mallory, Stephen R., 26.
Manassas (see First Battle of Bull Run),
Figs. 53-54.
Marshall, Humphrey, 118.
Maryland, 105.
Massachusetts, 105.
Maury & Company, R. H., Fig. 4.

Maxey, Maj. Gen. Samuel B., 99-100.
Mayers, A. G., 107.
medicines, 73, 91.
Memminger, Christopher G, 3-4, 11-
18, 23-35, 57, 75, 104-105, 127-28,
134, Figs. 9, 14.
Mexico, 5, 7-8, 30, 70, 76-77, 100-101,
116, 124.
Michigan, 105.
Miles, William P., 13.
militia:
in Choctaw Nation, 96.
in Tennessee, 49.
in Virginia, 51.
Mississippi: 27-30, 35, 45-48, 67, 91,
105, Figs. 18-19.
Jackson, 17, 29;
Meridian, 91.
Winston County Board of Police,
47-48.
Missouri: 70, 79-81, 87, 123, Figs. 38-
39.
Cassville, 79;
Jefferson City, 79;
Neosho, 79;
State Guard, 79-80.
Moffitt, Mr., 109.
Moore, Andrew B., 43-44.
Moore, Thomas O., 15, 25, 74-75, 128.
Morgan, Mr. & Mrs. La Verne E., xi.
Mosely, Samuel F., 100.
Murrah, Pendleton, 78.
Murray, Thomas H., 79.

McCullock, Brig. Gen. Benjamin, 86.
McGehee, John C., 64-65.

Nail, J. M., 100.
Nave, Andrew R., 87.
Nebraska Territory, 105.

New Jersey, 105;
Egg Harbor Bank, Egg Harbor City
Fig. 63.
New Mexico (see Confederate Ter-
ritory of Arizona), 95.
New York: 23, 105;
Bank of the Republic in New York
City, 23.
North Butte Mining Company, Fig. 2
North Carolina: 5, 7, 13-16, 42, 56, 6
63, 66, 71, 81, 90-91, 108, 131, Fig
26-27.
Charlotte mint, 3, 11, 14-16, 22;
assay office at, 3, 15-16;
Greensboro, 122;
Wilmington, 32.

Ohio, Cincinnati, 105-106.
Omnibus tickets, 5, 7, 25, 74, 129.
One Salmon, 87.

Patterson & Company, J. F., 44, Fig
17.
Pennsylvania, 105;
Philadelphia, 12, 34, Fig. 7;
Daily Inquirer, 34.
Perkins, John Jr., 27-28.
Peterson, A. N. M., 12.
Pettus, John J., 46.
Phillips, Dr. George D., 58.
Pike, Brig. Gen., Albert, 88, 90, 96-9
Pillow, Maj. Gen. Gideon J., 49.
Pitchlynn, Peter P., 98, 100, Fig. 46
Pollard, Edward A., 117.
Postage stamps: 5, 29, 107, 129.
counterfeit, 34;
Five Cents—Green, Fig. 55;
Five Cents—Pale Greenish Blue,
Fig. 56;
Ten Cents—Blue, Fig. 57;
Twenty Cents—Green, Fig. 58.

Post Office Department, 30, 107, 122.
Pressley, Benjamin C., 16.
printing press, 28, 35, 42, 56, 65, 67, 104, 132.
Provisional Congress, 4, 11-15, 17-18, 23-24, 26-27, 29, 31, 33-34, 80, 87, 90, 96, 101, 105, 110, 115, 127, 130-31, Fig. 10.

Quillian, Lewis W., 17-18.

Randolph, C. A., 76.
Reagan, John H., 29, 107, 122-23, Fig.
Rector, Maj. Elias, 97.
Rector, Henry M., 72, 85, Fig. 32.
Rhode Island, 105.
Rindley, S., 88.
Ross, John, 85-86, 89-90, 92, Fig. 41.
Rua, Filo E. de la., Fig. 30.
Rua & Company, Thomas de la., Fig. 56.

salt, 76.
Schmidt, Conrad, 12.
Scott, S. S., 91, 97-98.
Second Bank of the U. S., 1.
Semmes, Thomas J., 13-14.
Semple, James A., 123-24.
Sheveatt, Retonion, 57-58.
Shields, William, 79,80.
shinplasters: 4-5, 8, 13, 25, 33, 44, 47, 95, 108, 110, 115, 129-30.
in Arkansas, 71-72, 87;
in Cherokee Nation, 81, 88;
in Florida, 64-65;
in Georgia, 59;
in Louisiana, 74-75, 107, Figs. 59-60;

in Texas, 77, 107-108;
in Virginia, 51, 107.
Shorter, John Gill, 44, 105, Fig. 16.
silver, 2, 5-7, 14-15, 18, 25, 29-30, 43, 46, 51, 74, 77, 87-88, 105, 111, 121, 123, 132-33, 135; German, 106.
slaves, 34, 85-87, 110.
Snell, H. V., 64.
South Carolina: 3-4, 13, 16, 33, 42-43, 66, 80, 106, 117;
Bank of, 108;
Camden, 117;
Charleston, 2-4, 16, 22-23, 31, 86, 88, 106, 108-109;
banks in, 16;
Charleston Daily Courier, 105;
Columbia, 80, 109, 117;
Commercial Bank of, 28;
see Keatinge & Ball, 80;
Branch Bank of, 108;
Confederate Baptist, 109, 117.
Fort Sumter, 86.
Specie, x, 2-3, 5-7, 18, 22-23, 25, 28-32, 35, 42-44, 46-49, 51-52, 57-58, 61, 64-65, 70-78, 81-82, 87-88, 91-92, 96-97- 99-102, 104-108, 110-12, 116-17, 121-24, 128, 130-33.
Spence, James, 32.
Stames, E., 29.
Stone, Kate, 74.
Stone, William R., 74.
Straker & Sons, S., Fig. 64.
Strickland, Hardy, 18.

taxes, 6, 27, 29-31; 43-45, 47-48, 58, 63, 65-66, 71-72, 75, 77-78, 81, 01, 99, 102, 110, 115, 130-31, 134, 138.
war, 29, 51-52, 64, 71.

Taylor, F. F., 12.
Tennessee: 26, 48, 50, 89, Figs. 20-21, 40.
  Bank of, 49;
  Chattanooga, 50, Fig. 62;
  Cherry Valley, 50;
  Kingston, 50;
  Memphis, 49, 73;
  Nashville, 49, 106;
    fall of, Fig. 20;
  Planters Bank, 49;
  Smithville, 50.
Texas: 1-2, 5, 7, 27, 70, 75-79, 81, 95, 107-11, 116-17, 123-24, Figs. 36-37, 58.
  Austin (see *Tri-Weekly State Gazette*), 27;
  Brigade, 77;
  Commercial & Agriculture Bank of Galveston, 1;
  Houston (see *Tri-Weekly Telegraph*), 99;
  Jefferson, 100;
  Marshall, 10;
  Paris, 98;
  Tyler, 117.
Thompson, Brig. Gen. M. Jeff, 79.
tobacco, 5, 75, 110, 118-19.
Toombs, Robert, Fig. 9.
Trans-Mississippi:
  Confederacy, 5, 70, 78-79, 81, 85, 91-92, 99-101, 116, 124, 131, 138, Fig. 58;
  Department, 35, 123;
  River, 7-8.
Treasury Notes: 2, 4, 23, 25-27, 29-35, 40-42, 45, 49-50, 52, 57-59, 61, 63-64, 66, 71-73, 77-78, 88, 90, 99, 105, 107, 110-12, 115, 117-19, 122, 124, 127-33, 138, Figs. 65-66.

  counterfeit, 34-35, 48, Fig. 15;
  denominations, 5-6, 23-24, 28, 33-34, 43-44, 46-51, 58-59, 61-62, 6 65, 71-72, 74-75, 79-80, 88, 107 108, 115-16, 127, 131-32, 138, Figs. 12-13, 18-19, 23, 27.
  "Greenbacks," 117-18;
  Issued by Cherokee Nation, 2-3, 5; Issued by Choctaw Nation, 5;
  Kingston Issue, Fig. 21;
  military, 46-47;
  Smithville Issue, Fig. 20;
  use of Dollar Sign, 89, Figs. 21, 4(44.
Trenholm, George A., 30-31, 119, 12 22, *131, Fig. 9.*
Tri-Weekly State Gazette (see Austin Texas), 27.
Tri-Weekly Telegraph (see Houston, Texas), 77.
Tyler, John, Fig. 11.
Tyler, Robert, Fig. 11.

Upham, Samuel C., 34.

Vance, Zebulon, B., 63.
Vaughan's Brigade [also Vaughn; Bri Gen. John C. Vaughn], 123.
Vest, George G., 80.
Virginia: 27, 30, 45, 50-52, 63, 100, 107, 116, Fig. 21.
  Alexandria, Fig. 50;
  banks in, 1;
  Danville, 121-22;
  District of Henrico, 51;
  Petersburg, 111;
  Richmond, 50-52, 63, 75, 80, 91,9 100-101, 106, 108-109, 111, 116 17, 121-23, Figs. 7, 22, 24, 27, 3 44, 49, 55, 57-58.

Bank of the Commonwealth, 104;
banks in, 122-23;
Daily Richmond Enquirer, 13,
  110-16;
Daily Richmond Examiner, 13,
  51, 108-109, 117, 121;
Richmond Dispatch, 116, 121;
Tredegar Iron Works, 57;
Shenandoah Valley, 123.

Walker, James, x.
war costs, 7, 88, 131, 134-35.
warrants: 70-71, 90.
  Issued by Arkansas, 2, 5, 71-73,
    Figs. 32-33;
  Issued by Choctaw Nation, 2, 95,

  98-99, 101, Figs. 44, 46;
  Issued by Texas, 2, 5, 76, 78, Figs.
    36-37.
Washington, George, Fig. 21.
Watie, Stand, 86, 88-91, Figs. 41-43.
Watts, Thomas H., Fig. 9.
Western & Atlantic Railroad, 59.
Wigfall, Louis T., 77.
Wilbur, W. W., 106, Figs. 47-48.
Williams, F. E., 97.
Winder, Brig. Gen. John H., 51.
Wisconsin, 105.
wool cards, 73, 76, 78, 101-102.
Wright, Allen, 98, 100-101.

Young, William H., 57.